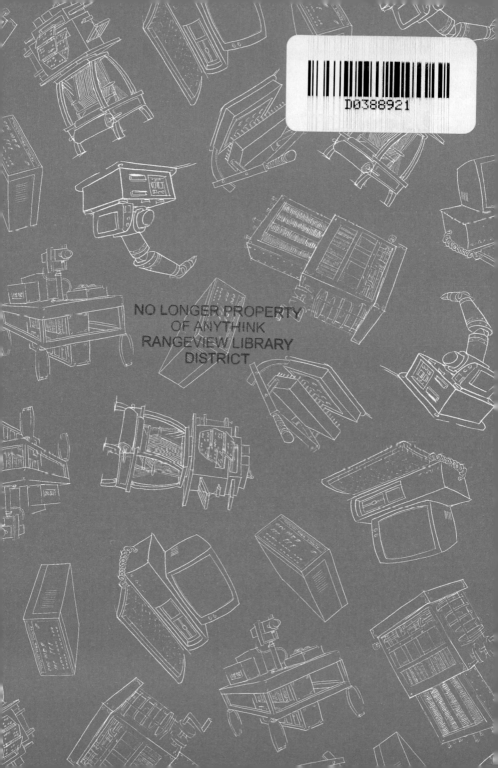

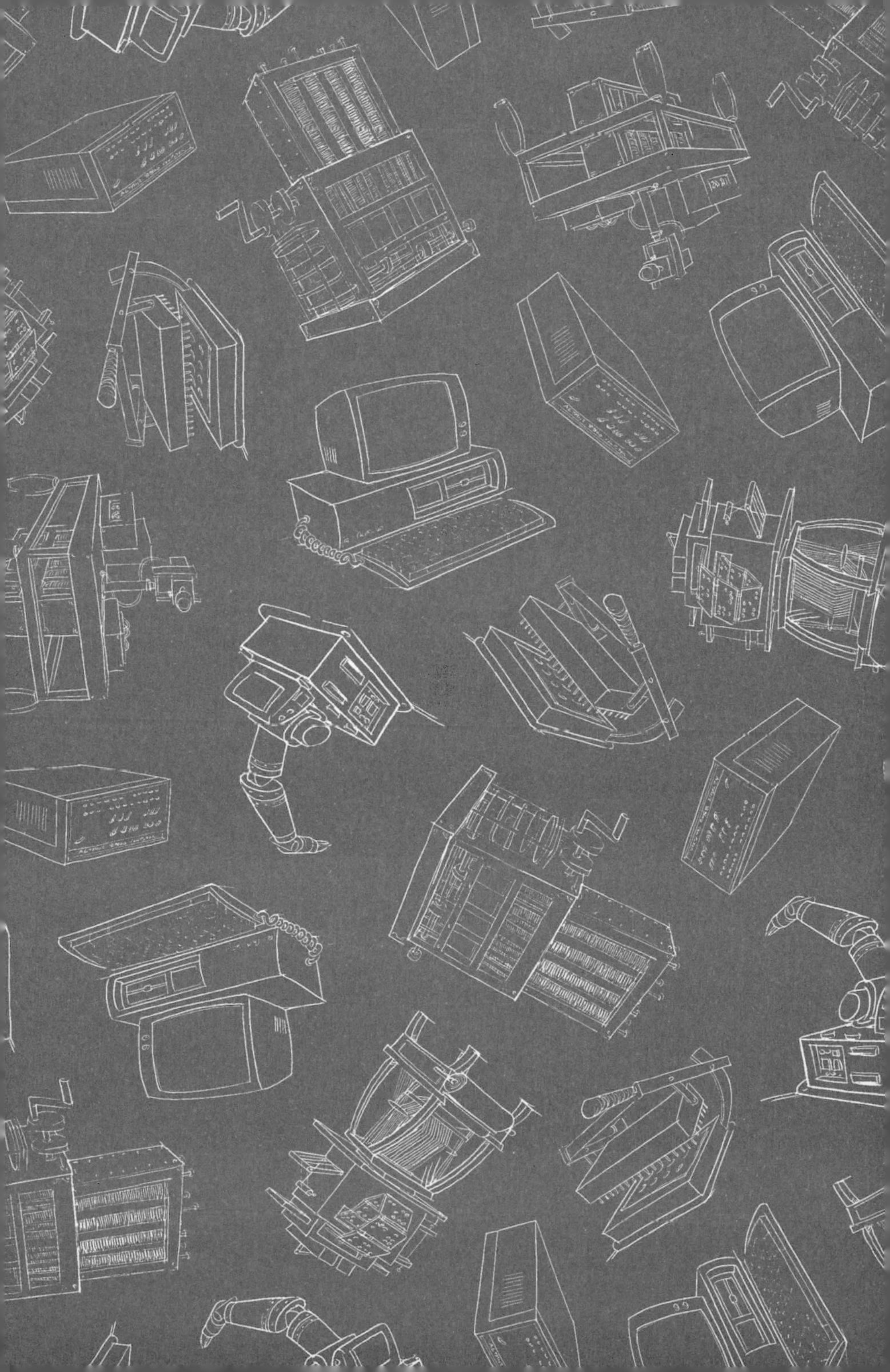

BIG IDEAS
THAT CHANGED THE WORLD

MACHINES THAT THINK!

DON BROWN

AMULET BOOKS • NEW YORK

The artwork in this book combines hand and digital drawing
with digital color collage and printing.

Cataloging-in-Publication Data has been applied for and may be obtained
from the Library of Congress.

ISBN 978-1-4197-4098-5

Text and illustrations copyright © 2020 Don Brown
Edited by Howard W. Reeves

Printed and bound in China

10 9 8 7 6 5 4 3 2 1

Amulet Books are available at special discounts when
purchased in quantity for premiums and promotions as well as fundraising
or educational use. Special editions can also be created to specification.
For details, contact specialsales@abramsbooks.com or the address below.

Amulet Books® is a registered trademark of Harry N. Abrams, Inc.

ABRAMS The Art of Books
195 Broadway, New York, NY 10007
abramsbooks.com

For Thom, a man who thinks

Note to reader: Unless otherwise noted, quotation marks signal actual quotes.
An explanation of "binary" and "bits" can be found on page 106.

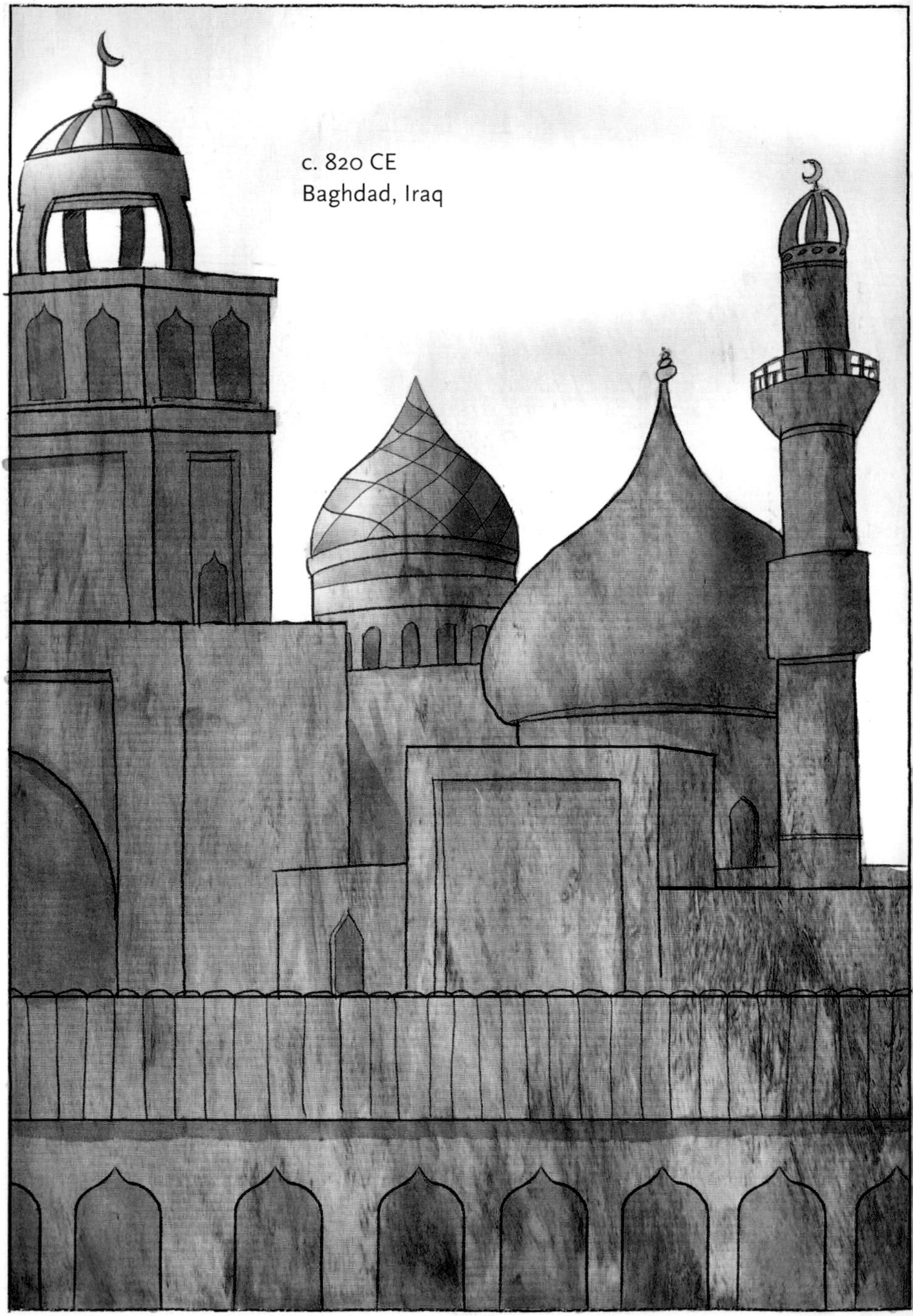
c. 820 CE
Baghdad, Iraq

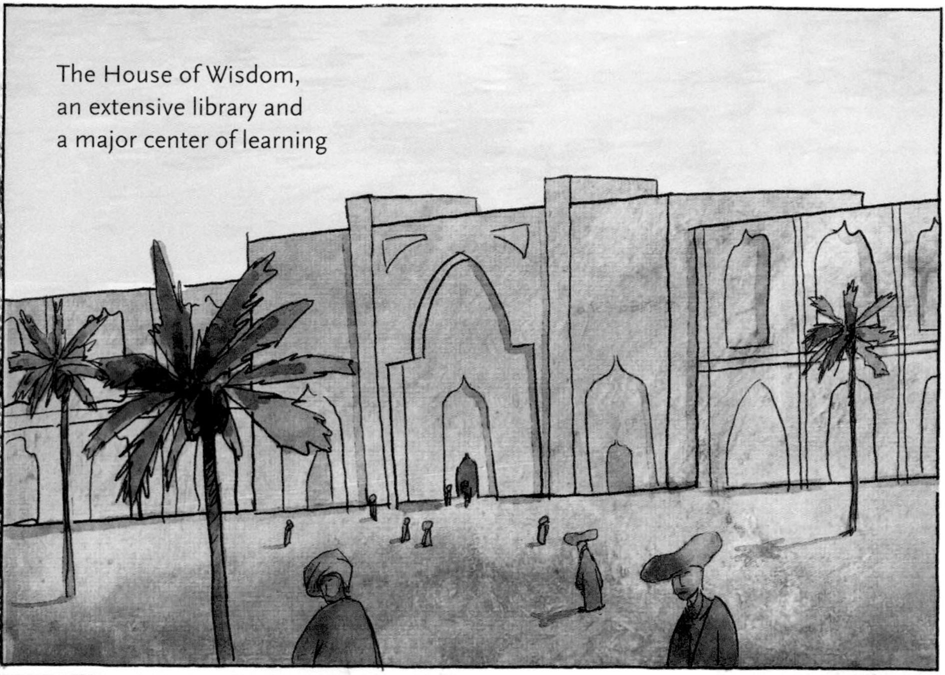
The House of Wisdom,
an extensive library and
a major center of learning

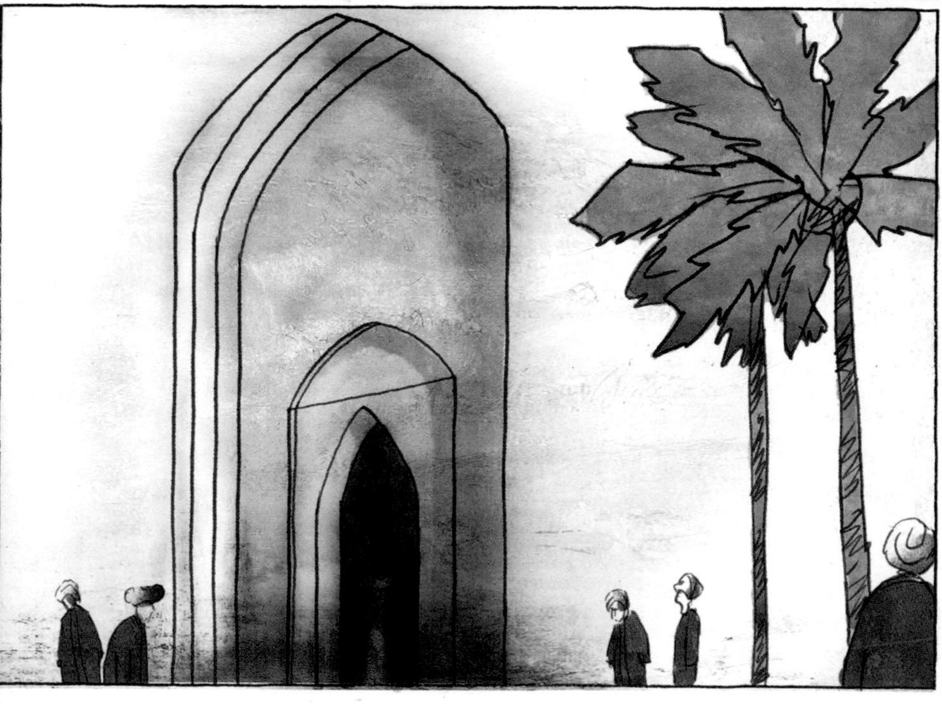

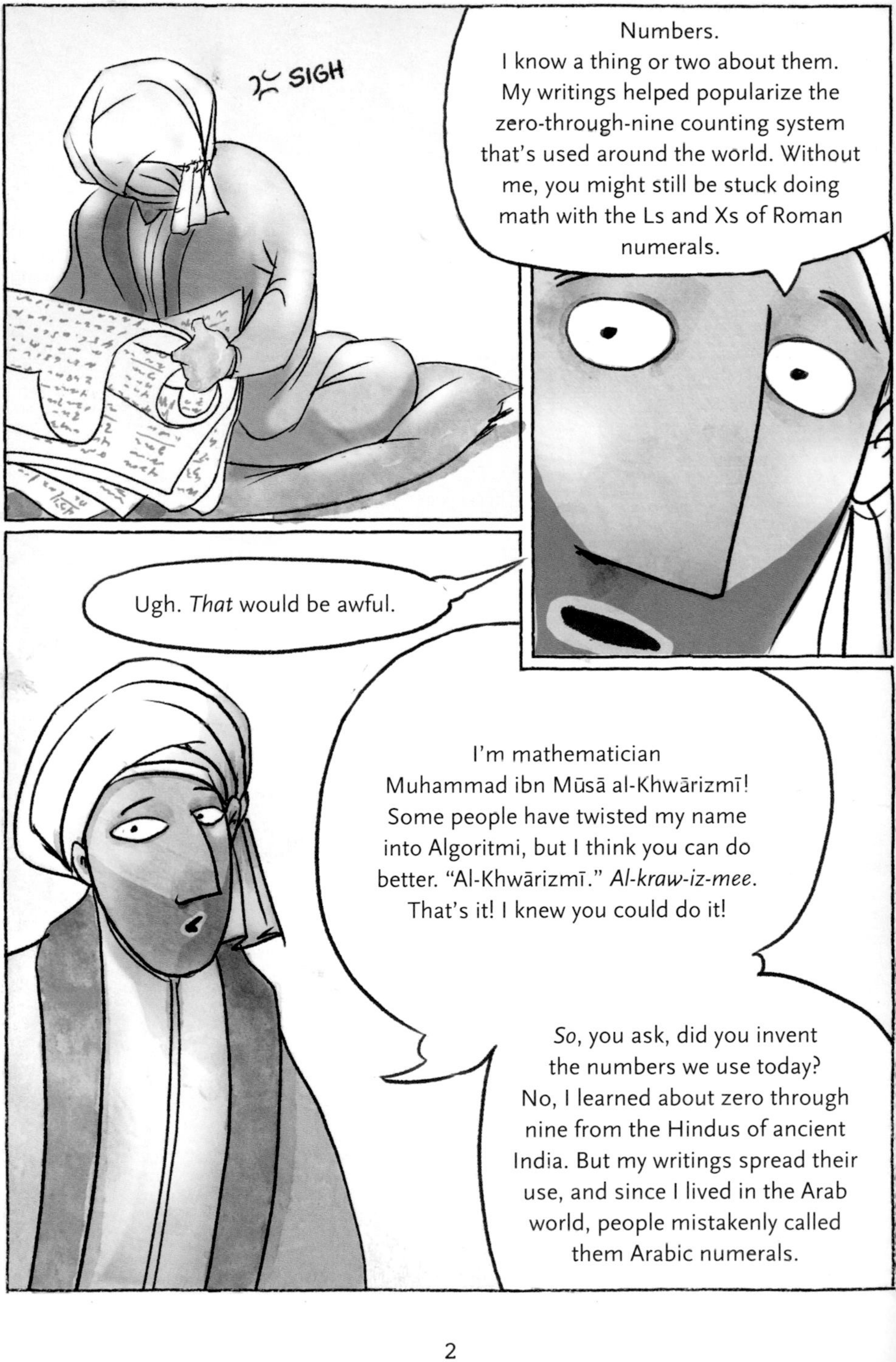
SIGH
Numbers. I know a thing or two about them. My writings helped popularize the zero-through-nine counting system that's used around the world. Without me, you might still be stuck doing math with the Ls and Xs of Roman numerals.
Ugh. *That* would be awful.
I'm mathematician Muhammad ibn Mūsā al-Khwārizmī! Some people have twisted my name into Algoritmi, but I think you can do better. "Al-Khwārizmī." *Al-kraw-iz-mee*. That's it! I knew you could do it!
So, you ask, did you invent the numbers we use today? No, I learned about zero through nine from the Hindus of ancient India. But my writings spread their use, and since I lived in the Arab world, people mistakenly called them Arabic numerals.

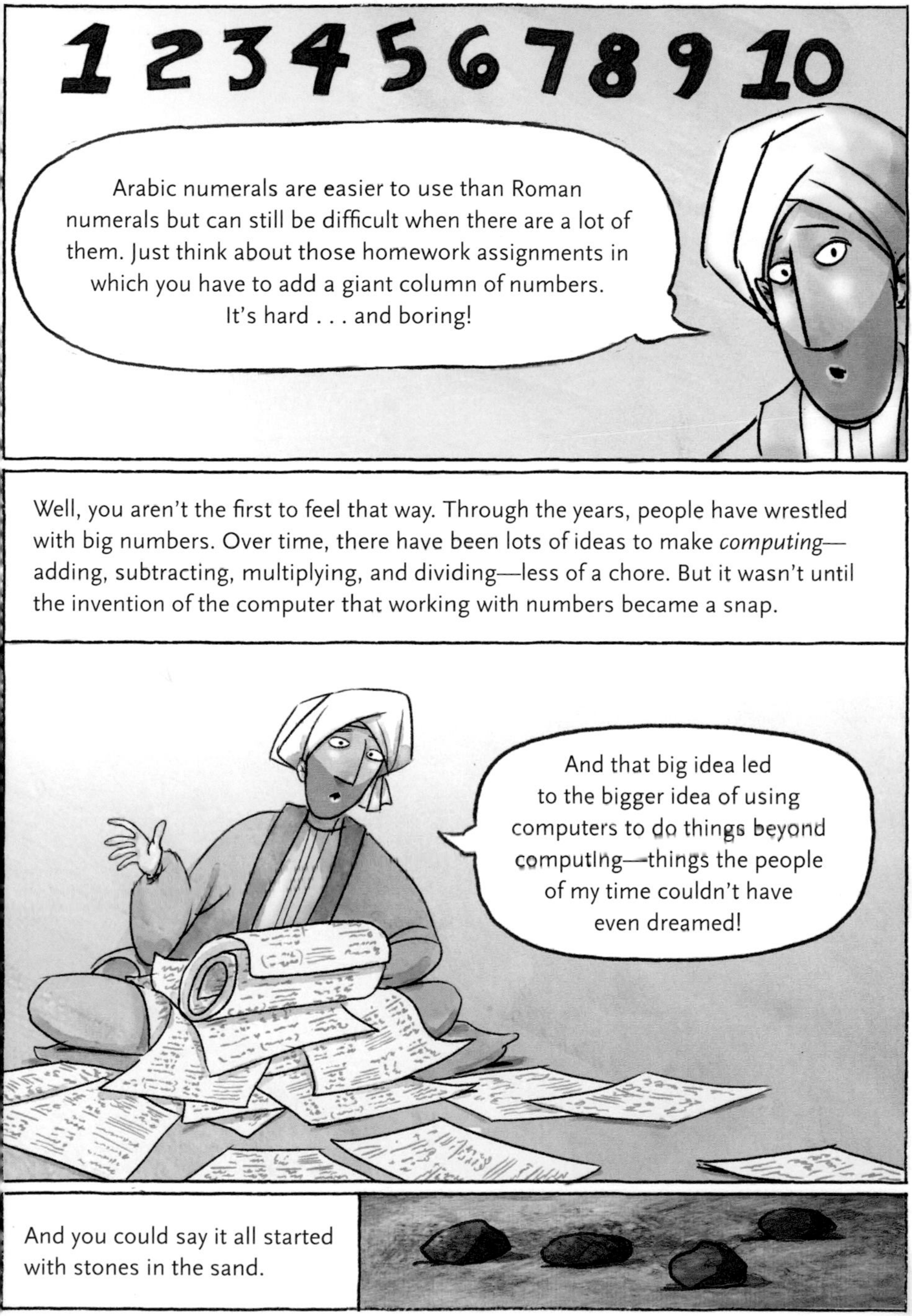
1 2 3 4 5 6 7 8 9 10
Arabic numerals are easier to use than Roman numerals but can still be difficult when there are a lot of them. Just think about those homework assignments in which you have to add a giant column of numbers. It's hard . . . and boring!
Well, you aren't the first to feel that way. Through the years, people have wrestled with big numbers. Over time, there have been lots of ideas to make *computing*—adding, subtracting, multiplying, and dividing—less of a chore. But it wasn't until the invention of the computer that working with numbers became a snap.
And that big idea led to the bigger idea of using computers to do things beyond computing—things the people of my time couldn't have even dreamed!
And you could say it all started with stones in the sand.

A long time ago—and I don't mean last month or last year, but about three thousand years ago—people had the idea to use pebbles and stones to calculate. Arranged in columns in the sand, the pebbles in each column were given a certain value: one, ten, or one hundred, for example.

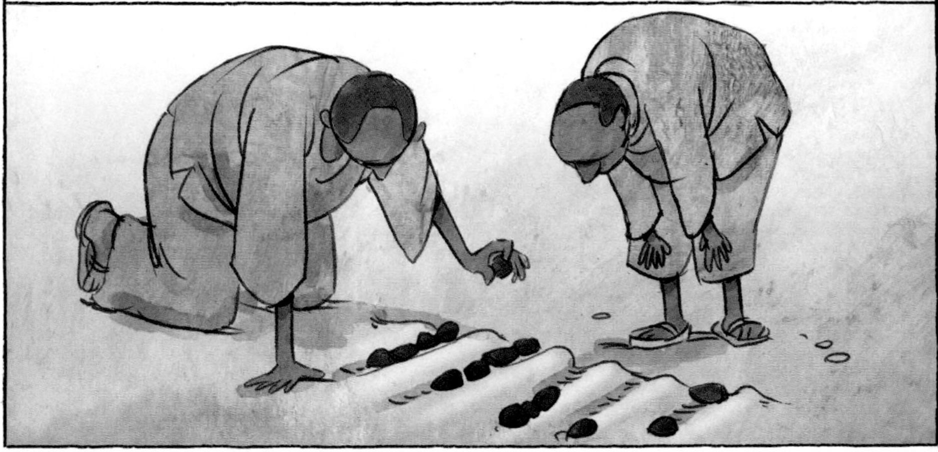

The user kept track of the pebbles in each of the columns. After ten pebbles were counted in the ones column, a pebble would be added to the tens column. When there were ten pebbles in the tens column, a pebble would be placed in the hundreds column. By moving pebbles into and out of the columns, the user could do arithmetic a lot easier than doing it in their head!

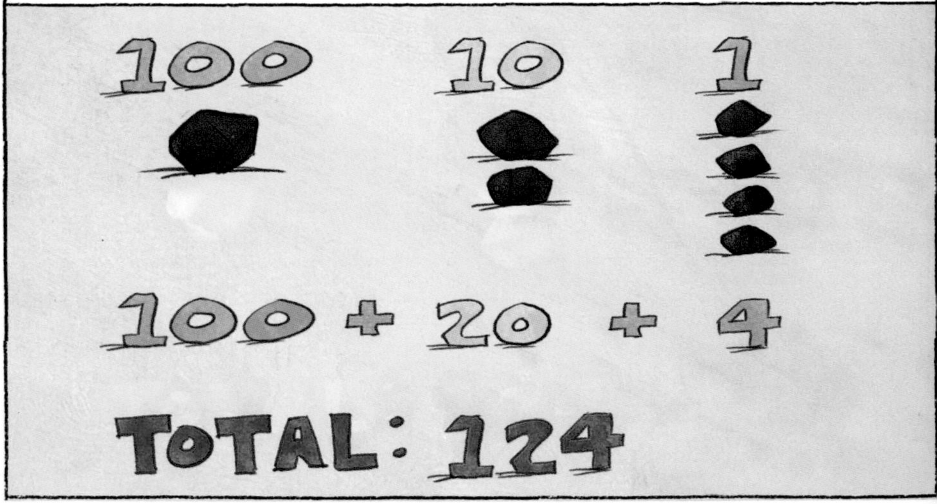
100
10
1
100 + 20 + 4
TOTAL: 124

Eventually people stopped counting in the sand and placed the stones on wooden boards. In time, the stones were replaced with metal counters or beads and the board was reduced to just a frame, called a counting board. We know it as the abacus.

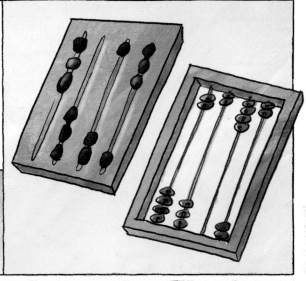

The ancient Greeks and Romans used the abacus, as did the Medieval Europeans. It's still widely used in Asia.

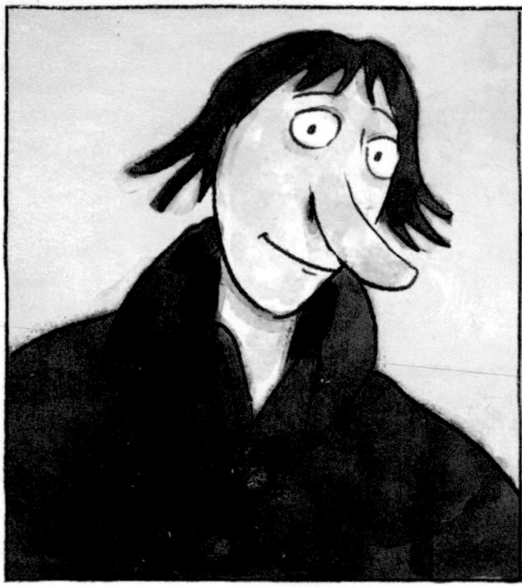

The world had to wait 2,500 years for another big idea to show up—the brainchild of the very brainy Blaise Pascal.

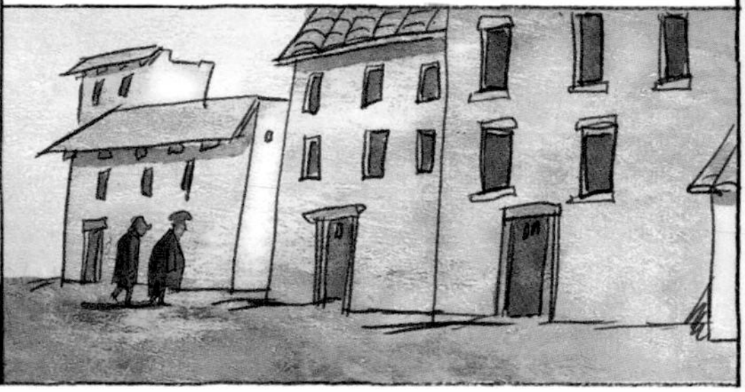

In 1642, Pascal, a nineteen-year-old Frenchman, was working beside his tax-collector father, Etienne.

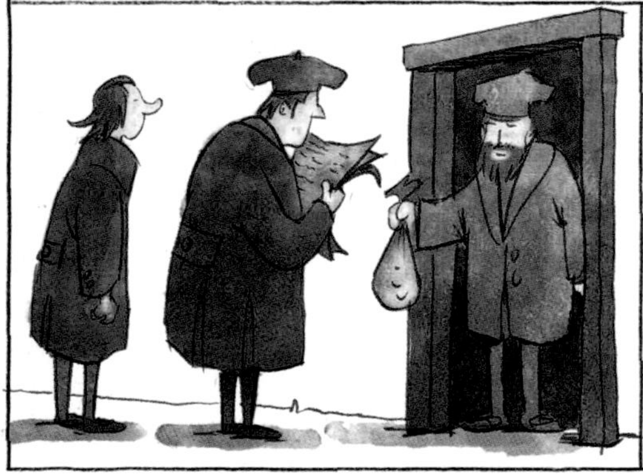

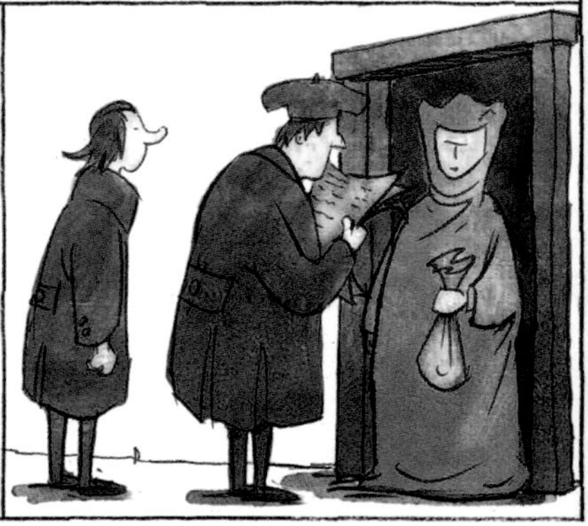

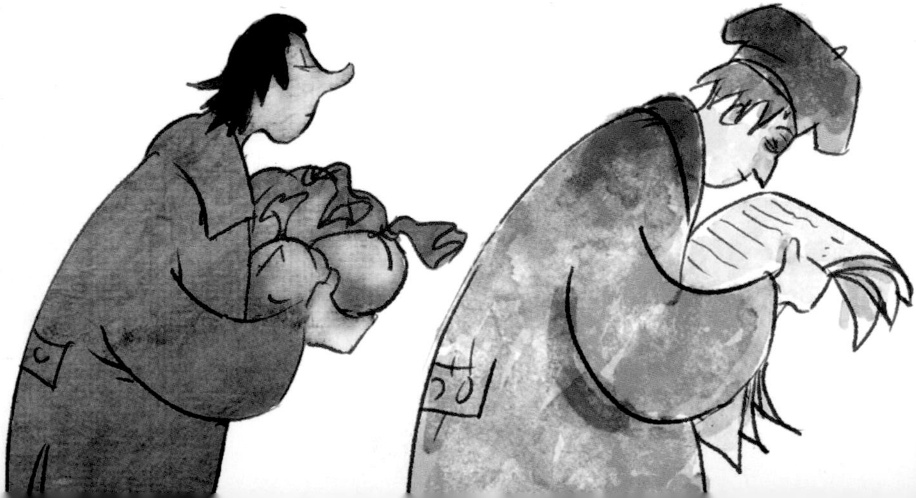

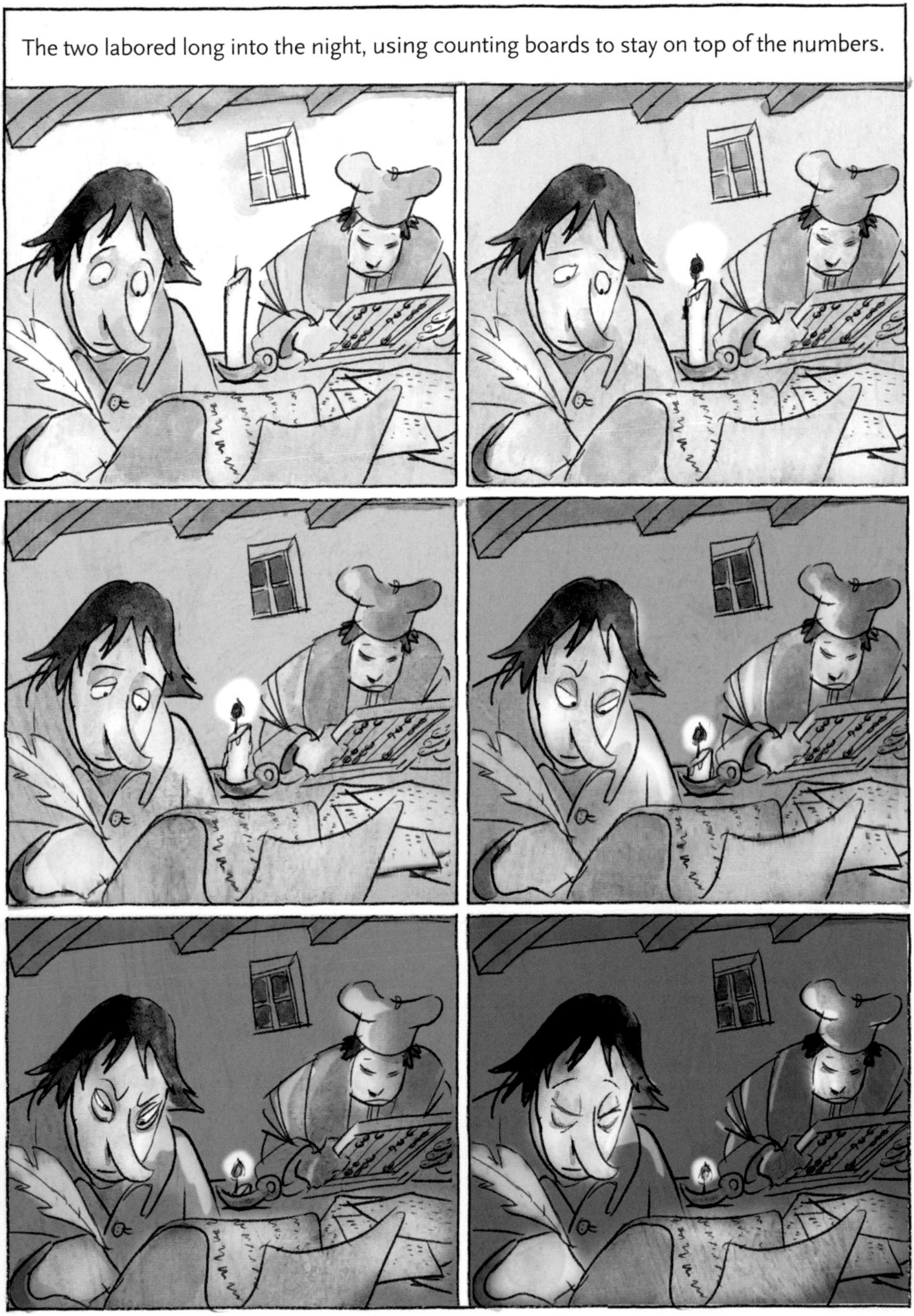
The two labored long into the night, using counting boards to stay on top of the numbers.

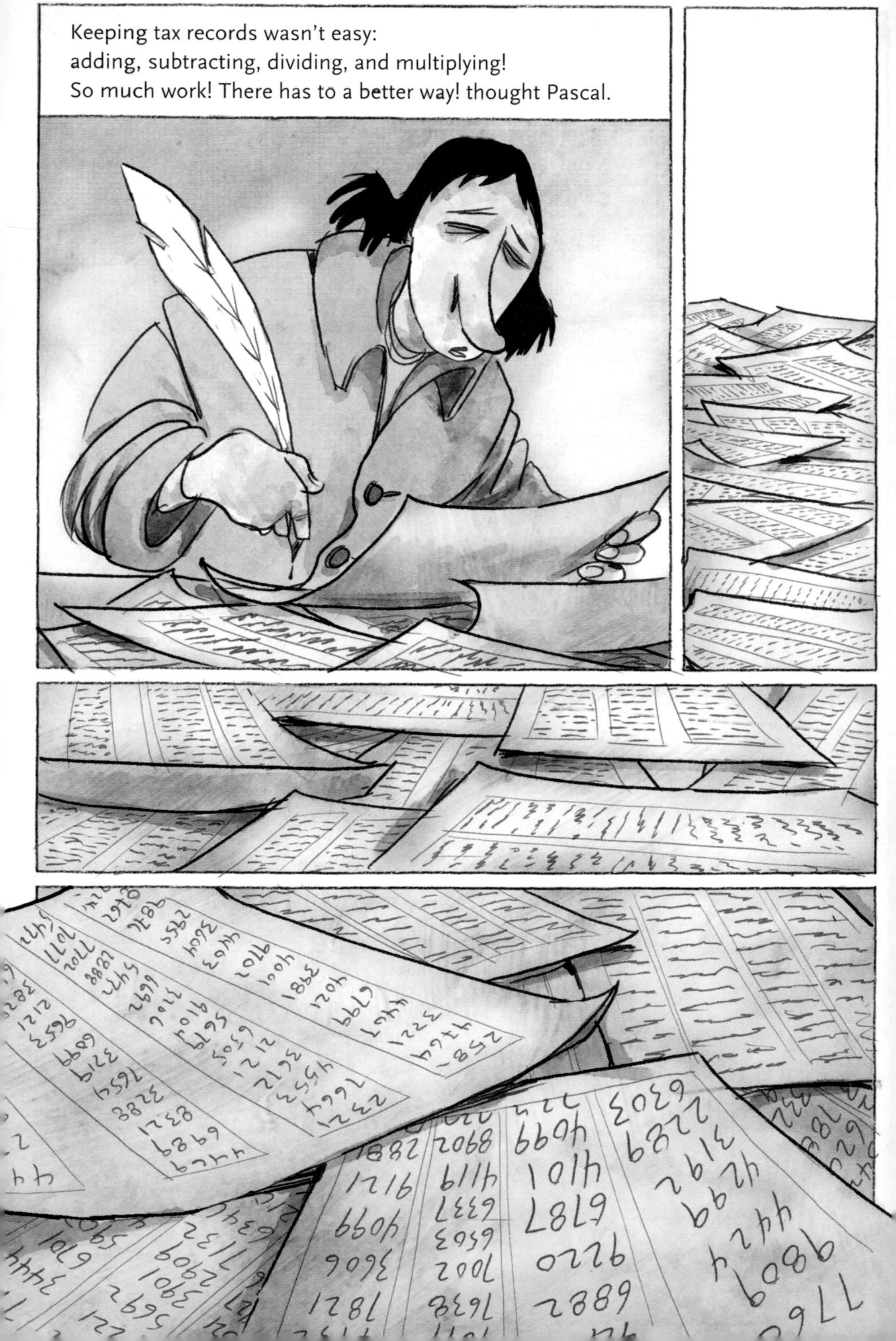
Keeping tax records wasn't easy:
adding, subtracting, dividing, and multiplying!
So much work! There has to a better way! thought Pascal.

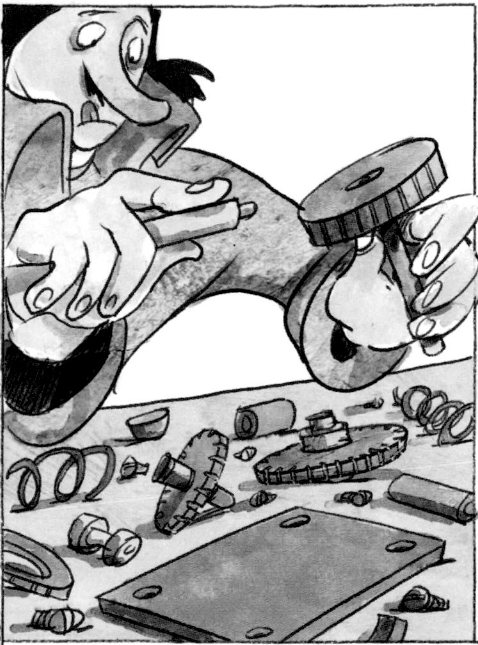

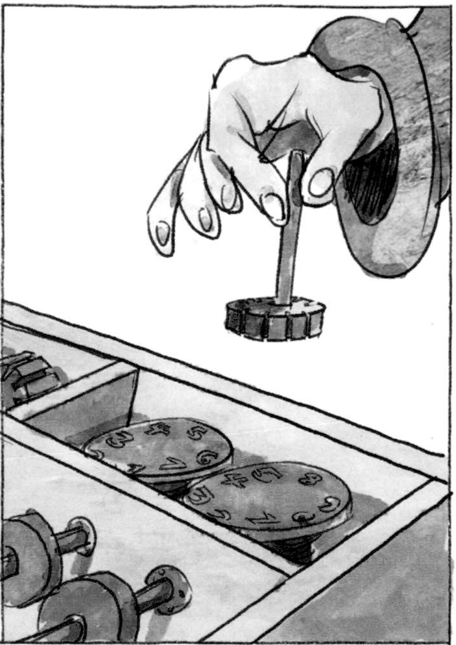

The Pascaline was born. It was a shoebox-sized gadget that used gears, wheels, axles, and dials to add numbers. Not bad for a self-taught engineer!

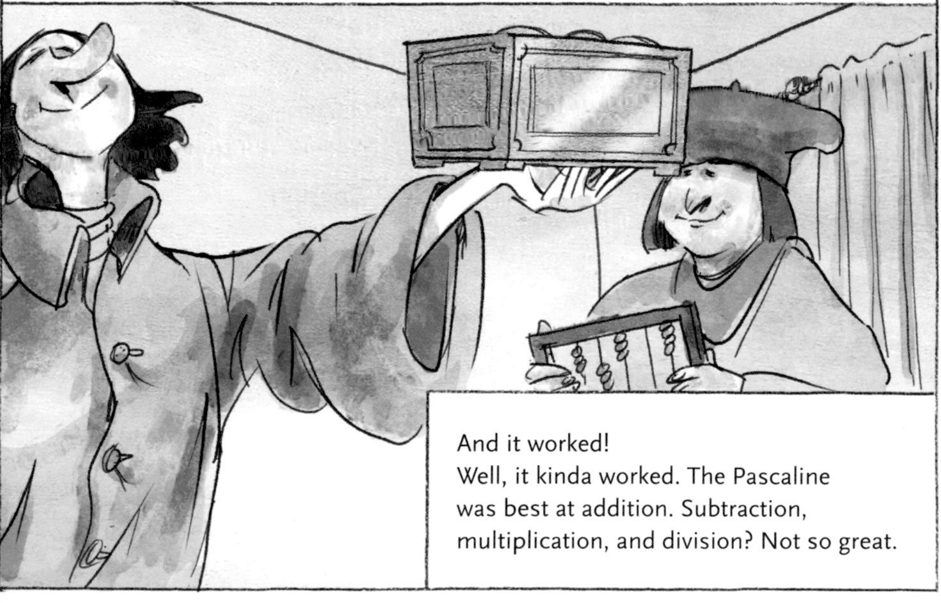
And it worked!
Well, it kinda worked. The Pascaline was best at addition. Subtraction, multiplication, and division? Not so great.

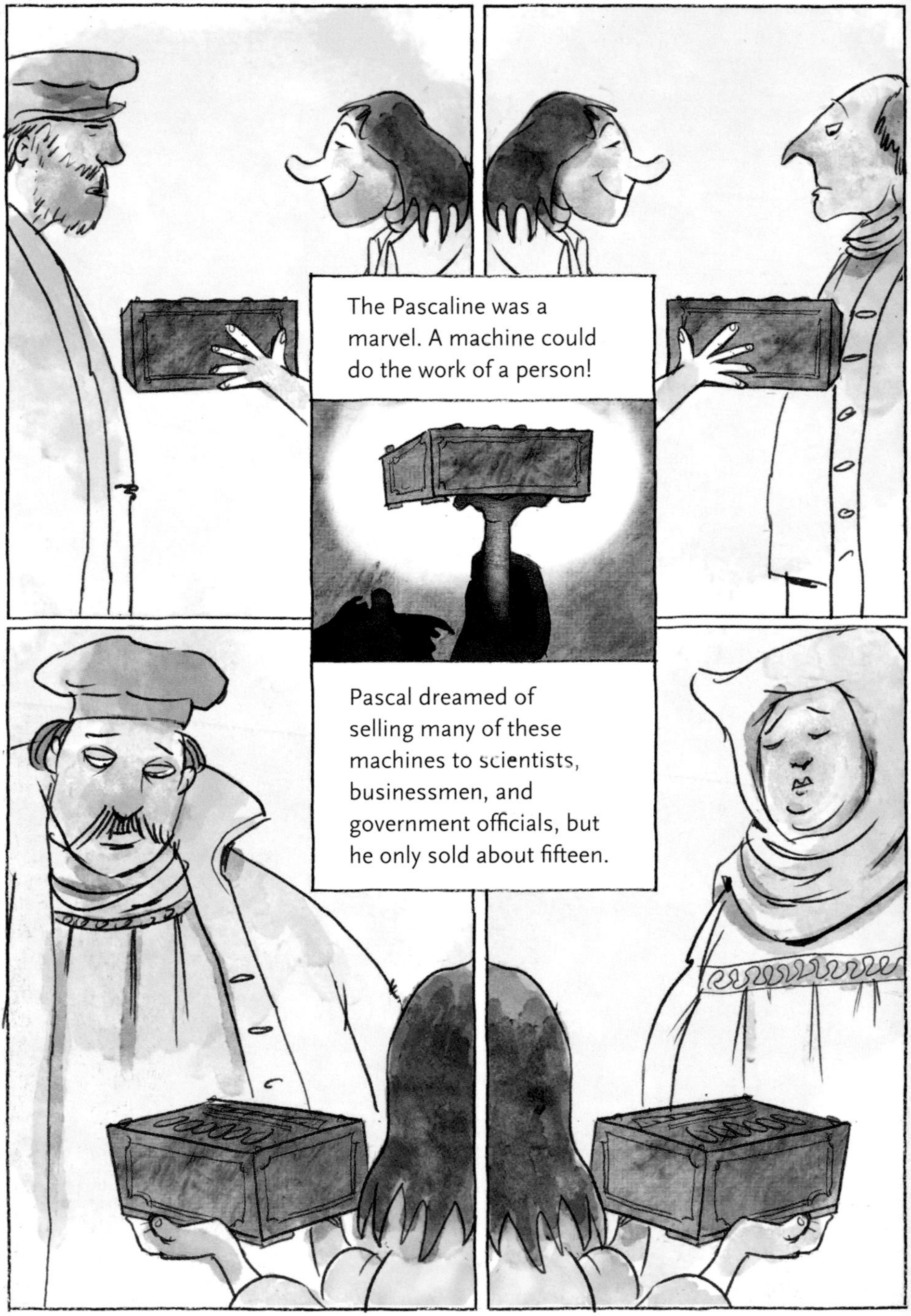
The Pascaline was a marvel. A machine could do the work of a person!
Pascal dreamed of selling many of these machines to scientists, businessmen, and government officials, but he only sold about fifteen.

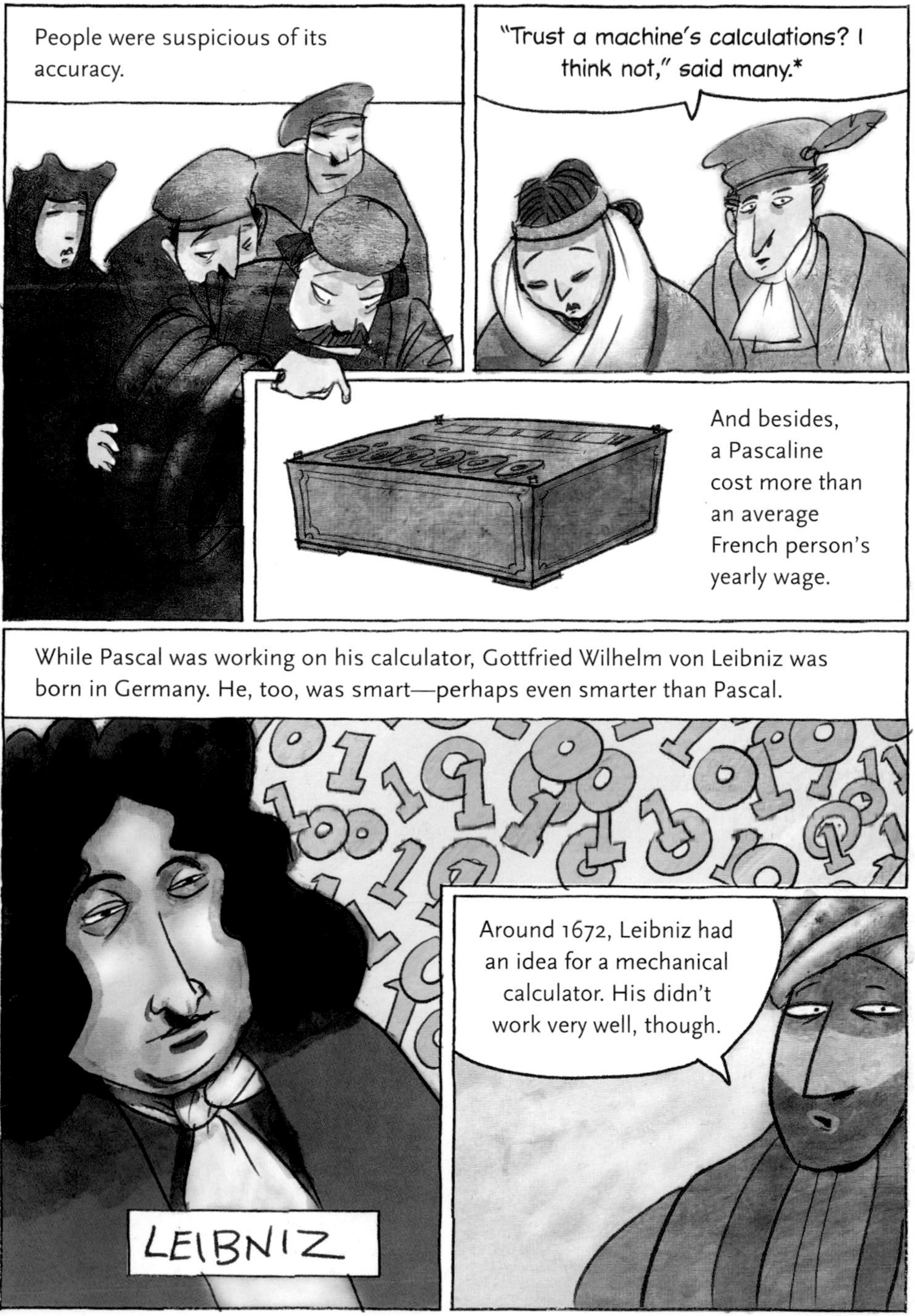
People were suspicious of its accuracy.
"Trust a machine's calculations? I think not," said many.*
And besides, a Pascaline cost more than an average French person's yearly wage.
While Pascal was working on his calculator, Gottfried Wilhelm von Leibniz was born in Germany. He, too, was smart—perhaps even smarter than Pascal.
LEIBNIZ
Around 1672, Leibniz had an idea for a mechanical calculator. His didn't work very well, though.

*Not a real quote

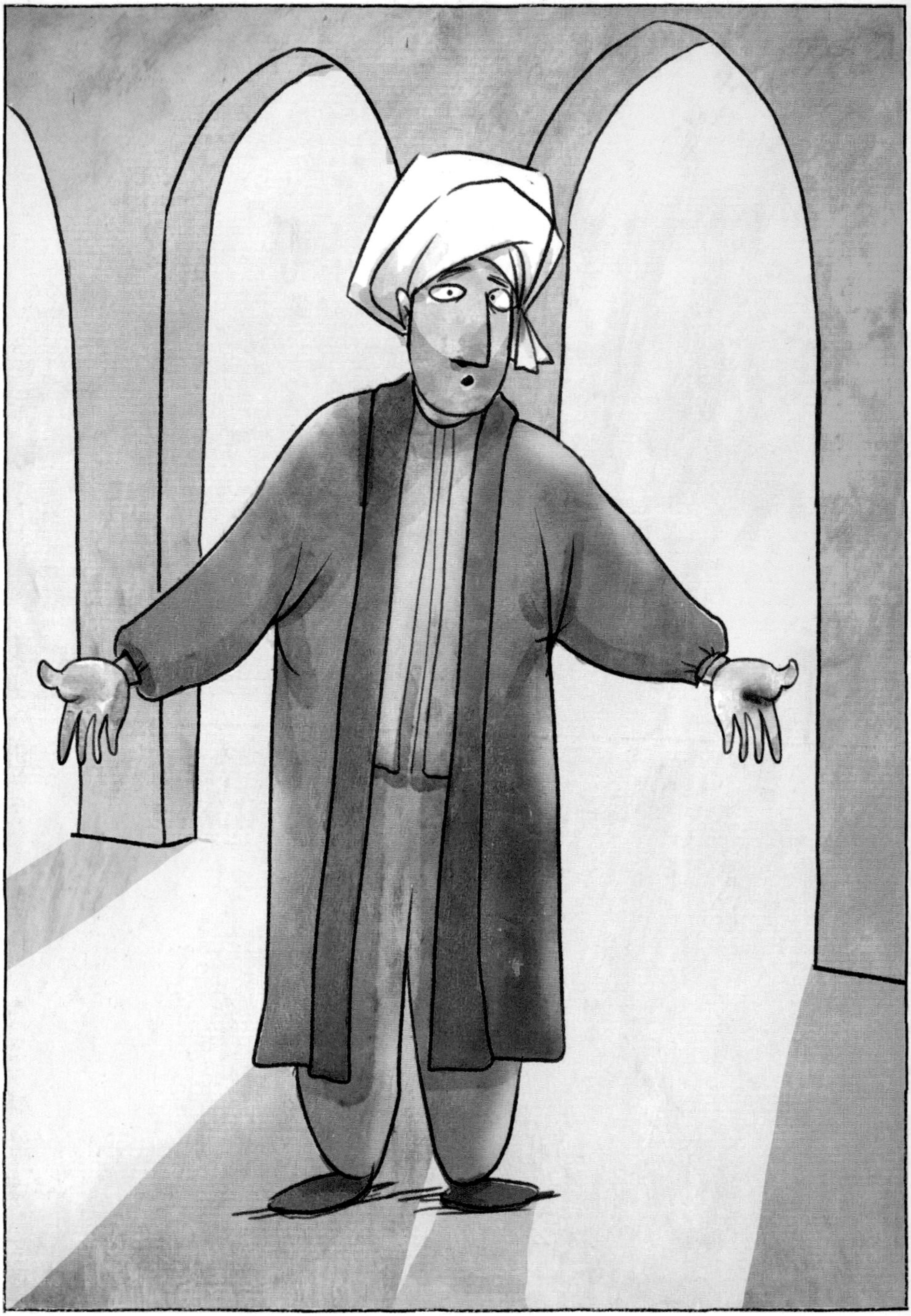

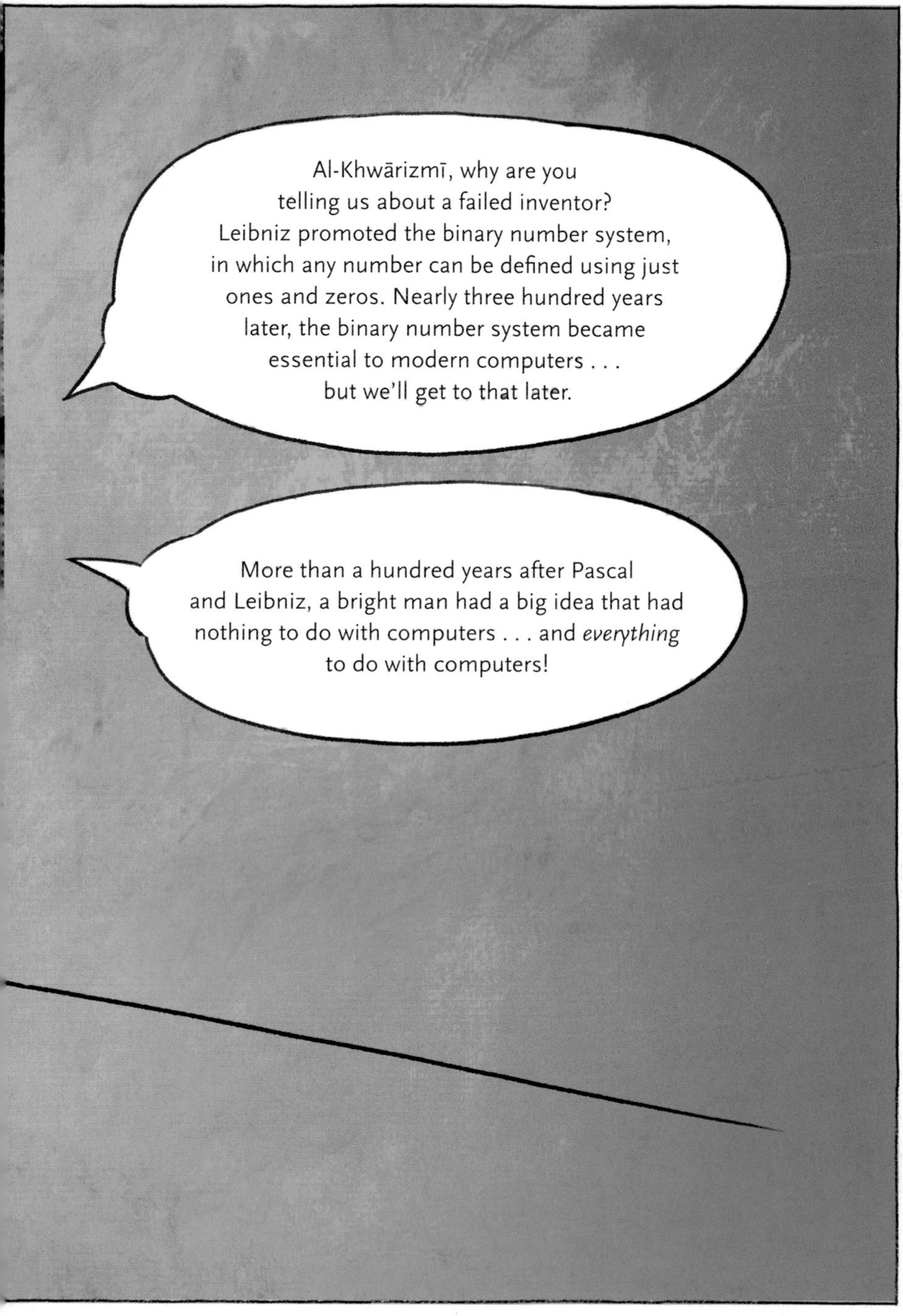
Al-Khwārizmī, why are you telling us about a failed inventor? Leibniz promoted the binary number system, in which any number can be defined using just ones and zeros. Nearly three hundred years later, the binary number system became essential to modern computers . . . but we'll get to that later.
More than a hundred years after Pascal and Leibniz, a bright man had a big idea that had nothing to do with computers . . . and *everything* to do with computers!

Around 1804, French weaver Joseph-Marie Jacquard invented a special loom.

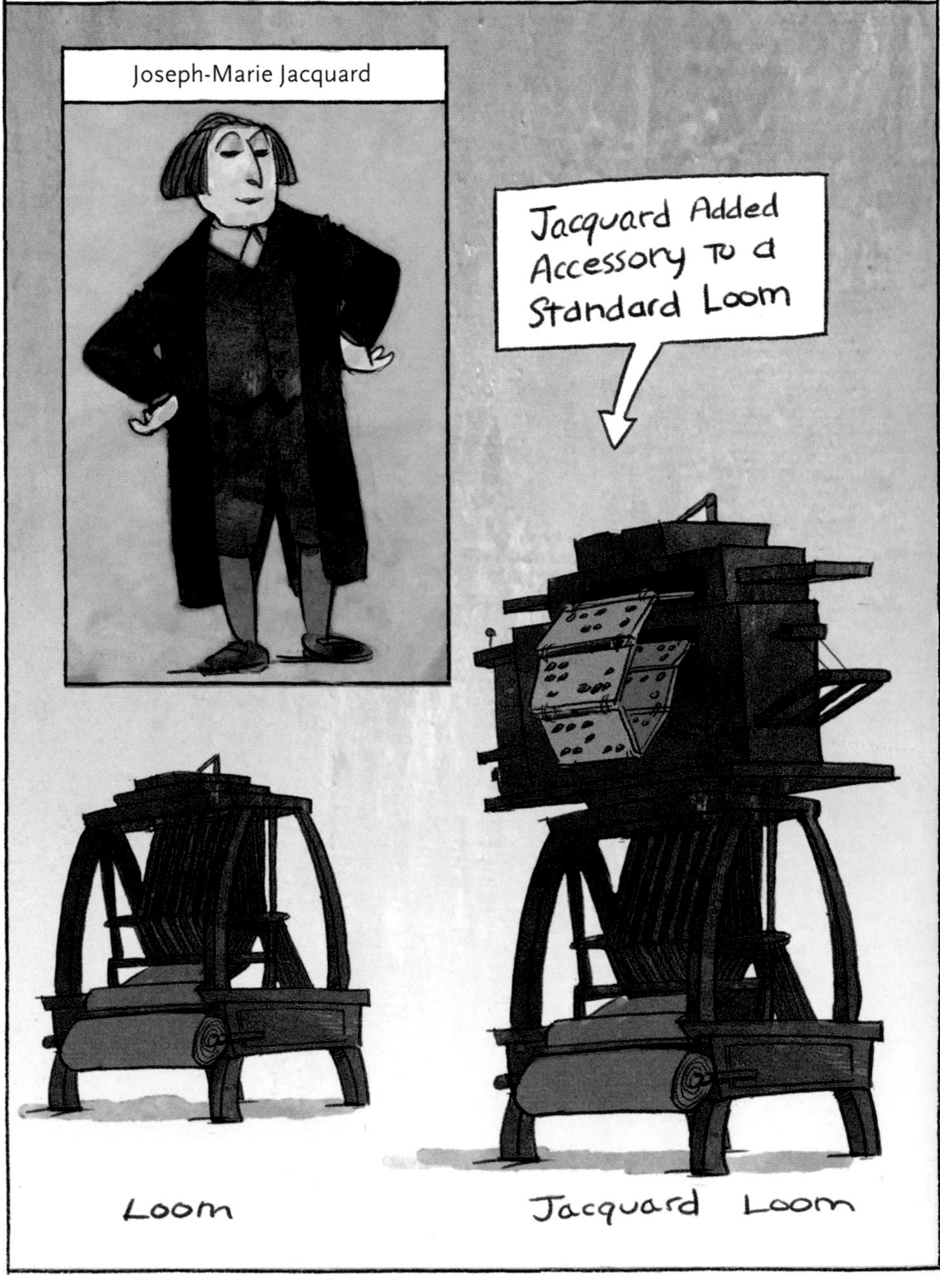
Joseph-Marie Jacquard
Jacquard Added Accessory To a Standard Loom
Loom
Jacquard Loom

A loom is a machine that weaves a set of threads through another set of threads. This is repeated again and again until a bolt of fabric is made.

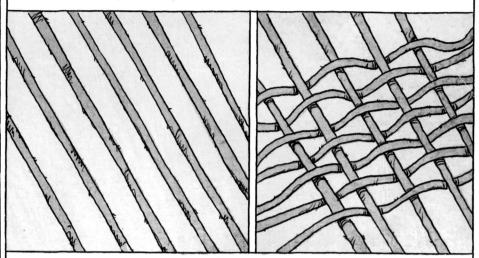

By cleverly using rods in the machine to tug under some threads and over others, a decorative image—a flower, for example—can be woven into the fabric. Jacquard knew that weaving any kind of image by hand was slow, tedious, and difficult. Elaborate images? Forget it! They took months, even years, to create. But Jacquard had a big idea.

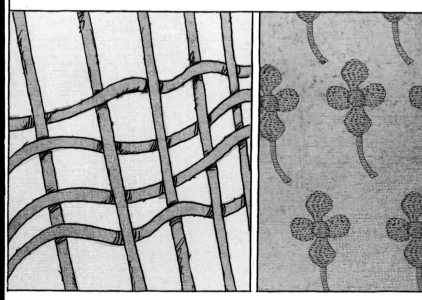

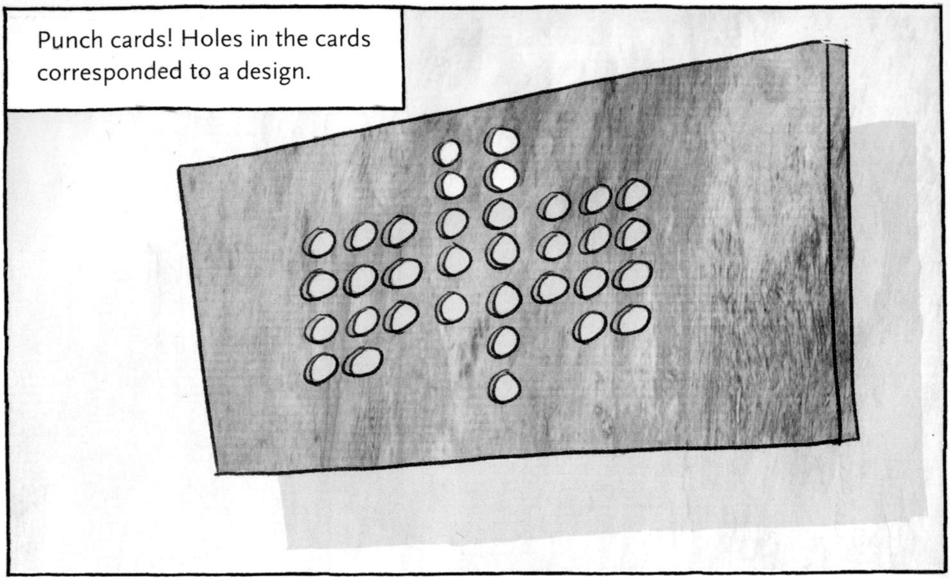
Punch cards! Holes in the cards corresponded to a design.

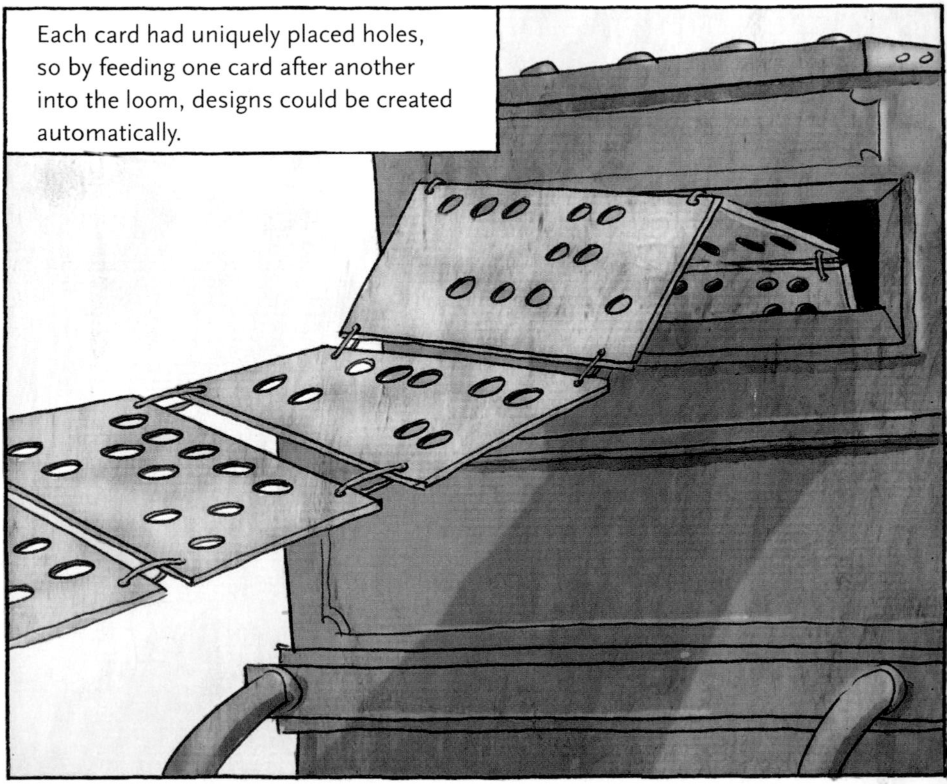
Each card had uniquely placed holes, so by feeding one card after another into the loom, designs could be created automatically.

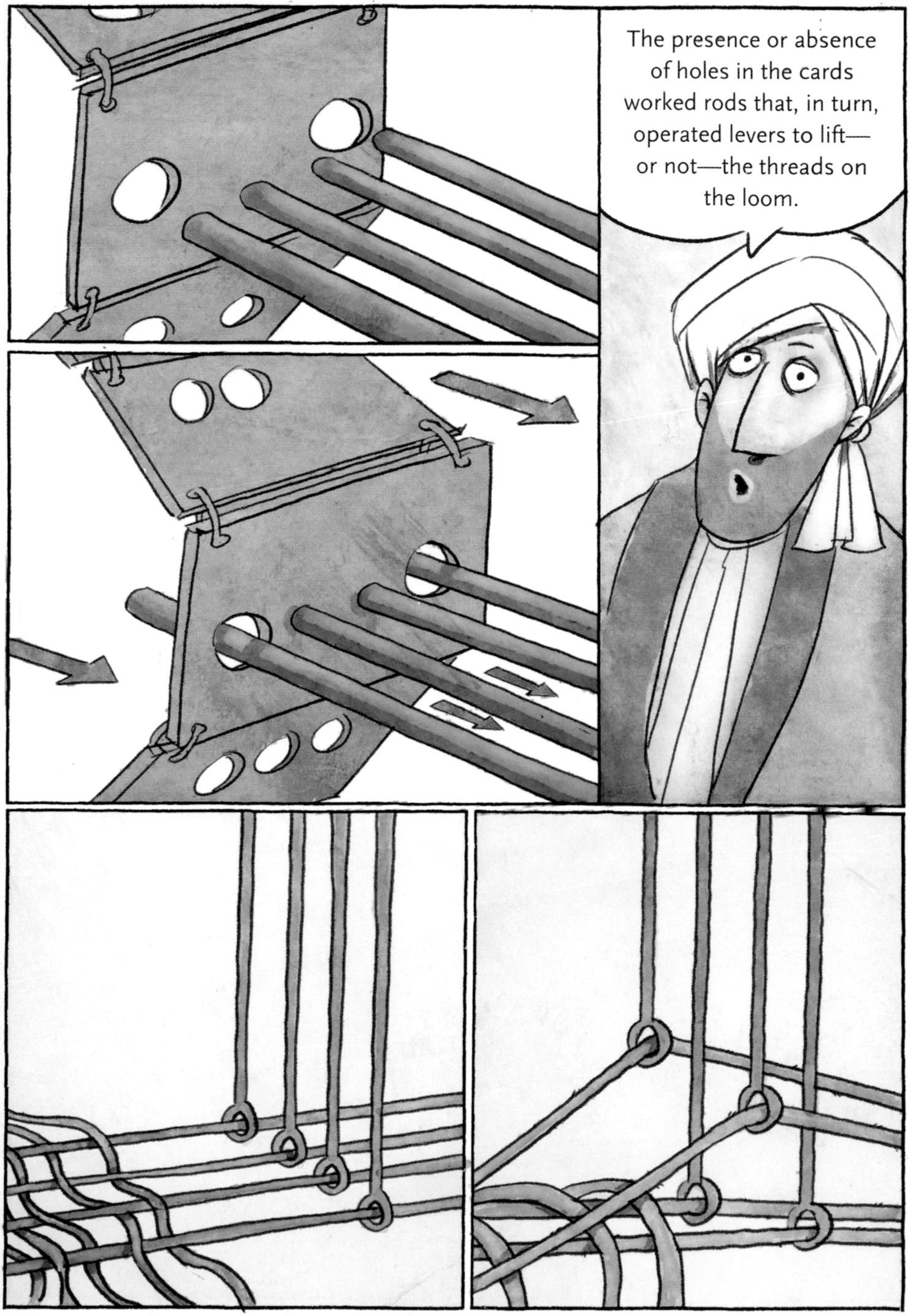
The presence or absence of holes in the cards worked rods that, in turn, operated levers to lift—or not—the threads on the loom.

Jacquard's new and improved loom was a wonder. The French government thought it was so important that it seized control of the machine. Don't worry, ol' Jacquard still received a royalty for every sale.

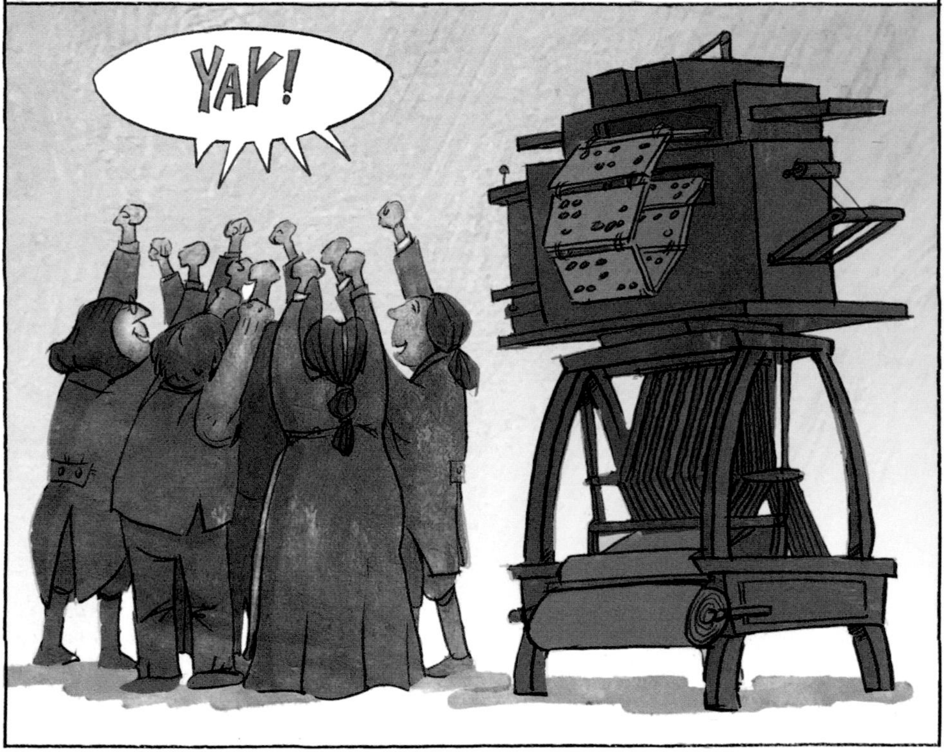
YAY!

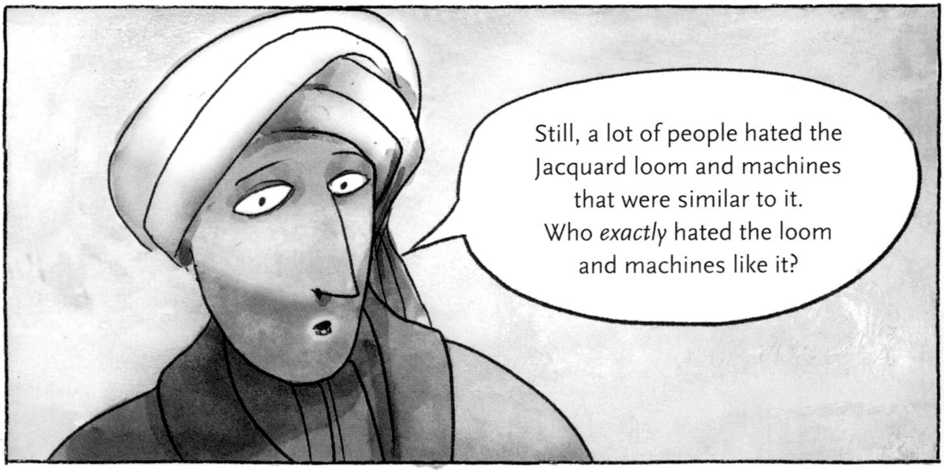
Still, a lot of people hated the Jacquard loom and machines that were similar to it. Who *exactly* hated the loom and machines like it?

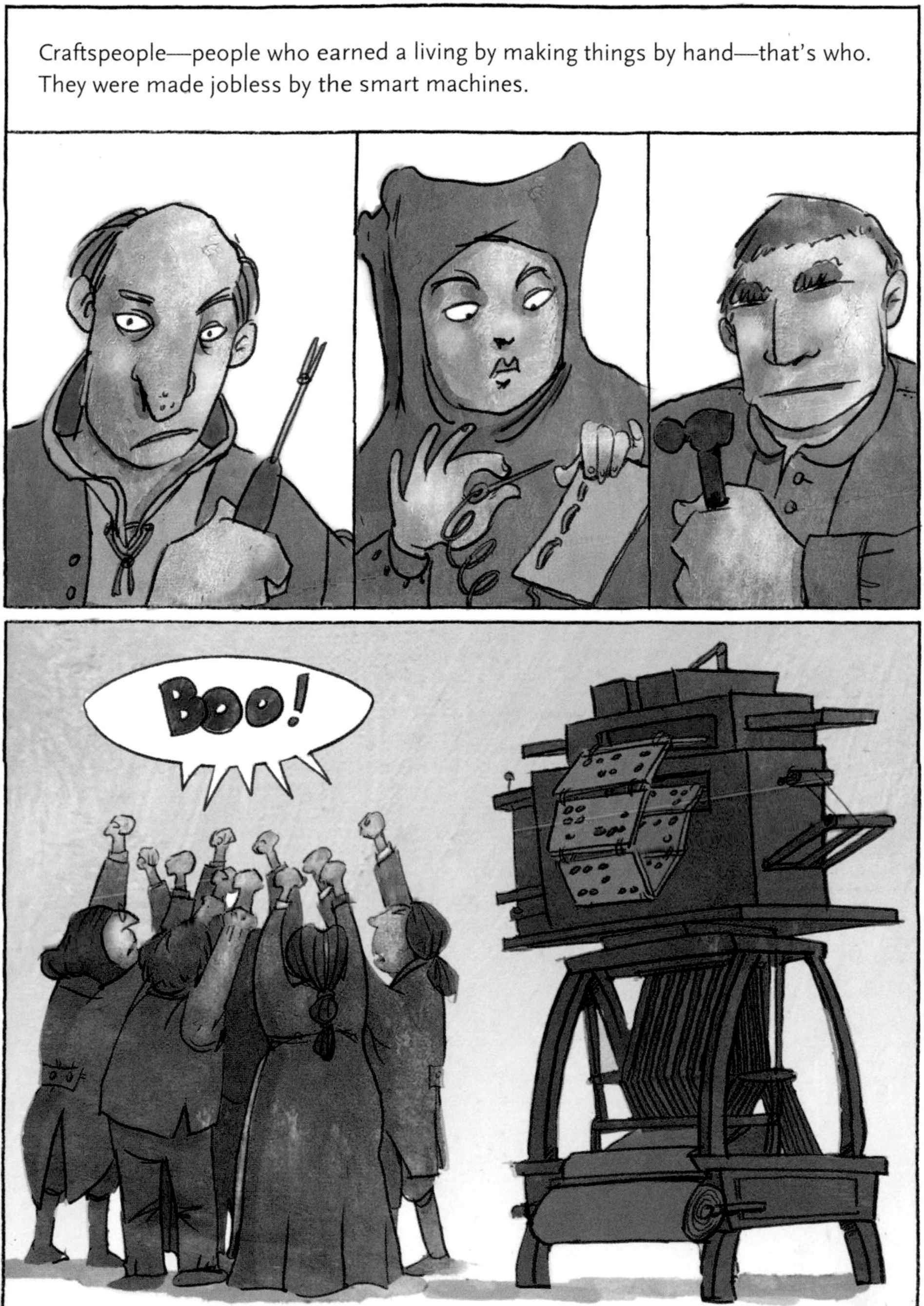
Craftspeople—people who earned a living by making things by hand—that's who. They were made jobless by the smart machines.
BOO!

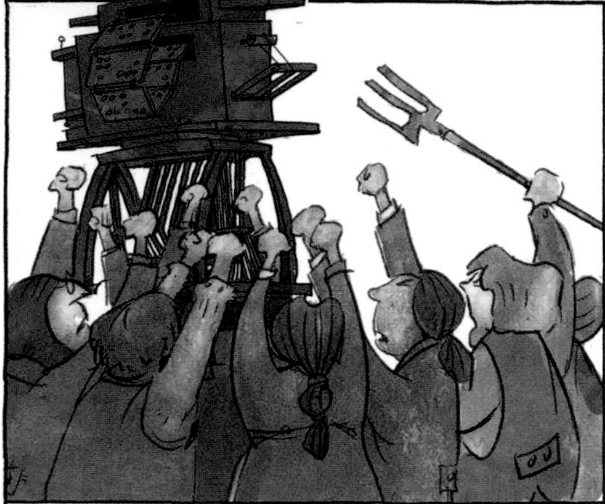

Some, known as Luddites, smashed the machines and even killed the machine owners. They drew their name from Ned Ludd, a weaver who was renowned for smashing knitting machinery. Or was it Ed Ludlam? No one is sure . . . in fact, no one's sure Ludd was real at all!

The Luddites found a sympathetic ear in Lord Byron, a minor member of the English royalty and a very famous poet. When he wasn't writing very famous poems, he declared that workmen were being . . .

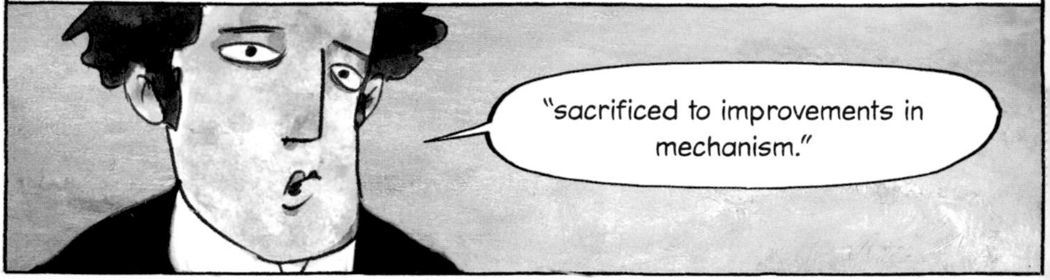
"sacrificed to improvements in mechanism."

That is interesting, but what does the poet Lord Byron have to do with computers?
Lord Byron, *nothing* . . .
but his *daughter* did.

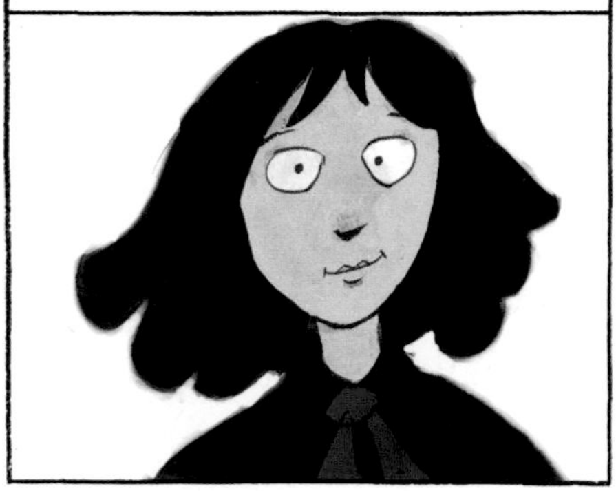

You see, Lord Byron was rowdy and unruly.

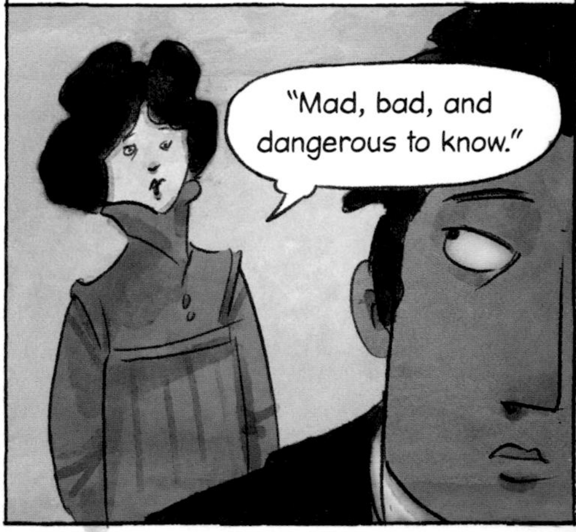
"Mad, bad, and dangerous to know."

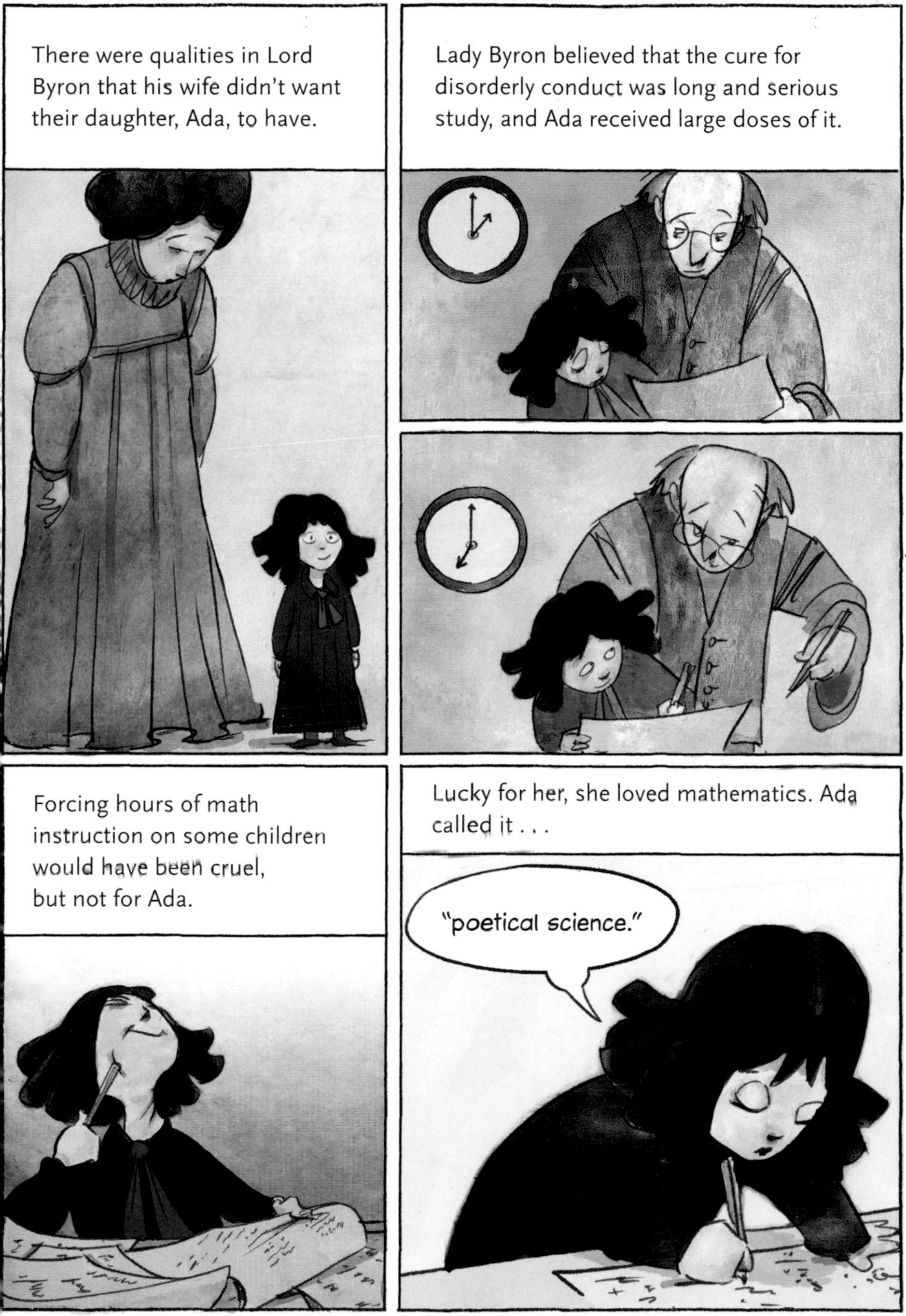
There were qualities in Lord Byron that his wife didn't want their daughter, Ada, to have.
Lady Byron believed that the cure for disorderly conduct was long and serious study, and Ada received large doses of it.
Forcing hours of math instruction on some children would have been cruel, but not for Ada.
Lucky for her, she loved mathematics. Ada called it . . .
"poetical science."

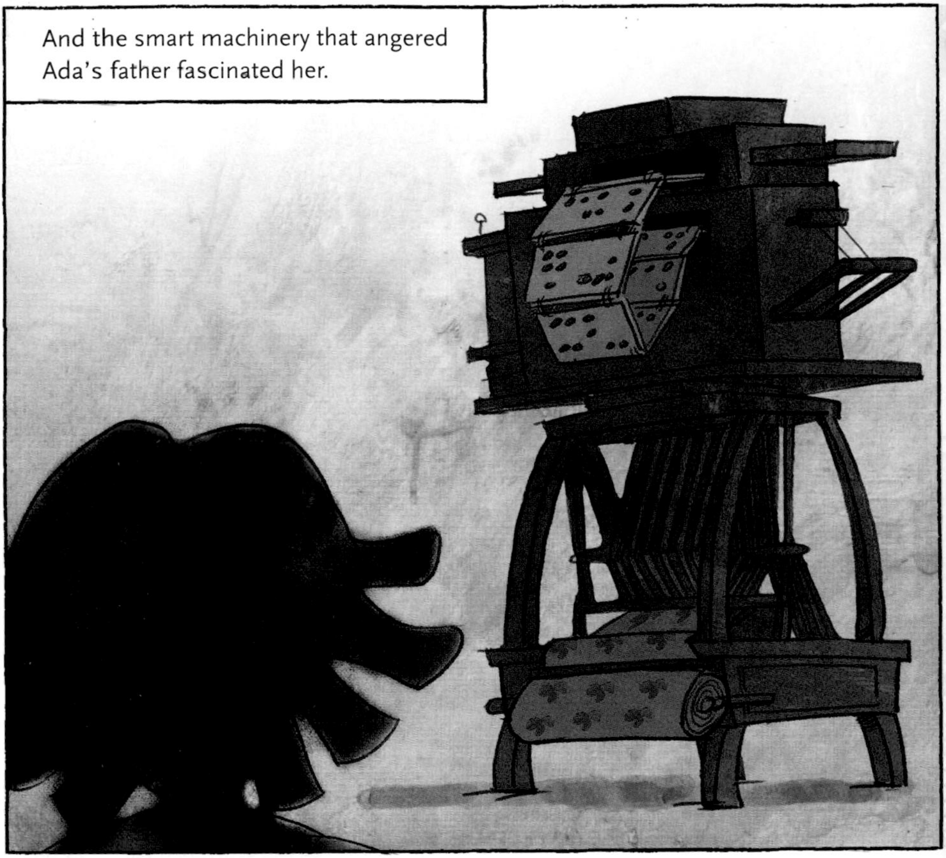
And the smart machinery that angered Ada's father fascinated her.

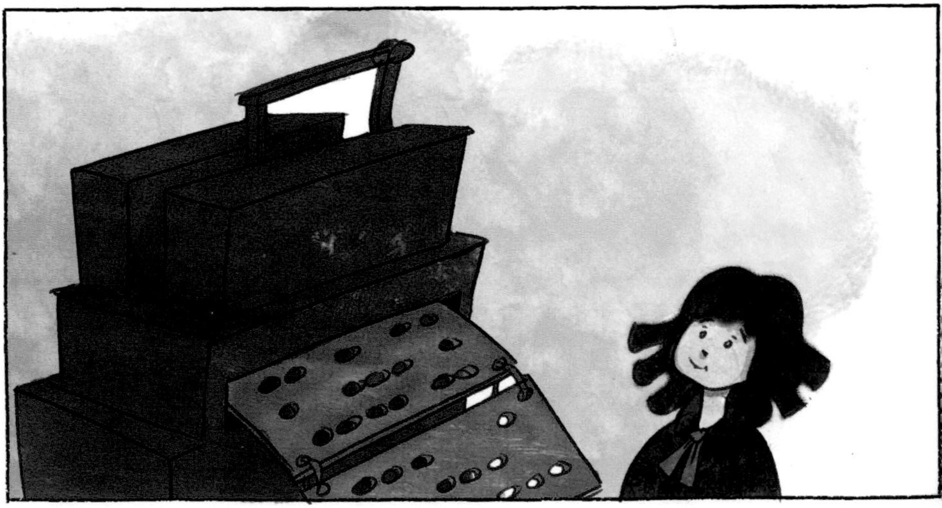

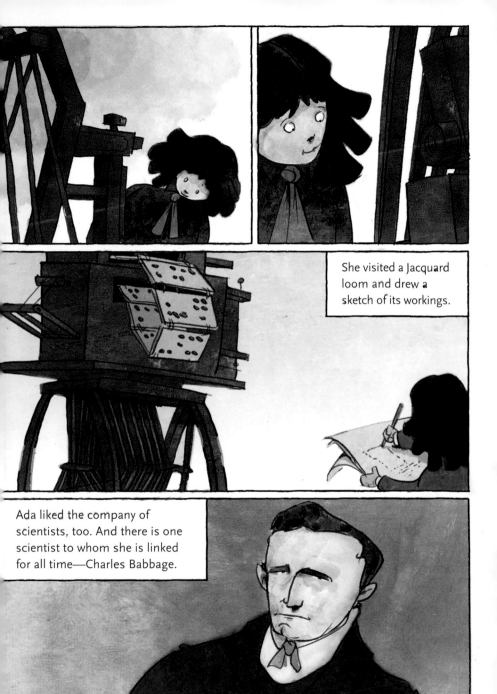

She visited a Jacquard loom and drew a sketch of its workings.

Ada liked the company of scientists, too. And there is one scientist to whom she is linked for all time—Charles Babbage.

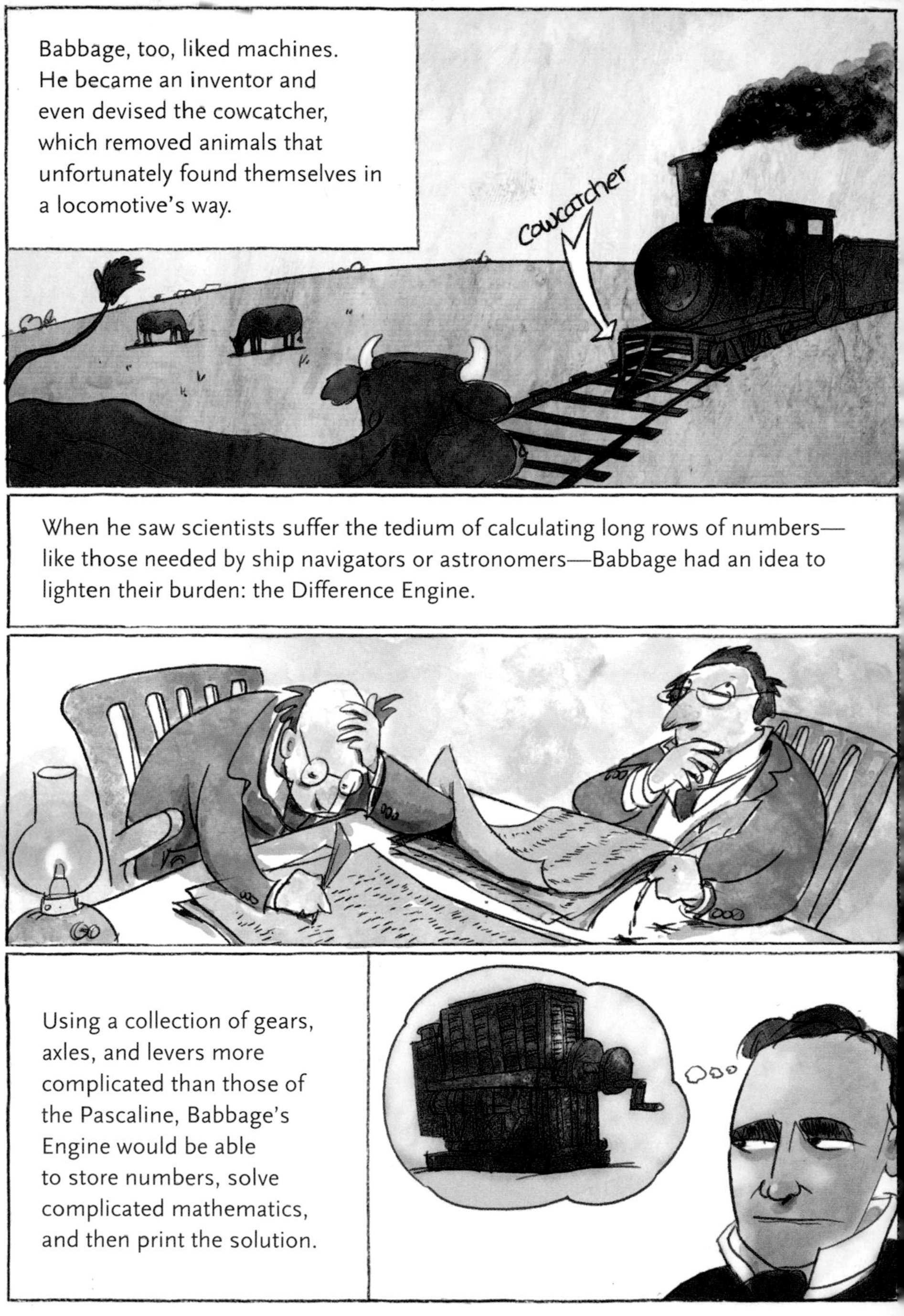
Babbage, too, liked machines. He became an inventor and even devised the cowcatcher, which removed animals that unfortunately found themselves in a locomotive's way.
Cowcatcher
When he saw scientists suffer the tedium of calculating long rows of numbers—like those needed by ship navigators or astronomers—Babbage had an idea to lighten their burden: the Difference Engine.
Using a collection of gears, axles, and levers more complicated than those of the Pascaline, Babbage's Engine would be able to store numbers, solve complicated mathematics, and then print the solution.

It promised to be astonishing, and the English government paid for its construction, spending more on it than they would have for a warship.

But after ten years, there was little to show.

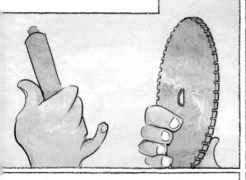

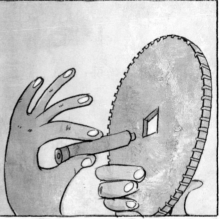

The precisely made gears, levers, axles, and wheels needed to make the Engine work were beyond the skills of metalworkers of the day.

But Babbage wasn't discouraged. He bubbled with ideas and hit upon something even better! The Analytical Engine.

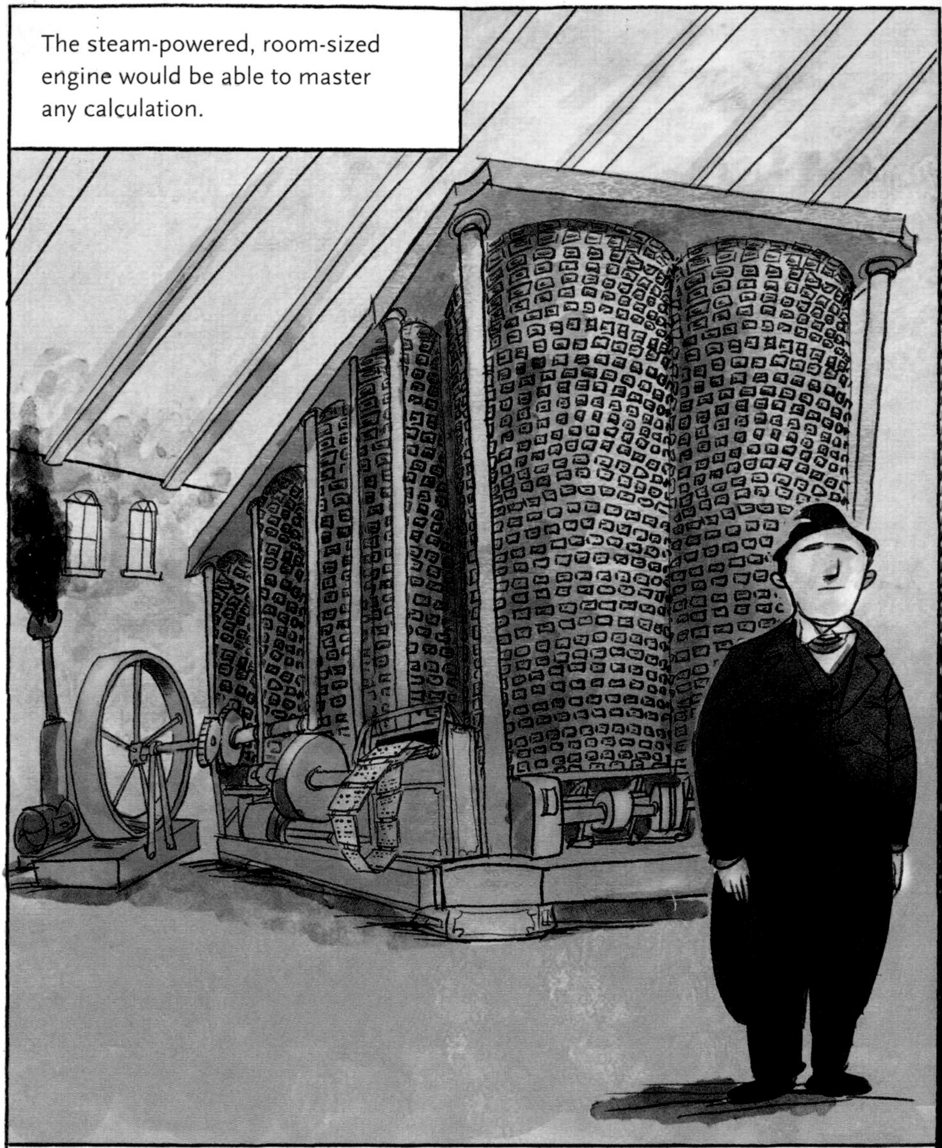
The steam-powered, room-sized engine would be able to master any calculation.

Babbage envisioned it to have four parts: the *reader*, where data—information—could be entered into the machine; the *store*, where data would be kept; the *mill*, where calculations would take place; and the *printer* that would print the solution to the calculations . . . all the elements we find in a modern computer!

The Analytical Engine would be controlled by . . . punch cards!
Inspired by Jacquard's loom, Babbage intended to use the holes in punch cards to set functions, make calculations, and print results.

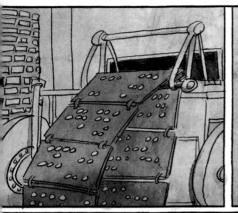
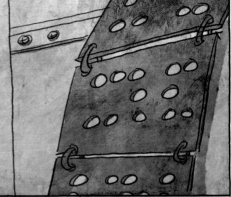

Babbage's cards were more inventive than the Frenchman's. By restricting or allowing rods and pins in the machine to engage levers, gears, and switches, the cards could instruct the machine to enter numbers, compute, and even change its course of action based on the outcome of its calculation!

All this talk about punch cards brings us back to Ada Byron.

What, you thought I had forgotten about her?

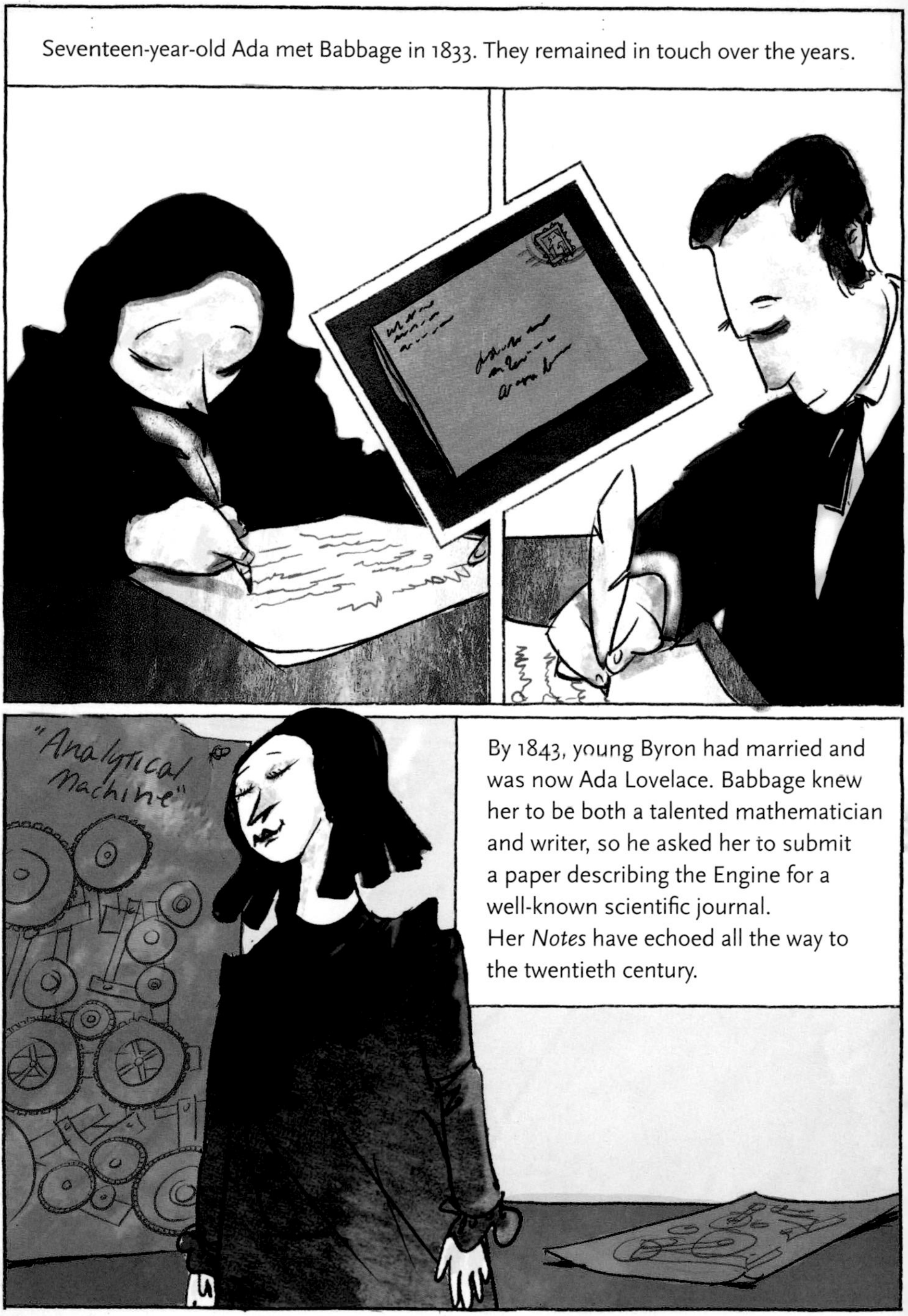
Seventeen-year-old Ada met Babbage in 1833. They remained in touch over the years.
"Analytical machine"
By 1843, young Byron had married and was now Ada Lovelace. Babbage knew her to be both a talented mathematician and writer, so he asked her to submit a paper describing the Engine for a well-known scientific journal.
Her *Notes* have echoed all the way to the twentieth century.

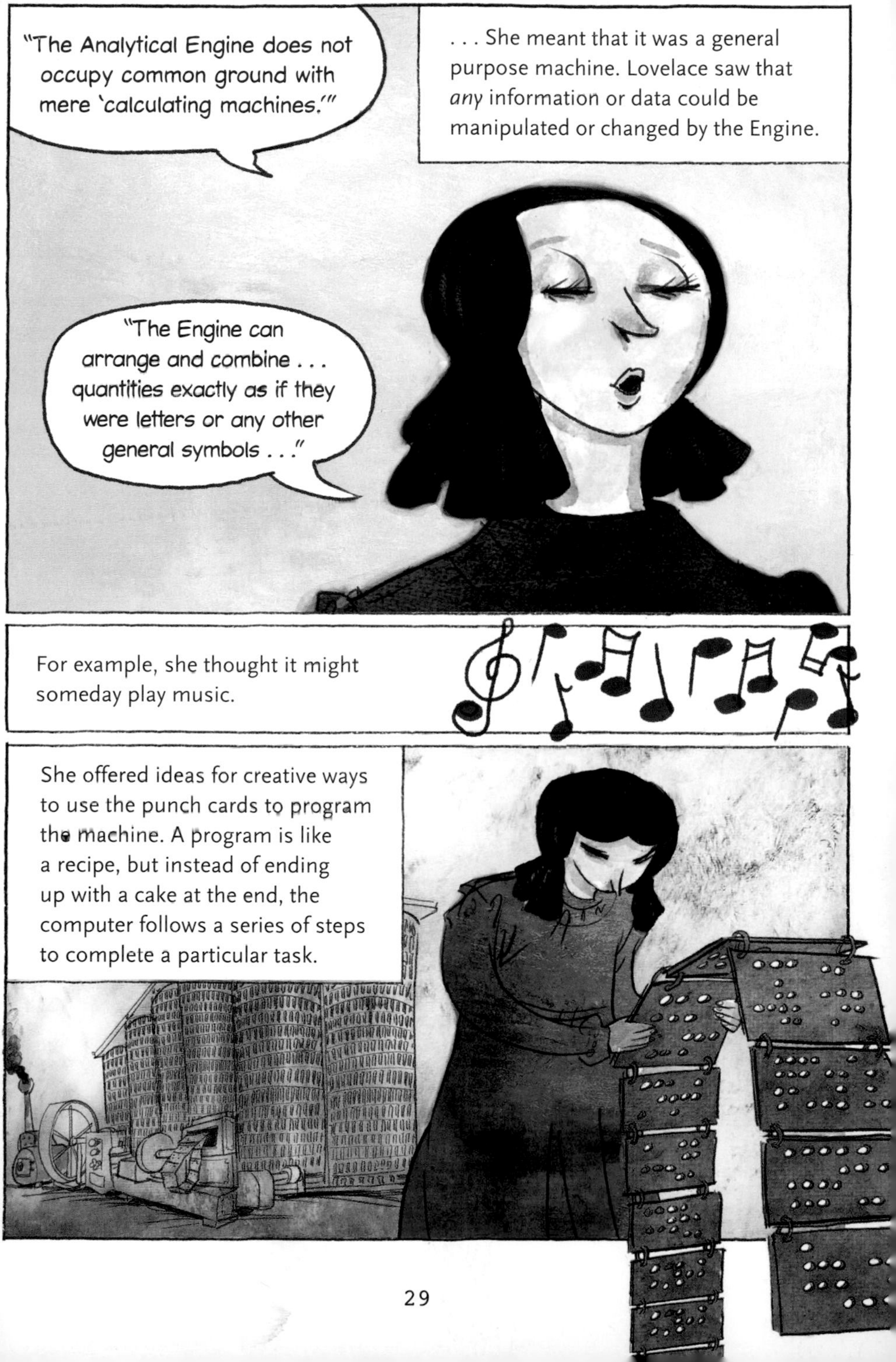
"The Analytical Engine does not occupy common ground with mere 'calculating machines.'"
. . . She meant that it was a general purpose machine. Lovelace saw that *any* information or data could be manipulated or changed by the Engine.
"The Engine can arrange and combine . . . quantities exactly as if they were letters or any other general symbols . . ."
For example, she thought it might someday play music.
She offered ideas for creative ways to use the punch cards to program the machine. A program is like a recipe, but instead of ending up with a cake at the end, the computer follows a series of steps to complete a particular task.

Lovelace fell ill and died at age thirty-six. Babbage lived to seventy-nine, closing out his life as a bit of a crank.

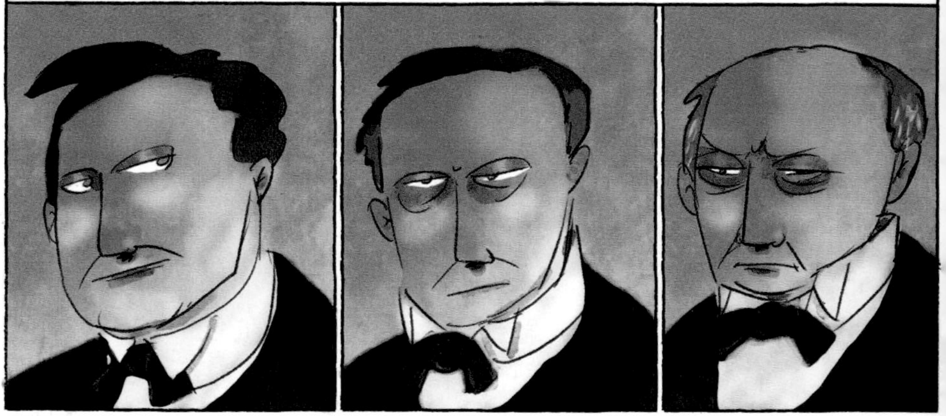

He and his friend, writer Charles Dickens, worked to outlaw street musicians and the noise they made.

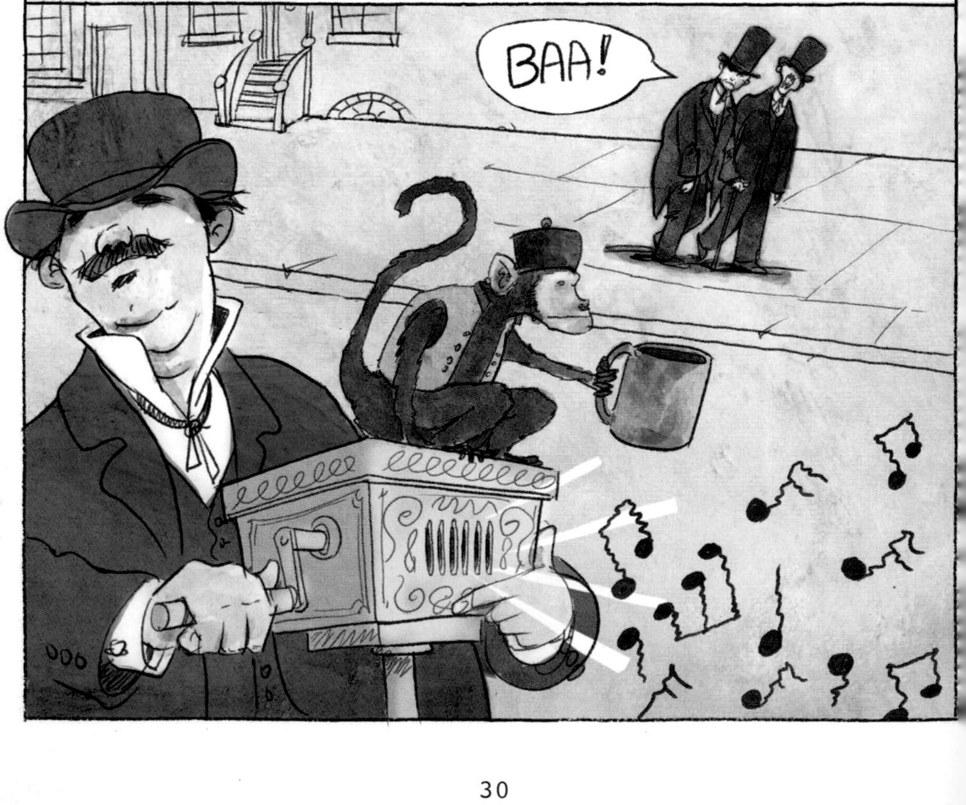
BAA!

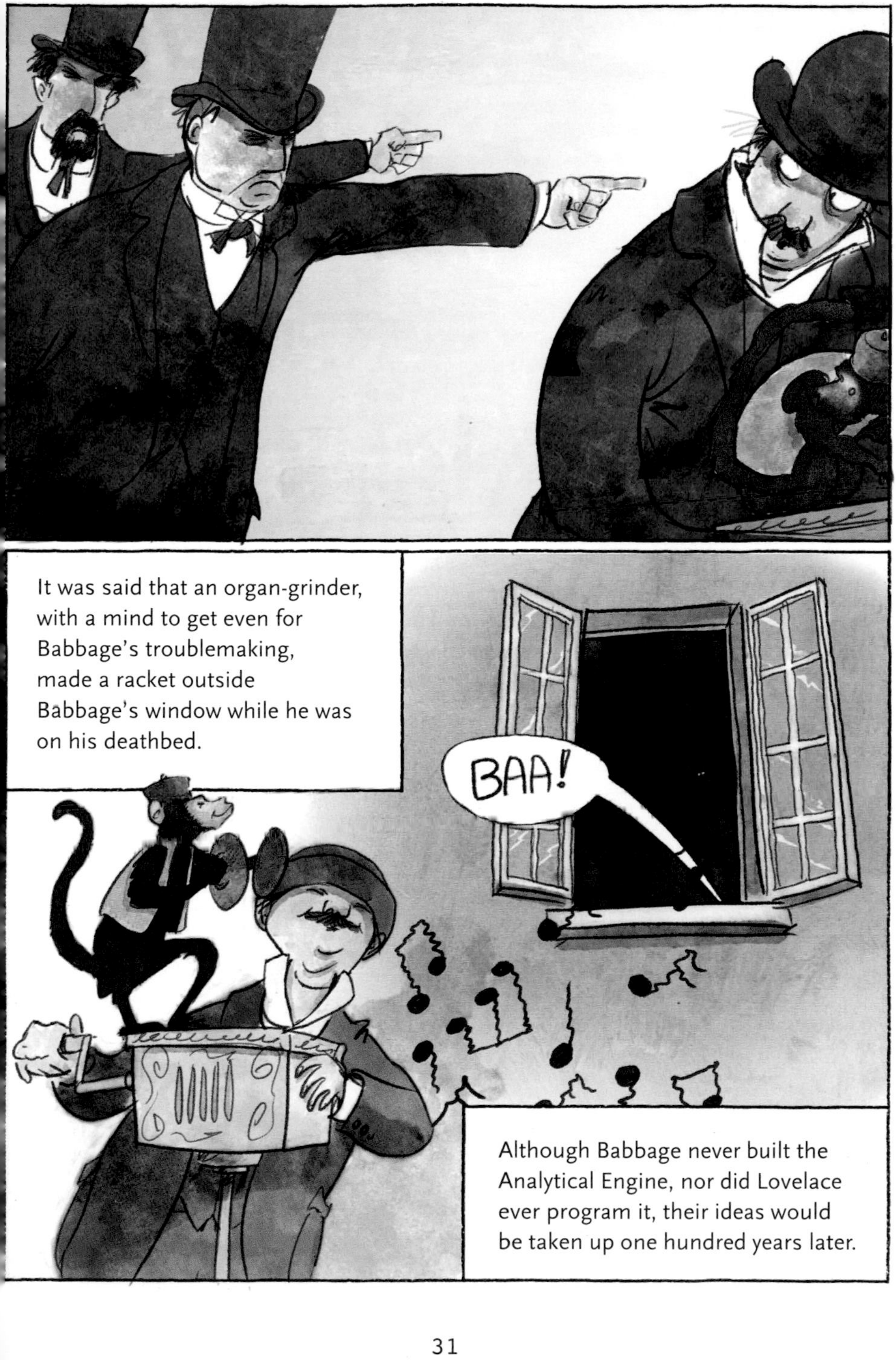
It was said that an organ-grinder, with a mind to get even for Babbage's troublemaking, made a racket outside Babbage's window while he was on his deathbed.
BAA!
Although Babbage never built the Analytical Engine, nor did Lovelace ever program it, their ideas would be taken up one hundred years later.

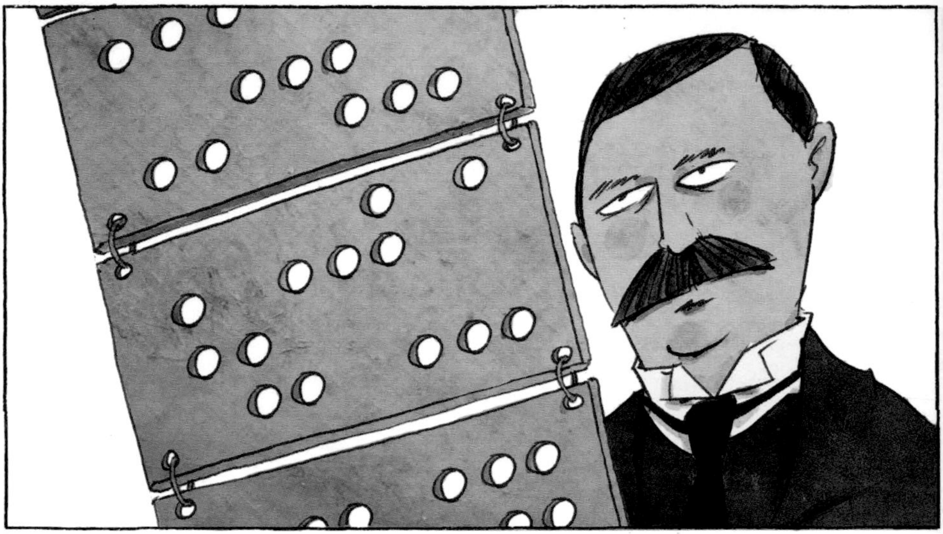

In the meantime, punch cards proved important to American engineer Herman Hollerith and the United States Census Office. Before Hollerith, the Census Office counted America's population every ten years entirely by hand, including details within the count such as gender—that is, man or woman—birthplace, and job.

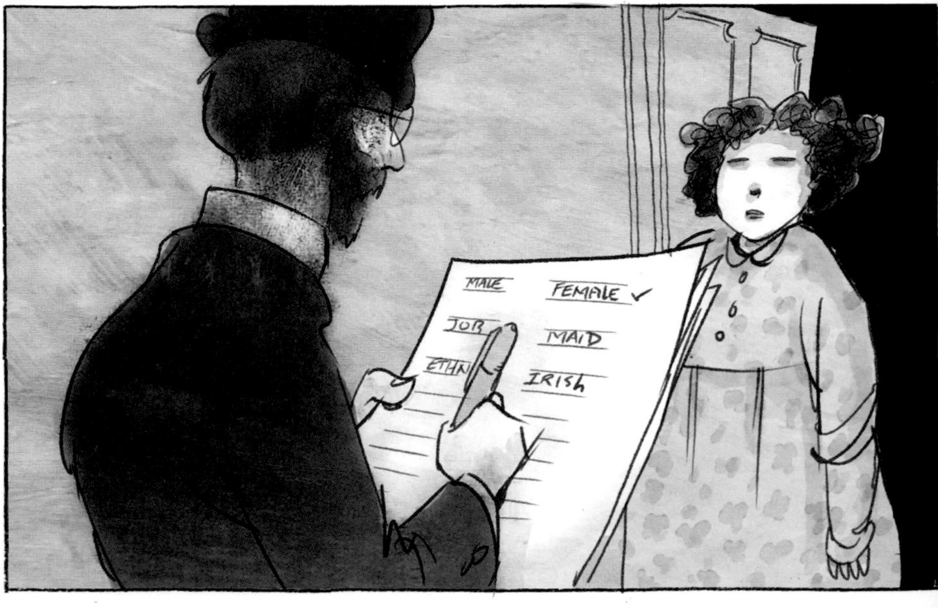
MALE
FEMALE ✓
JOB
MAID
ETHN
IRISH

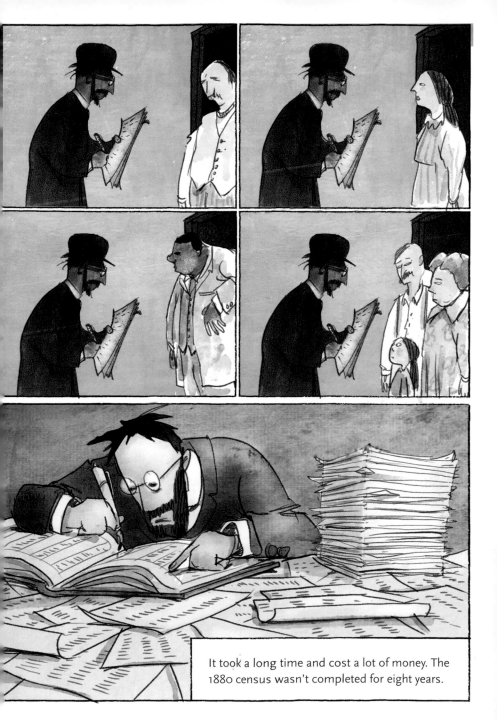

It took a long time and cost a lot of money. The 1880 census wasn't completed for eight years.

Instead of entering the data on sheets of paper, Hollerith entered it as exact positions on punch cards. For example, a specially placed hole in the card showed the person was a farmer. Other holes might indicate the person was female or had been born in Ireland.

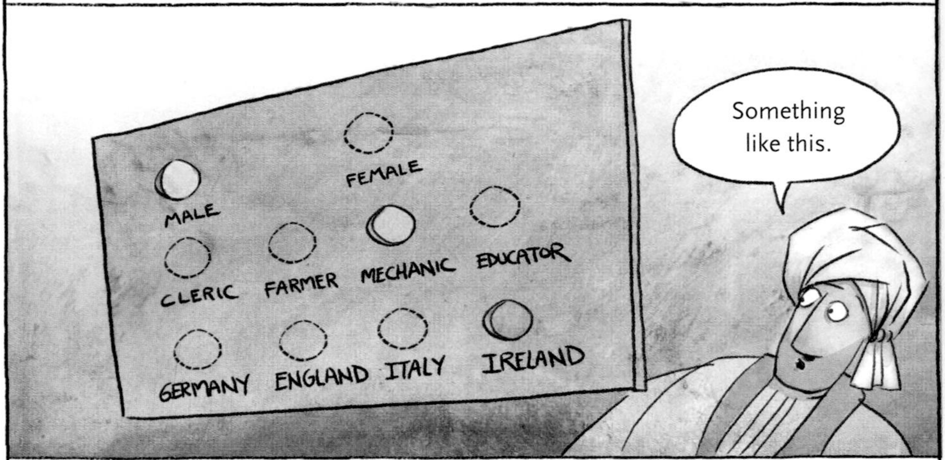
FEMALE
MALE
CLERIC
FARMER
MECHANIC
EDUCATOR
GERMANY
ENGLAND
ITALY
IRELAND
Something like this.

Hollerith then built a machine that read the cards by noting where electrical connections were completed at the holes, and then tabulated the results.

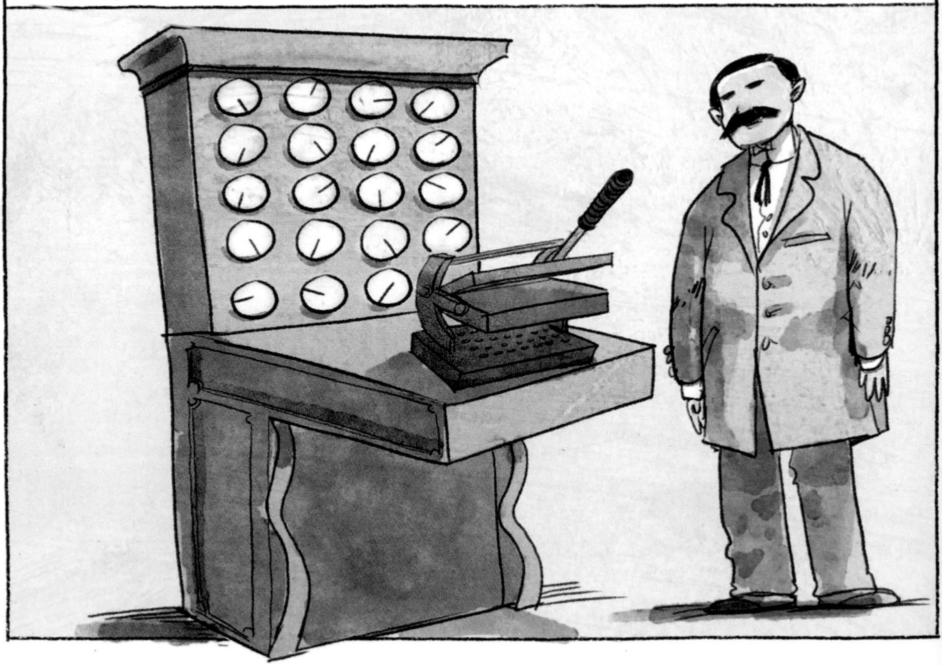

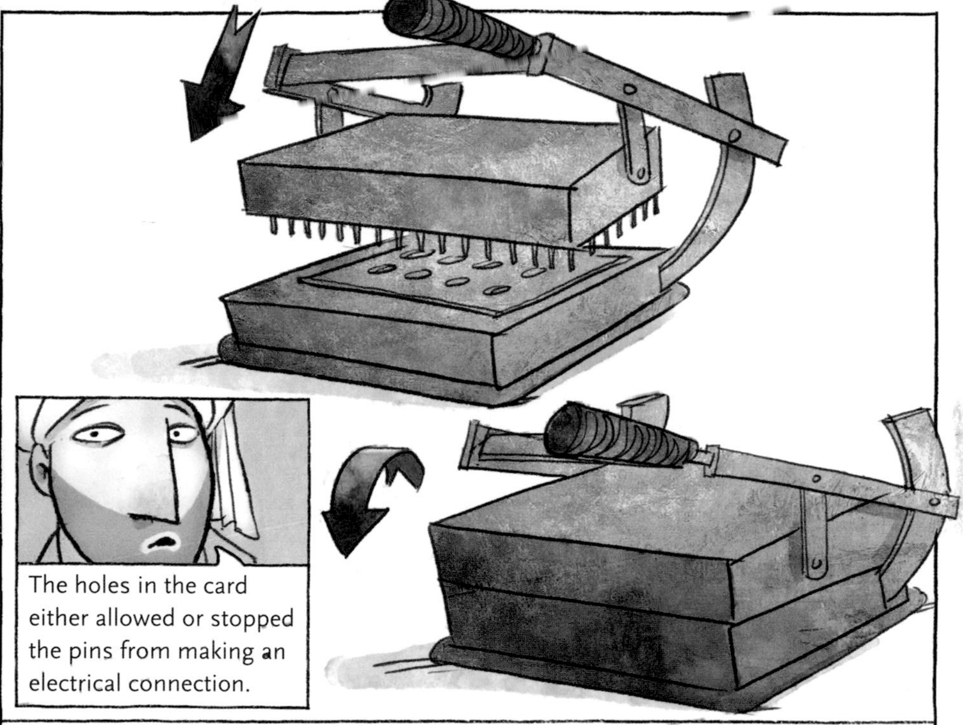
The holes in the card either allowed or stopped the pins from making an electrical connection.

His machine outpaced hand tabulating and allowed more detailed study of the population. Let's say you wanted to know how many Italian immigrants born before 1870 were miners. For calculations like these, Hollerith's machine proved to be the jackrabbit of tabulators, and a big sensation.

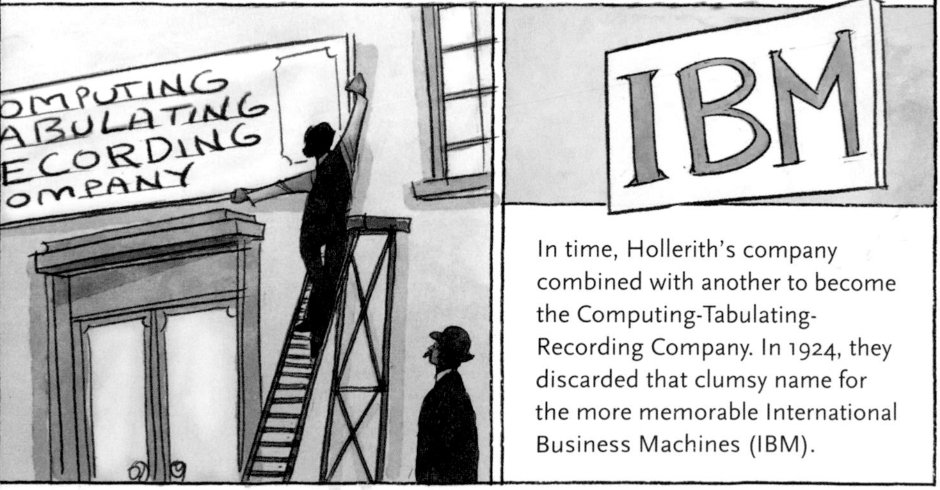
OMPUTING
ABULATING
ECORDING
OMPANY
IBM
In time, Hollerith's company combined with another to become the Computing-Tabulating-Recording Company. In 1924, they discarded that clumsy name for the more memorable International Business Machines (IBM).

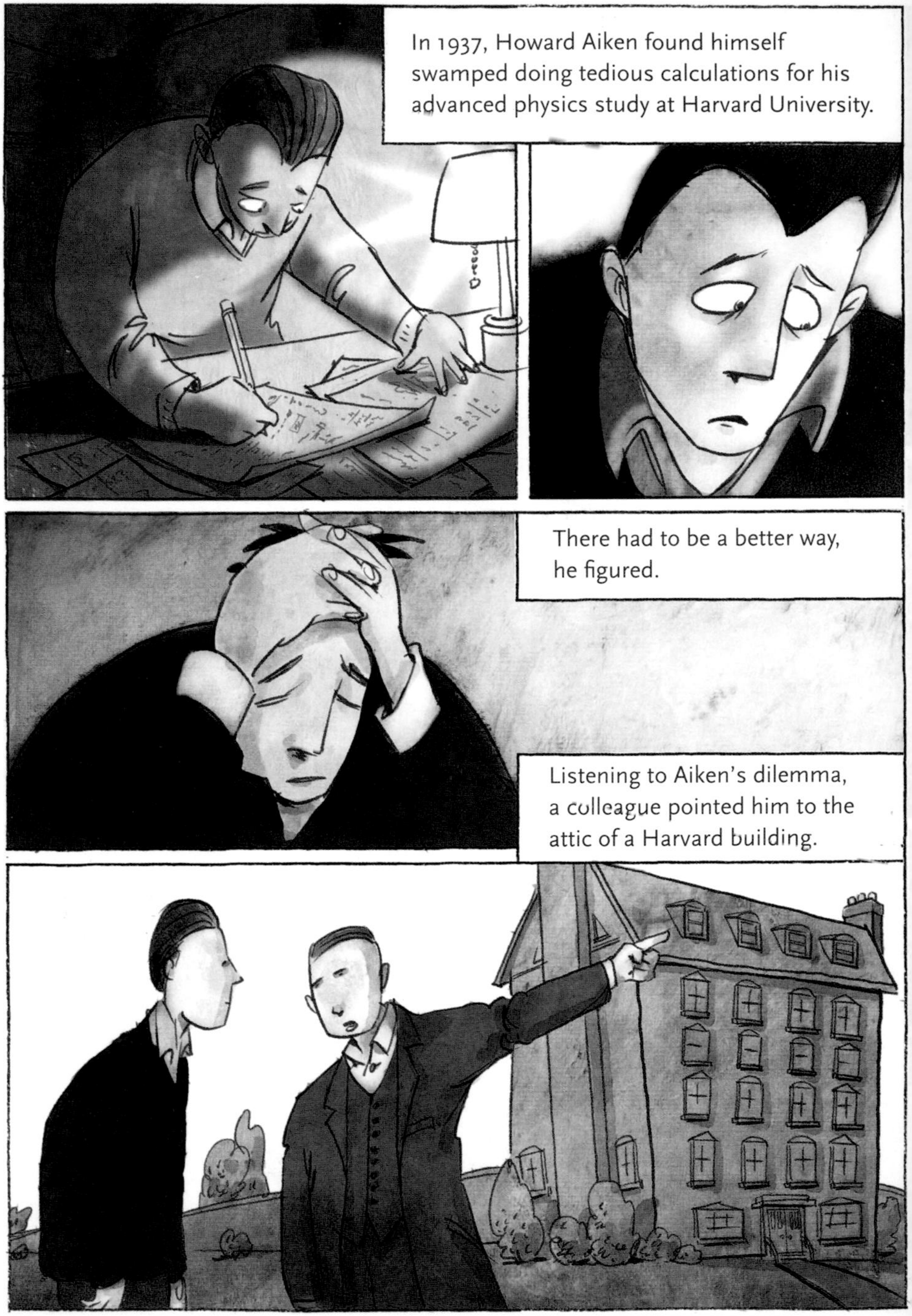
In 1937, Howard Aiken found himself swamped doing tedious calculations for his advanced physics study at Harvard University.
There had to be a better way, he figured.
Listening to Aiken's dilemma, a colleague pointed him to the attic of a Harvard building.

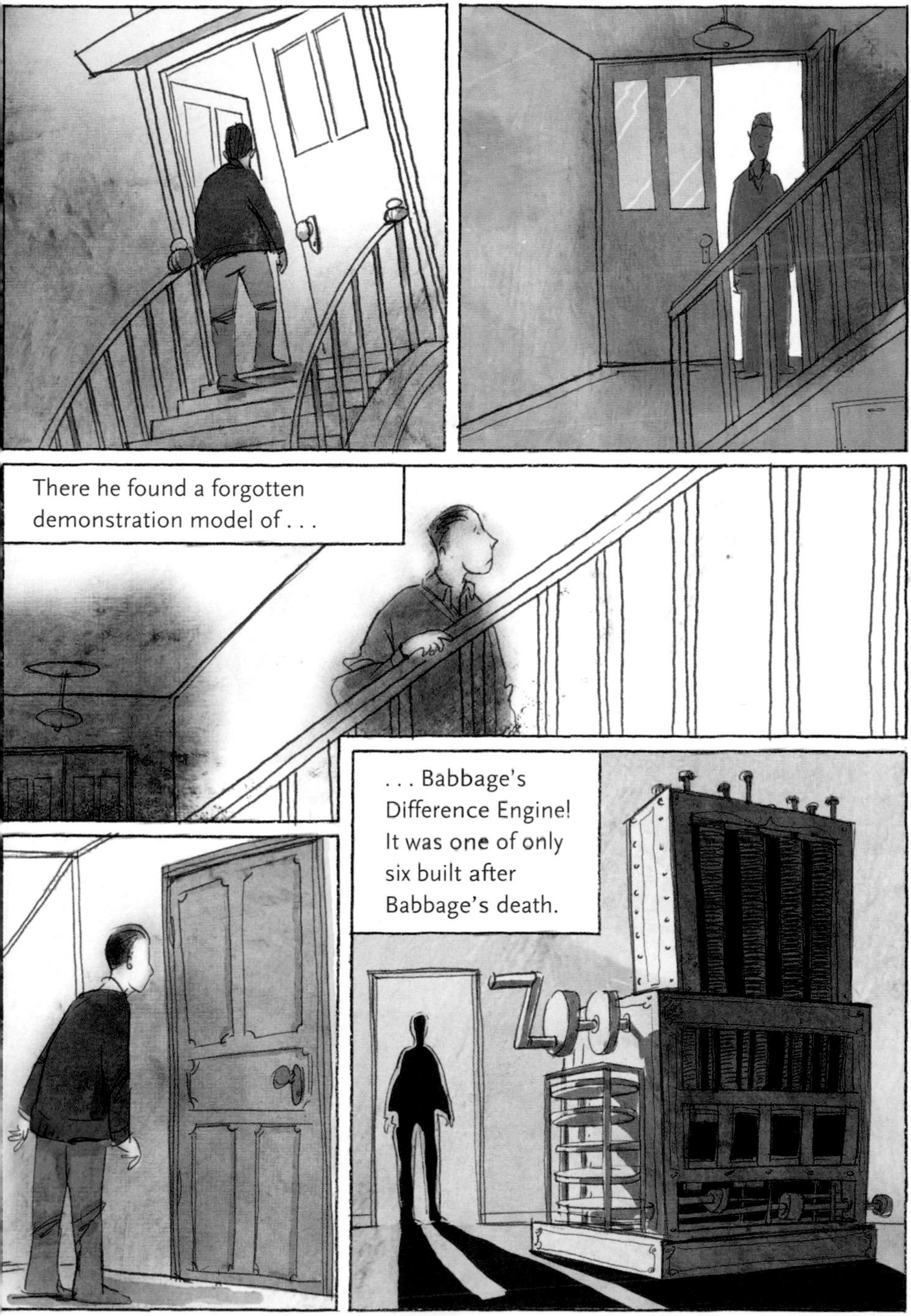
There he found a forgotten demonstration model of . . .
. . . Babbage's Difference Engine! It was one of only six built after Babbage's death.

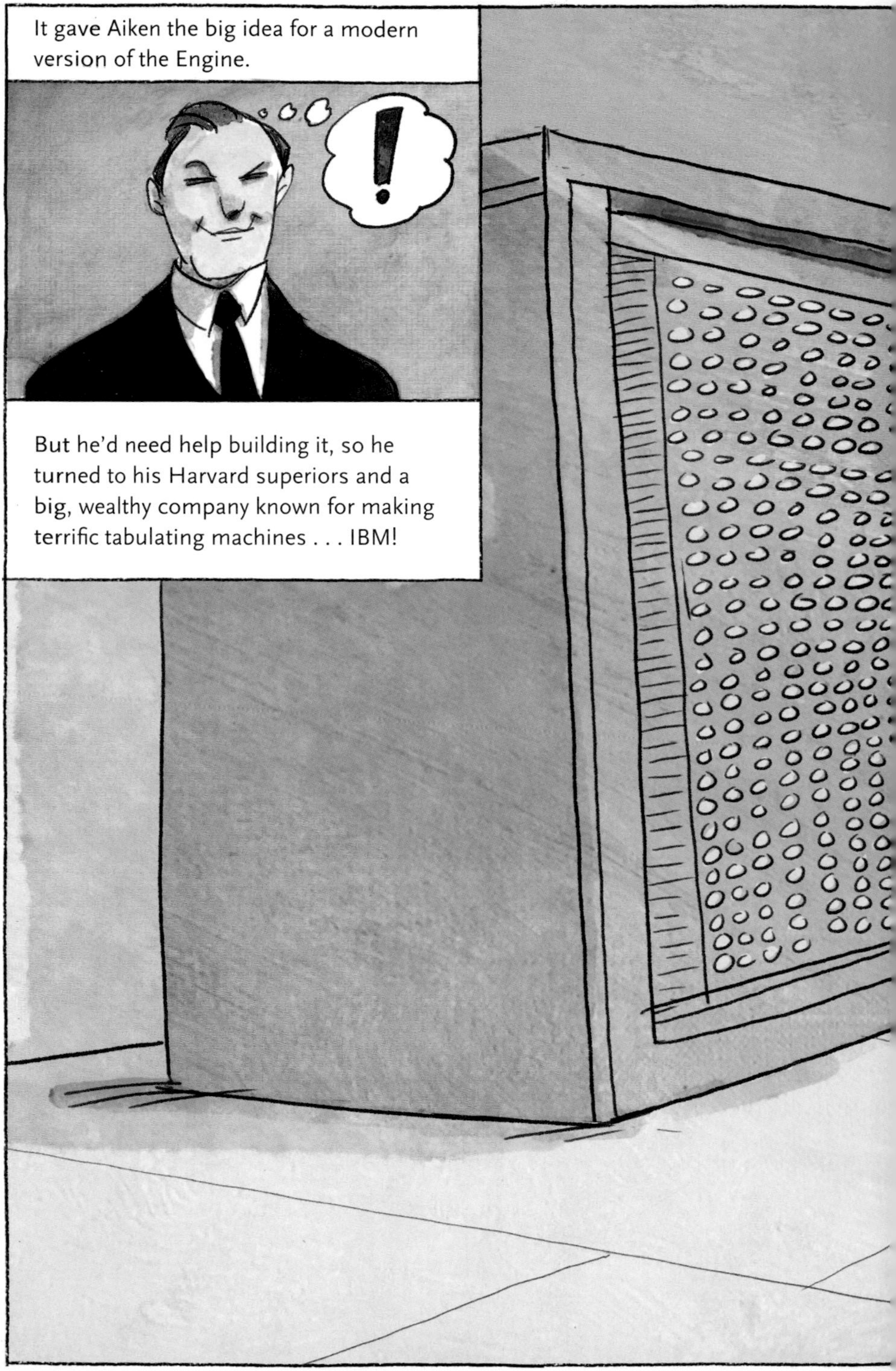
It gave Aiken the big idea for a modern version of the Engine.
!
But he'd need help building it, so he turned to his Harvard superiors and a big, wealthy company known for making terrific tabulating machines . . . IBM!

Together they built the Harvard Mark I, an 8 ft (2 m) tall, 5 short ton (4 long ton) monster with 750,000 parts. It could multiply figures that were each twenty-three numbers long in one second!

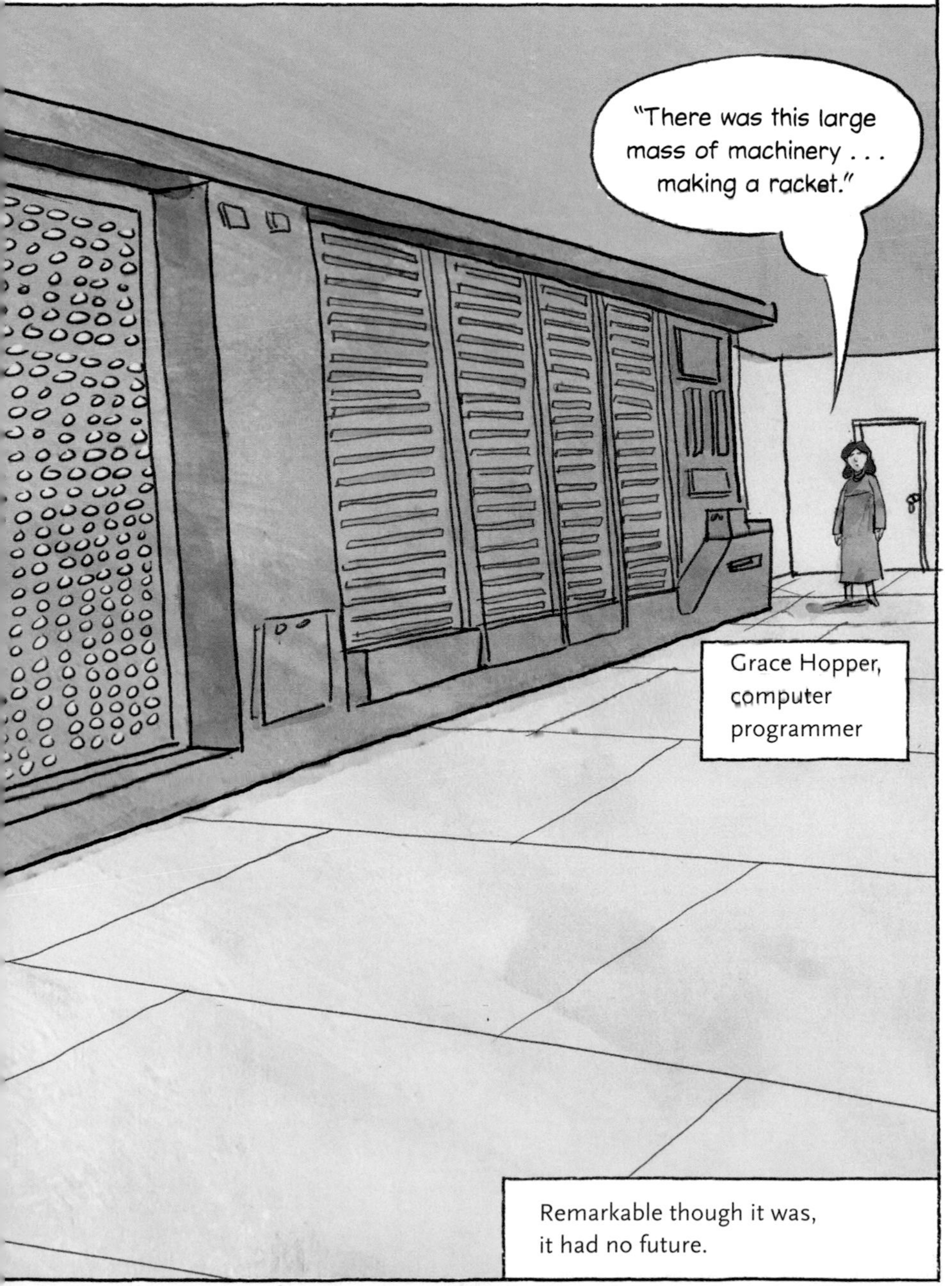
"There was this large mass of machinery . . . making a racket."
Grace Hopper, computer programmer
Remarkable though it was, it had no future.

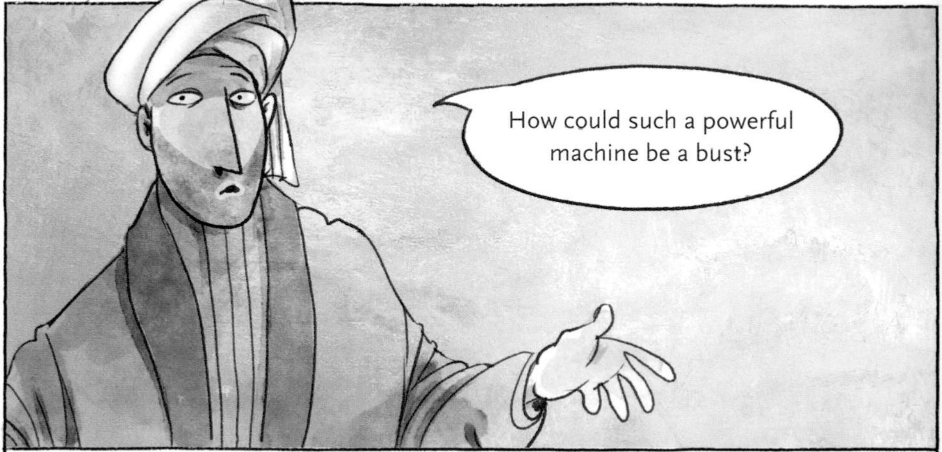
How could such a powerful machine be a bust?

Here's why: It had shafts, axles, and wheels—three thousand wheels!—and many switches. The Mark I was mostly a collection of *mechanical* switches, objects that physically opened and closed. The future of the computer would be *electronic*, with switches that moved at the superfast speed of electricity stopping and starting.

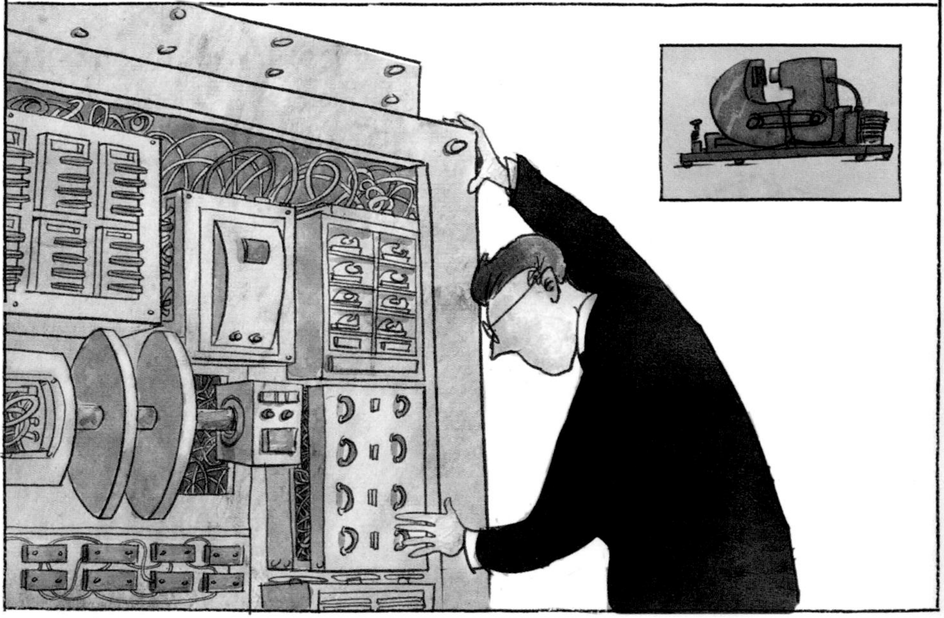

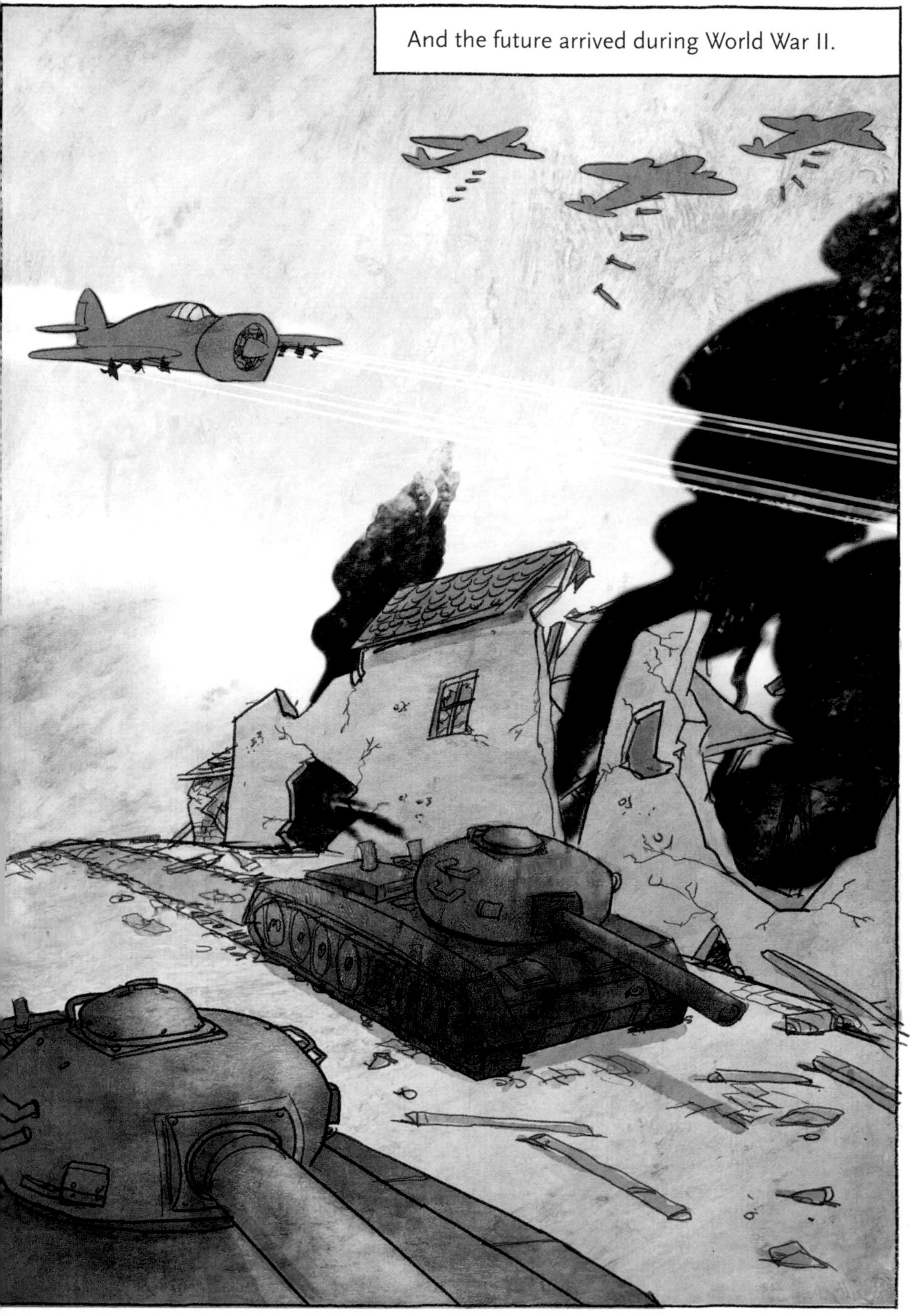
And the future arrived during World War II.

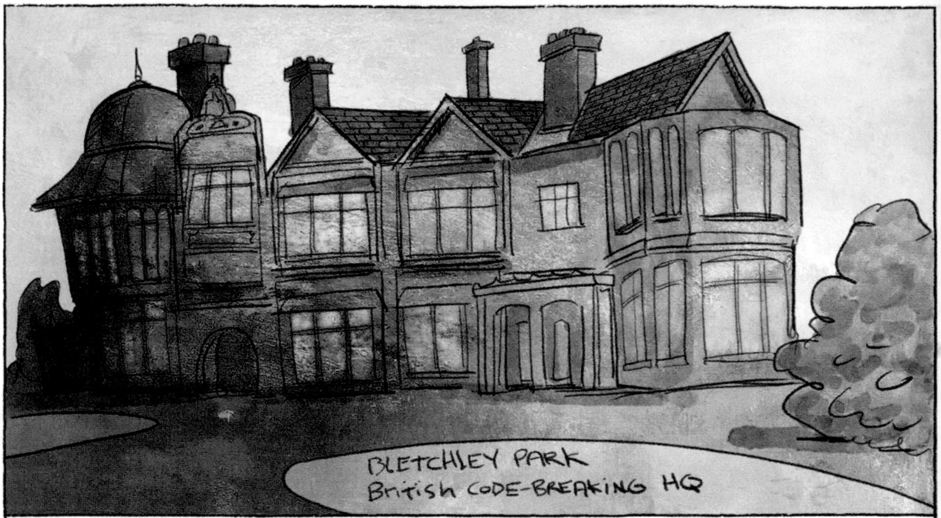
BLETCHLEY PARK
British CODE-BREAKING HQ

During England's fight against Germany, British scientists had the idea to build an electronic computer to break the enemy's secret message codes. They called it Colossus. It was used to uncover German war plans and helped achieve victory for England and its allies.

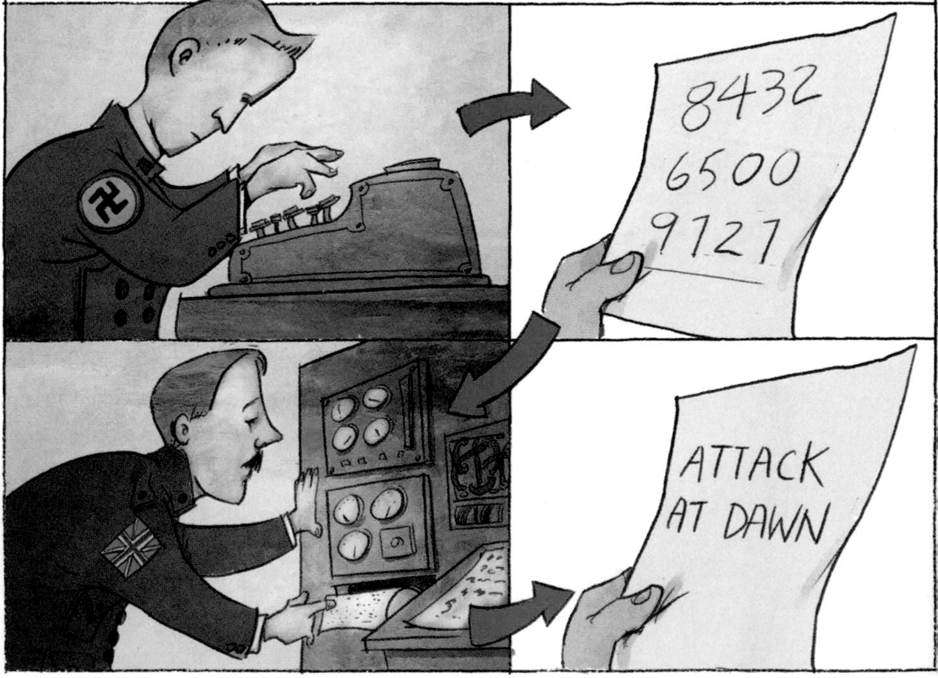
8432
6500
9127
ATTACK
AT DAWN

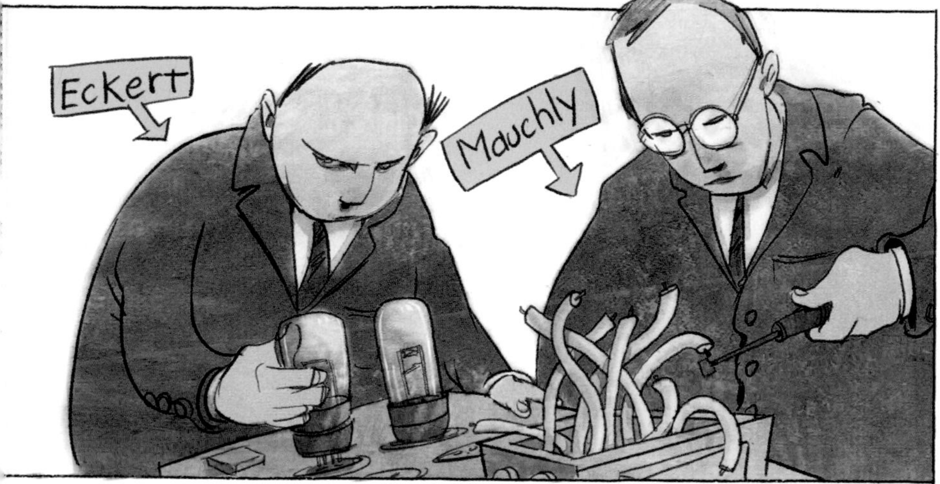
Eckert
Mauchly

Meanwhile, wartime America worked on its own all-electronic computer. In 1943, University of Pennsylvania scientists John William Mauchly and J. Presper Eckert began making the Electronic Numerical Integrator and Computer—ENIAC for short. It, like Colossus, used vacuum tube switches instead of mechanical ones.

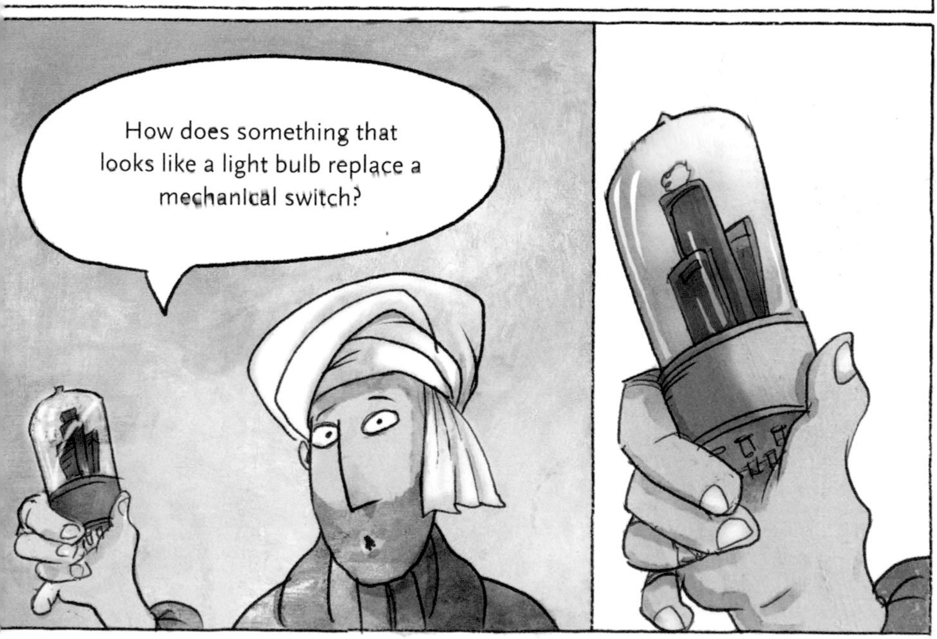
How does something that looks like a light bulb replace a mechanical switch?

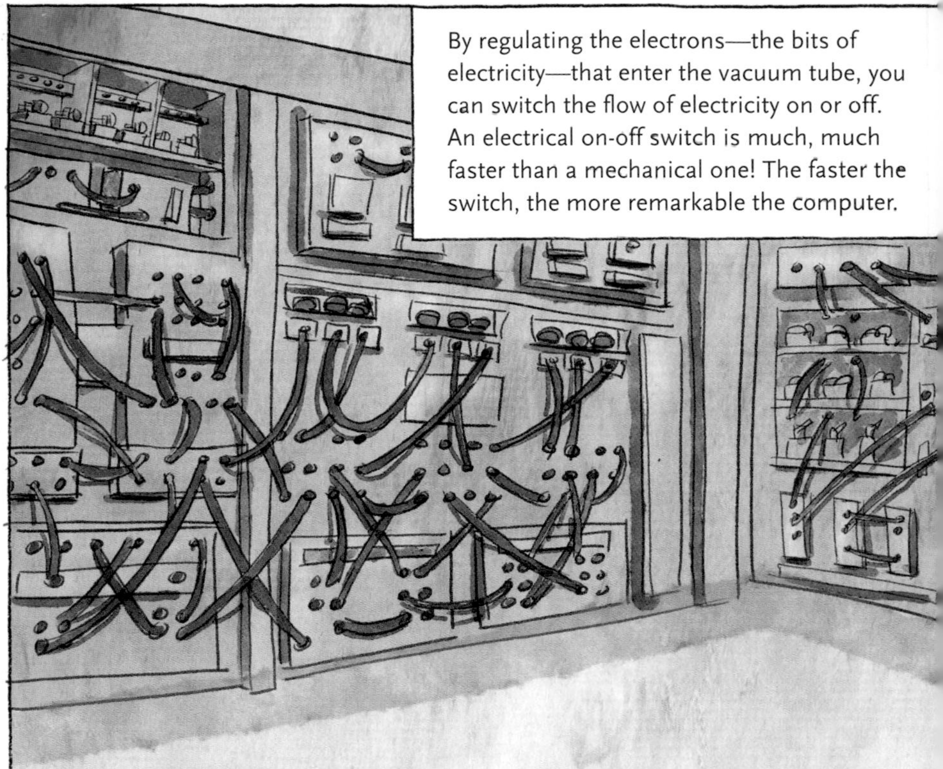
By regulating the electrons—the bits of electricity—that enter the vacuum tube, you can switch the flow of electricity on or off. An electrical on-off switch is much, much faster than a mechanical one! The faster the switch, the more remarkable the computer.

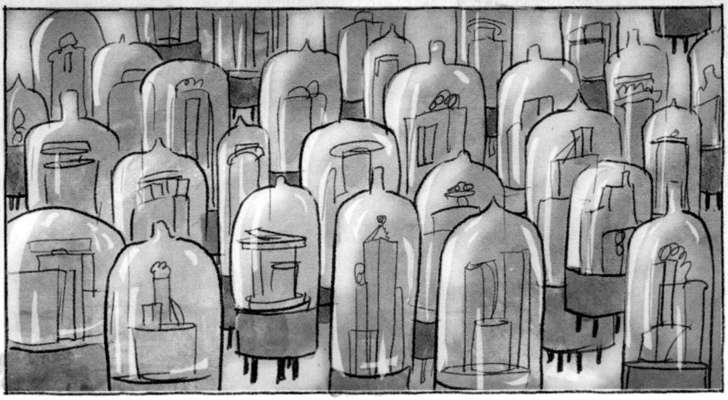

ENIAC's 17,500 vacuum tubes helped make it one thousand times faster than Aiken's Mark I.

The vacuum tubes were remarkable, but they became very hot. Computers had to be kept cool. Otherwise, the vacuum tubes would melt the guts of the machine.

The fast-operating, vacuum-tube on-off switch was crucial to the computer.

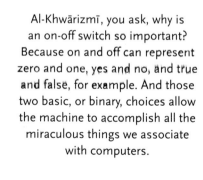

Al-Khwārizmī, you ask, why is an on-off switch so important? Because on and off can represent zero and one, yes and no, and true and false, for example. And those two basic, or binary, choices allow the machine to accomplish all the miraculous things we associate with computers.

0 1
NO YES
FALSE TRUE

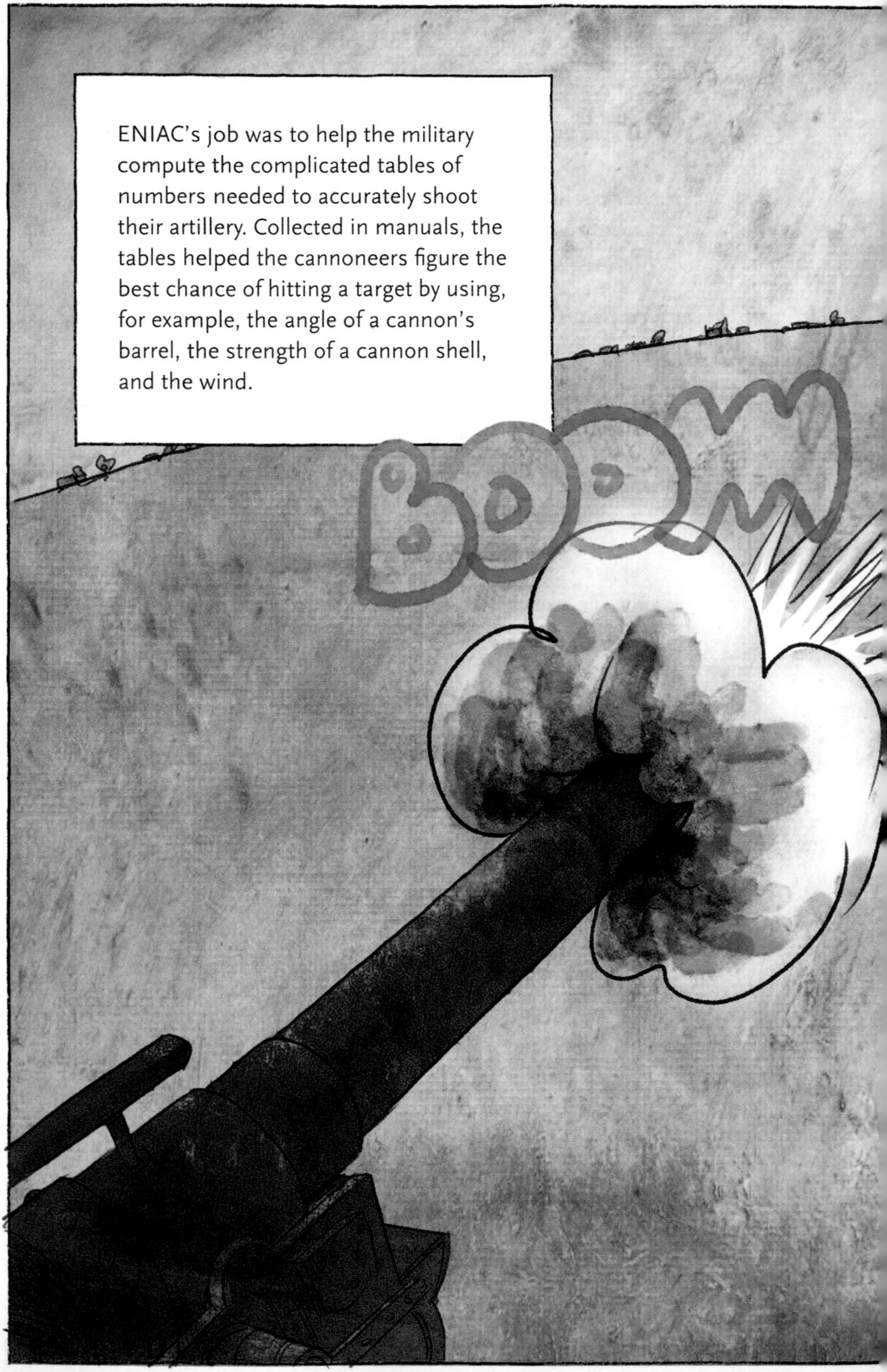
ENIAC's job was to help the military compute the complicated tables of numbers needed to accurately shoot their artillery. Collected in manuals, the tables helped the cannoneers figure the best chance of hitting a target by using, for example, the angle of a cannon's barrel, the strength of a cannon shell, and the wind.
BOOM

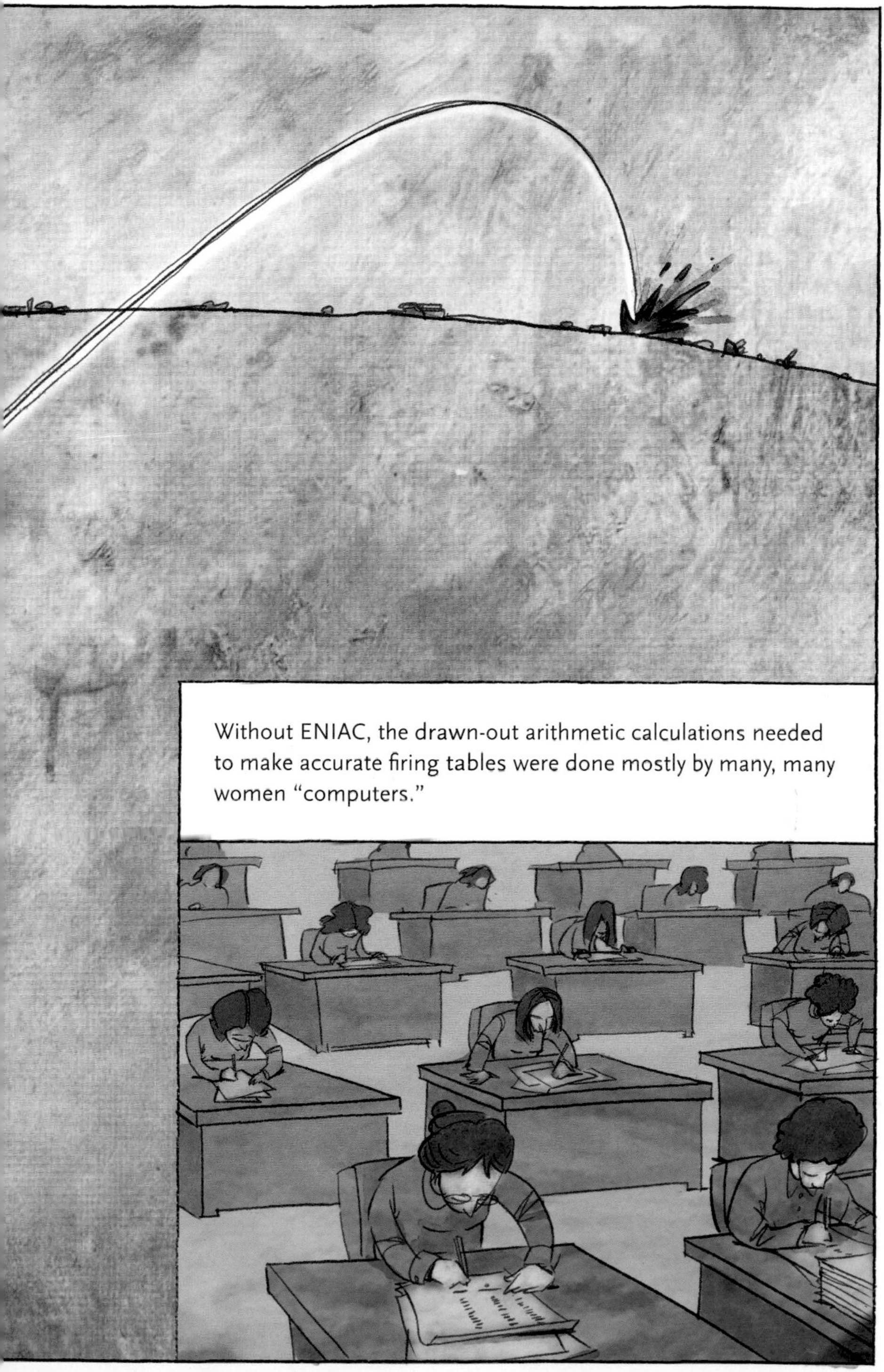
Without ENIAC, the drawn-out arithmetic calculations needed to make accurate firing tables were done mostly by many, many women "computers."

Giving the ENIAC operating instructions, also known as programming, meant resetting the spaghetti-like collection of wires that covered the computer. They were plugged or unplugged in different arrangements depending on the job the ENIAC was required to complete.

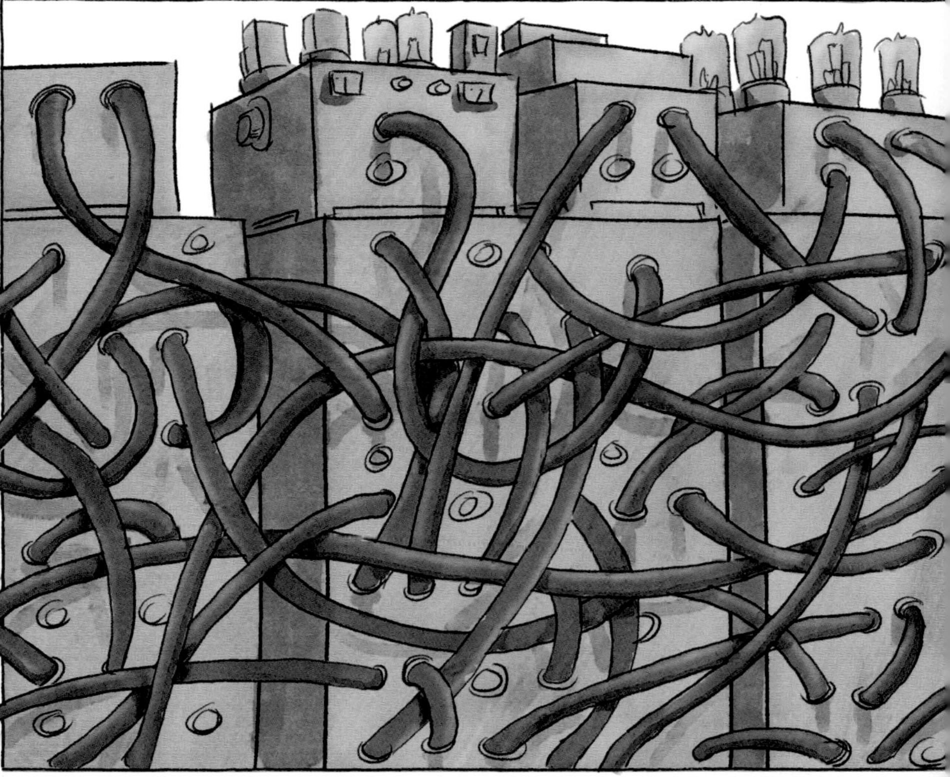

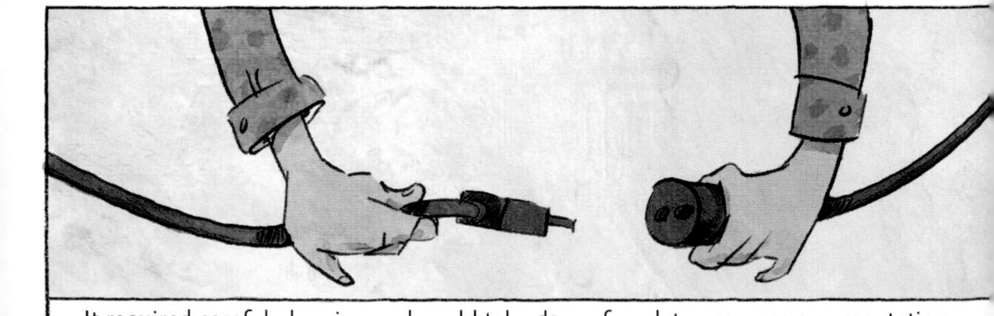

It required careful planning and could take days of work to program a computation that ENIAC would complete in seconds.

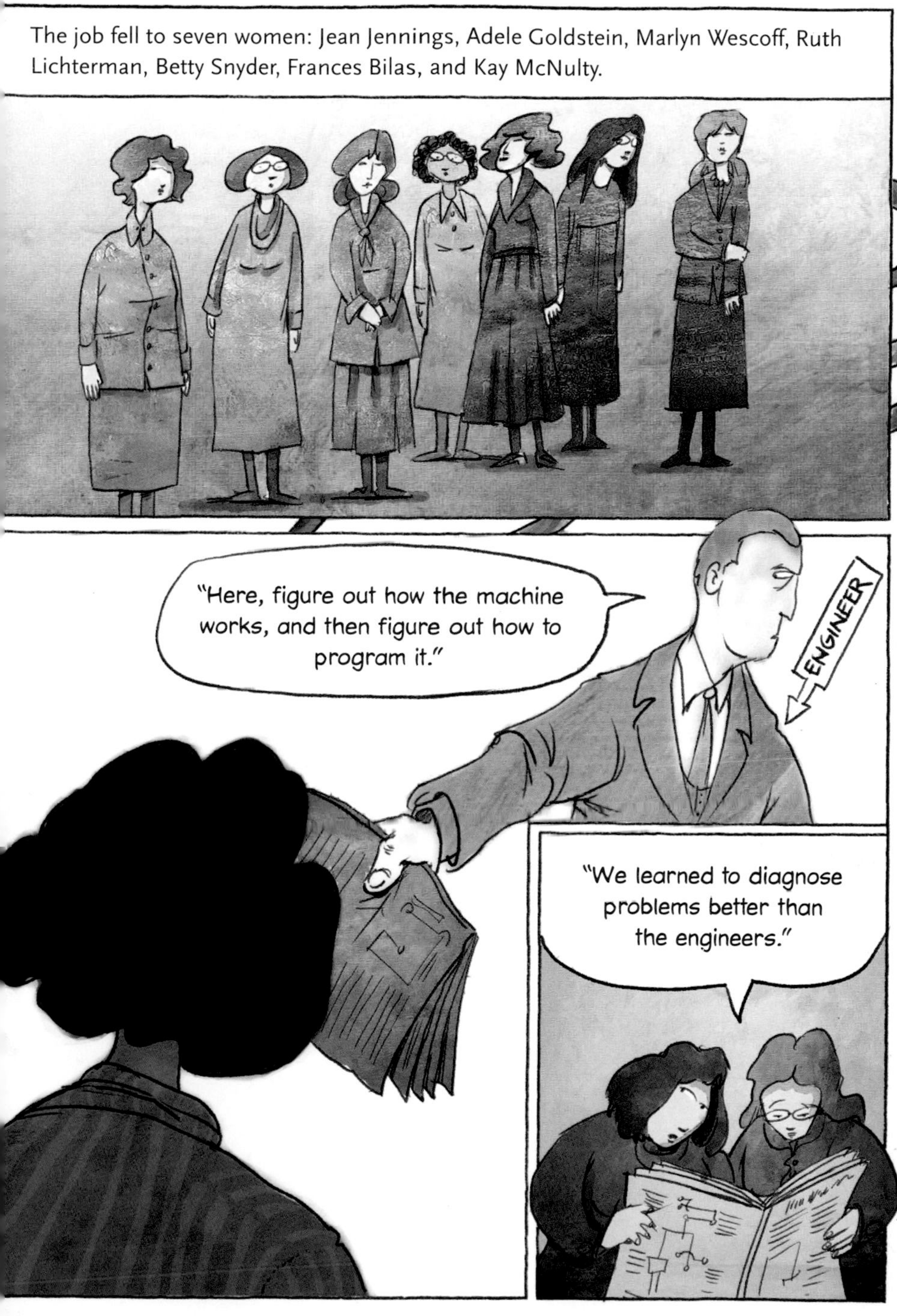
The job fell to seven women: Jean Jennings, Adele Goldstein, Marlyn Wescoff, Ruth Lichterman, Betty Snyder, Frances Bilas, and Kay McNulty.
"Here, figure out how the machine works, and then figure out how to program it."
ENGINEER
"We learned to diagnose problems better than the engineers."

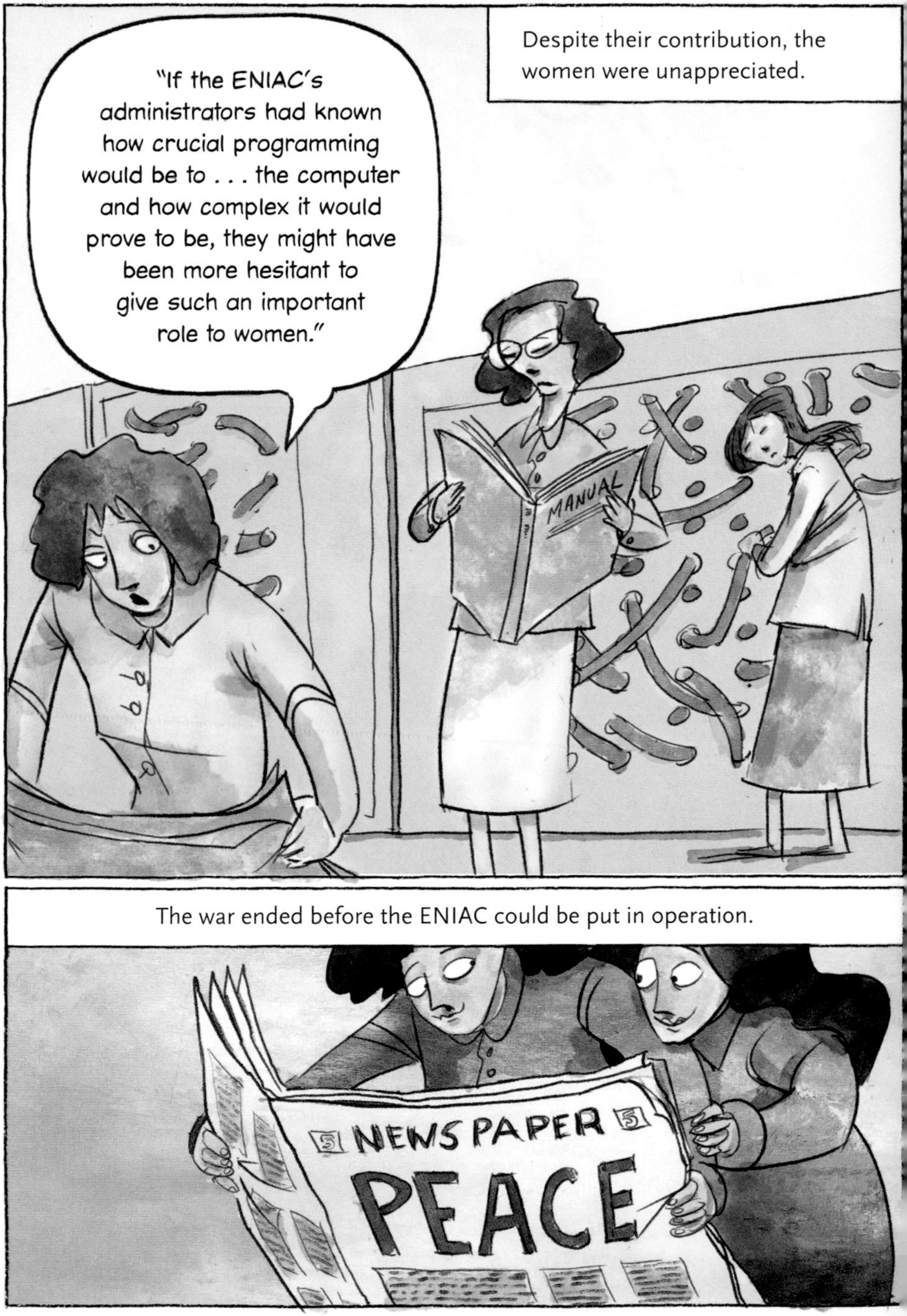
Despite their contribution, the women were unappreciated.
"If the ENIAC's administrators had known how crucial programming would be to . . . the computer and how complex it would prove to be, they might have been more hesitant to give such an important role to women."
MANUAL
The war ended before the ENIAC could be put in operation.
NEWSPAPER
PEACE

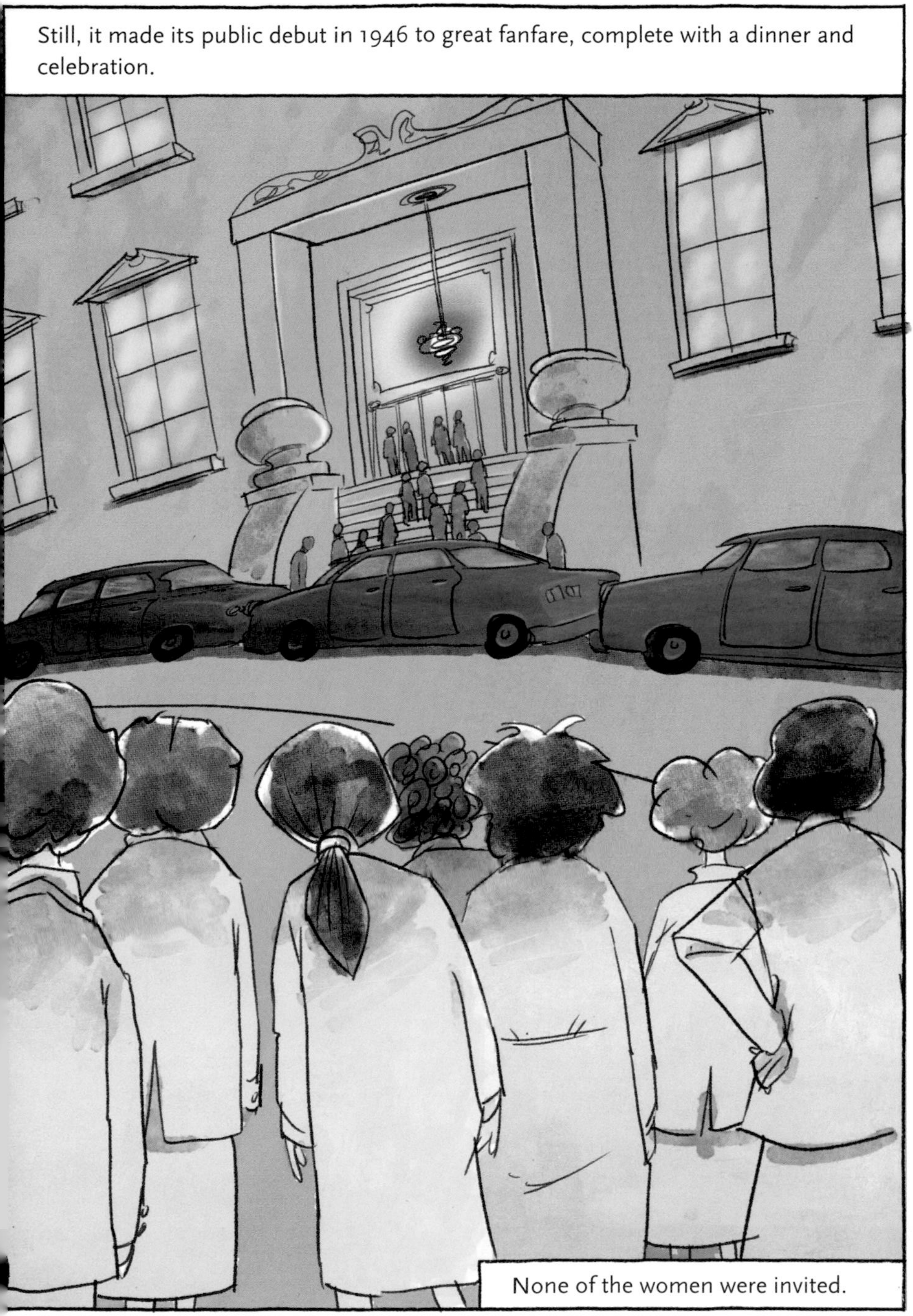
Still, it made its public debut in 1946 to great fanfare, complete with a dinner and celebration.
None of the women were invited.

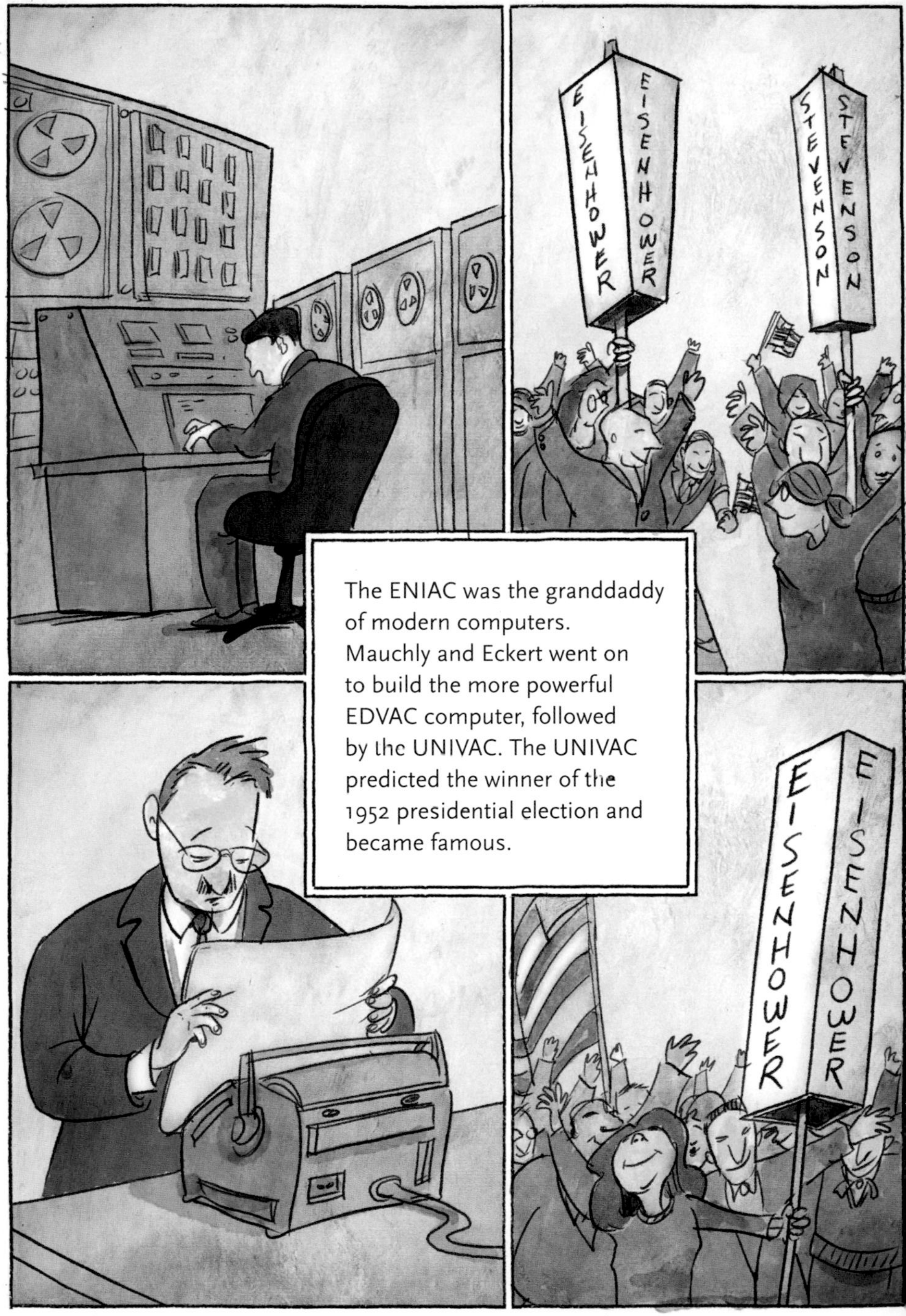
EISENHOWER
EISENHOWER
STEVENSON
STEVENSON
The ENIAC was the granddaddy of modern computers. Mauchly and Eckert went on to build the more powerful EDVAC computer, followed by the UNIVAC. The UNIVAC predicted the winner of the 1952 presidential election and became famous.
EISENHOWER
EISENHOWER

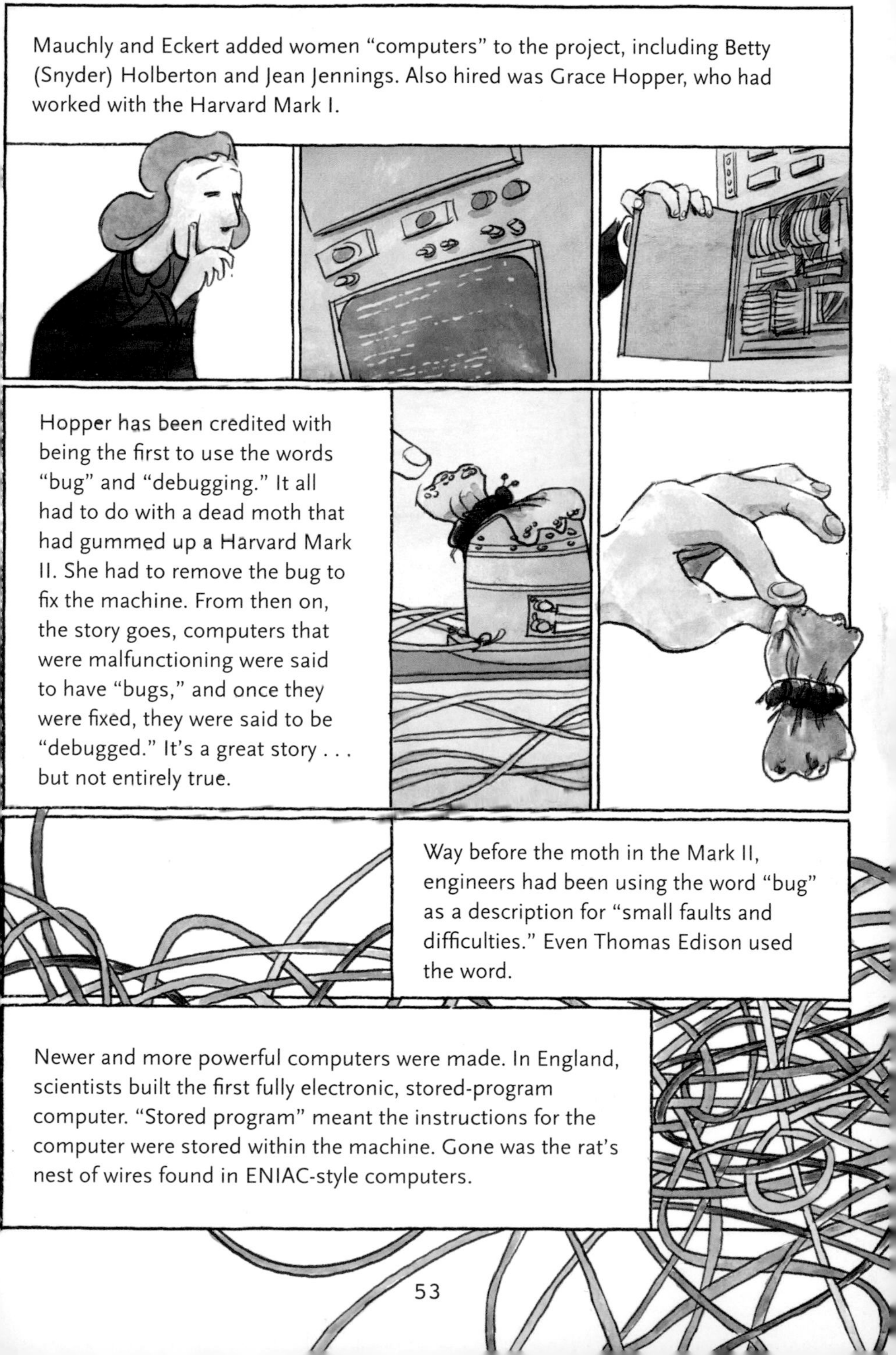
Mauchly and Eckert added women "computers" to the project, including Betty (Snyder) Holberton and Jean Jennings. Also hired was Grace Hopper, who had worked with the Harvard Mark I.
Hopper has been credited with being the first to use the words "bug" and "debugging." It all had to do with a dead moth that had gummed up a Harvard Mark II. She had to remove the bug to fix the machine. From then on, the story goes, computers that were malfunctioning were said to have "bugs," and once they were fixed, they were said to be "debugged." It's a great story . . . but not entirely true.
Way before the moth in the Mark II, engineers had been using the word "bug" as a description for "small faults and difficulties." Even Thomas Edison used the word.
Newer and more powerful computers were made. In England, scientists built the first fully electronic, stored-program computer. "Stored program" meant the instructions for the computer were stored within the machine. Gone was the rat's nest of wires found in ENIAC-style computers.

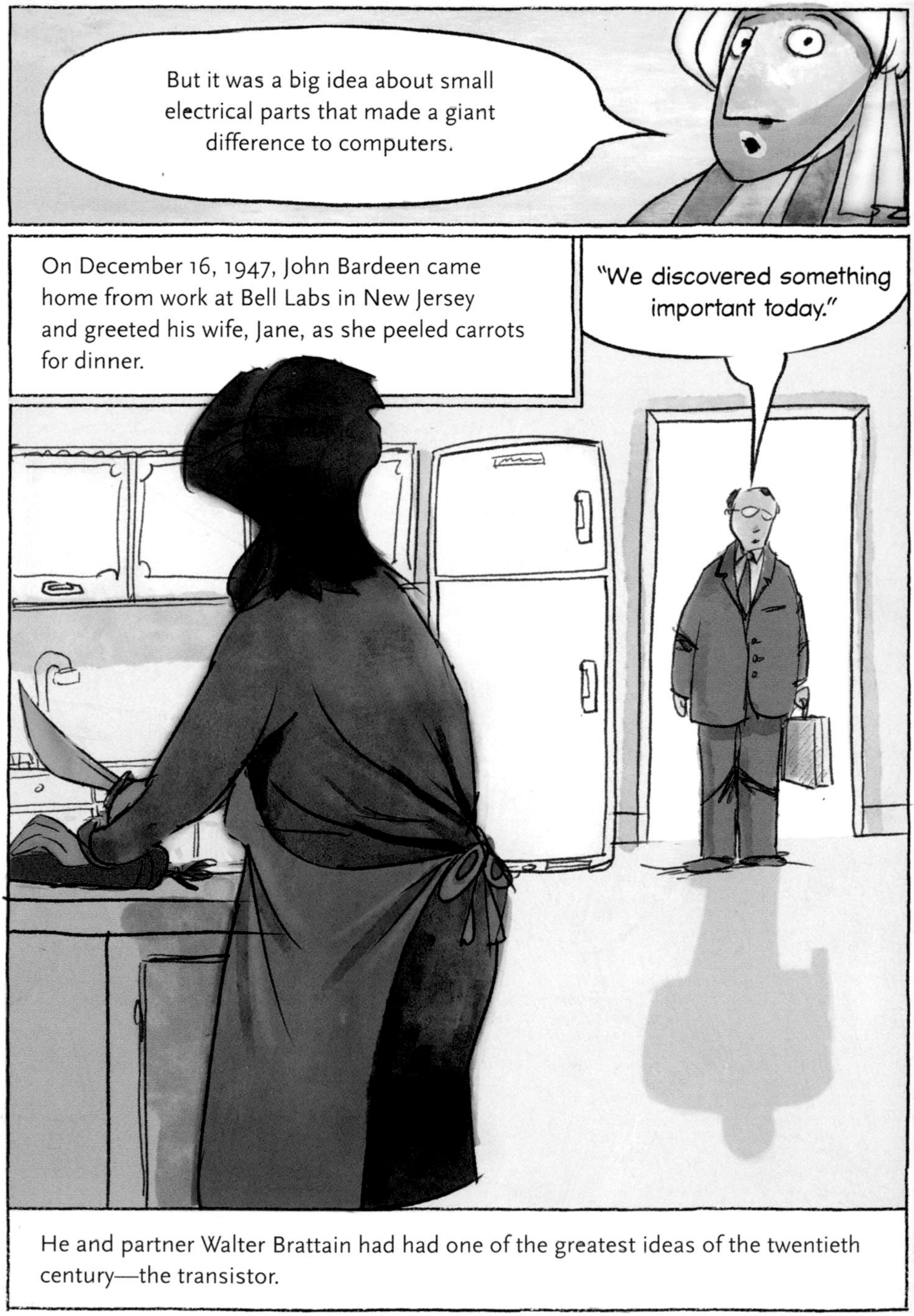
But it was a big idea about small electrical parts that made a giant difference to computers.
On December 16, 1947, John Bardeen came home from work at Bell Labs in New Jersey and greeted his wife, Jane, as she peeled carrots for dinner.
"We discovered something important today."
He and partner Walter Brattain had had one of the greatest ideas of the twentieth century—the transistor.

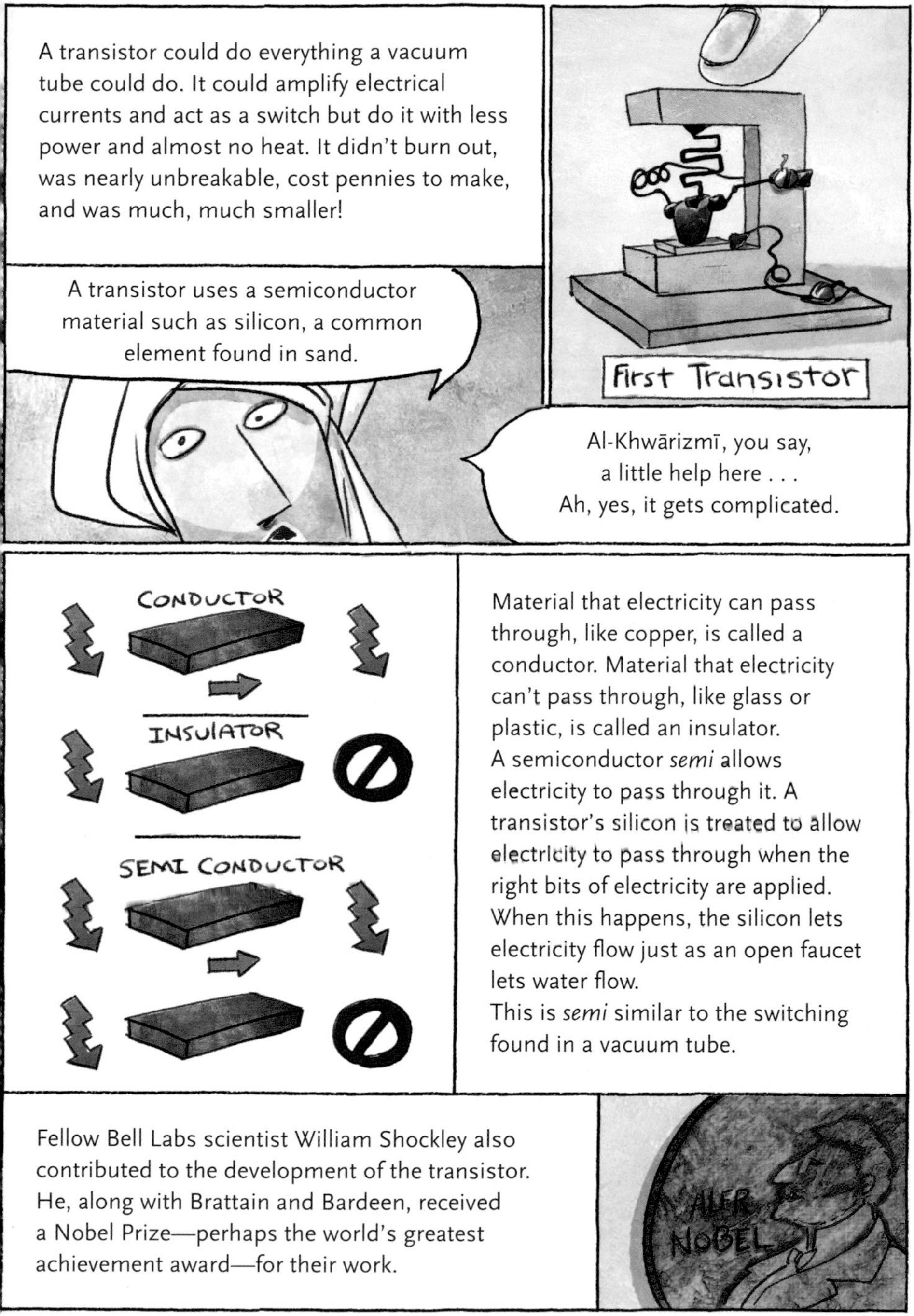

A transistor could do everything a vacuum tube could do. It could amplify electrical currents and act as a switch but do it with less power and almost no heat. It didn't burn out, was nearly unbreakable, cost pennies to make, and was much, much smaller!

First Transistor

A transistor uses a semiconductor material such as silicon, a common element found in sand.

Al-Khwārizmī, you say, a little help here . . . Ah, yes, it gets complicated.

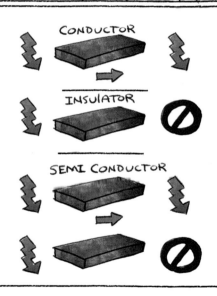

CONDUCTOR

INSULATOR

SEMI CONDUCTOR

Material that electricity can pass through, like copper, is called a conductor. Material that electricity can't pass through, like glass or plastic, is called an insulator. A semiconductor *semi* allows electricity to pass through it. A transistor's silicon is treated to allow electricity to pass through when the right bits of electricity are applied. When this happens, the silicon lets electricity flow just as an open faucet lets water flow.

This is *semi* similar to the switching found in a vacuum tube.

Fellow Bell Labs scientist William Shockley also contributed to the development of the transistor. He, along with Brattain and Bardeen, received a Nobel Prize—perhaps the world's greatest achievement award—for their work.

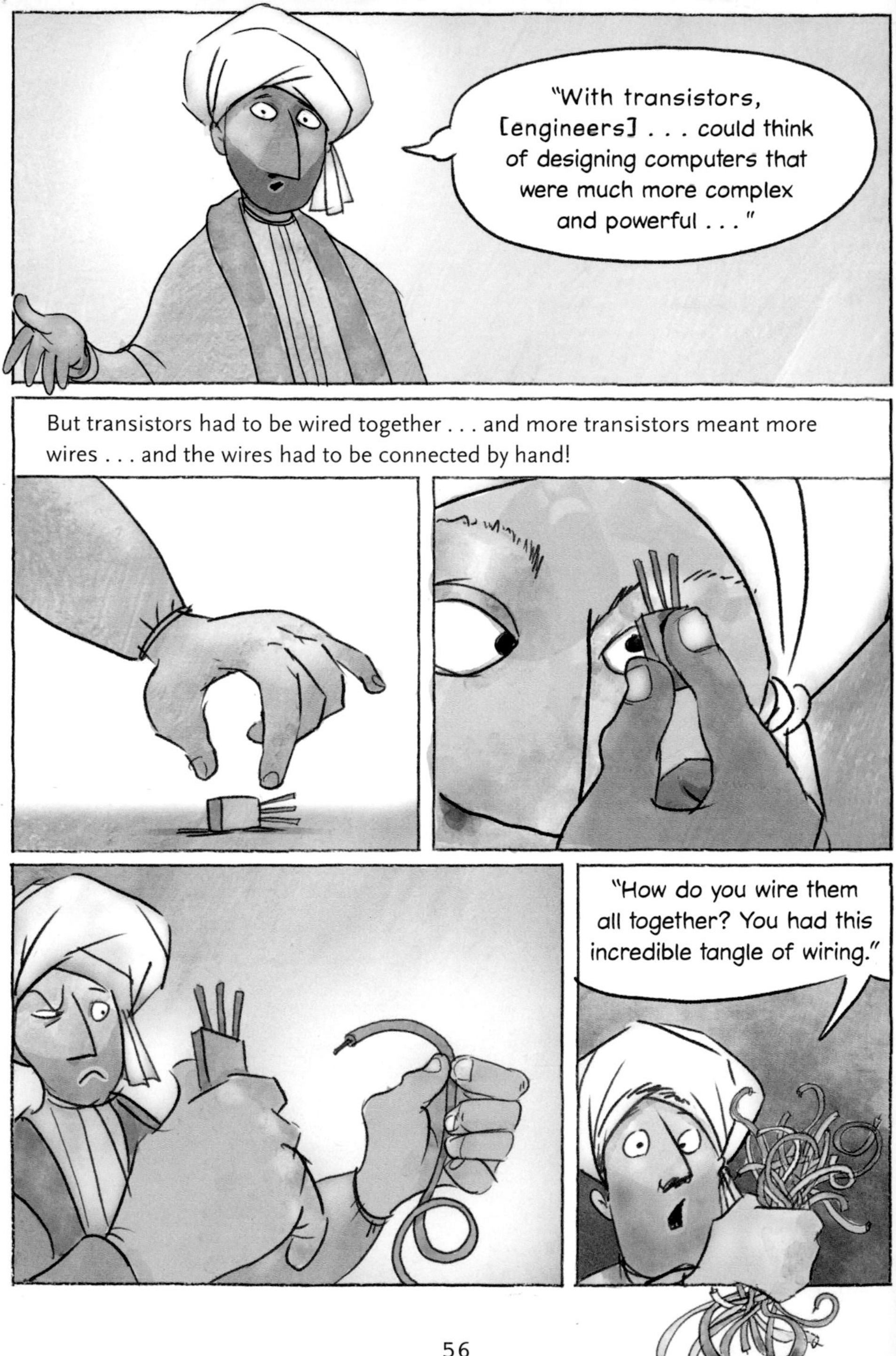
"With transistors, [engineers] . . . could think of designing computers that were much more complex and powerful . . ."
But transistors had to be wired together . . . and more transistors meant more wires . . . and the wires had to be connected by hand!
"How do you wire them all together? You had this incredible tangle of wiring."

It seemed like future computers would be swamped with wires. This was a problem that crippled computer design, and until engineers solved it, there would be no fantastic computers. Then Robert Noyce had a big idea.

In 1959, Noyce altered a chip of silicon so that it held several computer parts, including a transistor. Instead of clumsy wires, the tiny parts were joined by metal that was layered over the chip. In this way, everything on the chip is in one piece, or integrated. The device was called an integrated circuit.

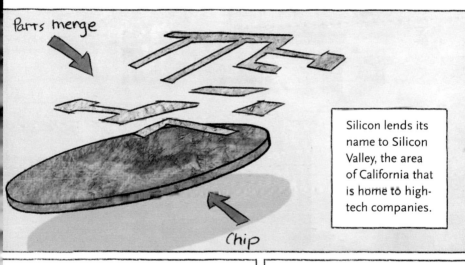

Parts merge

Silicon lends its name to Silicon Valley, the area of California that is home to high-tech companies.

Chip

Noyce wasn't the first to have the idea for an integrated circuit. Working independently, scientist Jack Kilby had thought of it months earlier. But Noyce's idea was more practical and could be mass-produced. It was Noyce who beat back the jungle of wires that had tripped up computer improvement.

Don't feel bad about Kilby. He won a Nobel Prize for his contribution.

In 1960, the first integrated circuit had fewer than ten transistors and cost $1,000. By 1970, you could buy an integrated circuit that was a thousand times more powerful for just pennies.

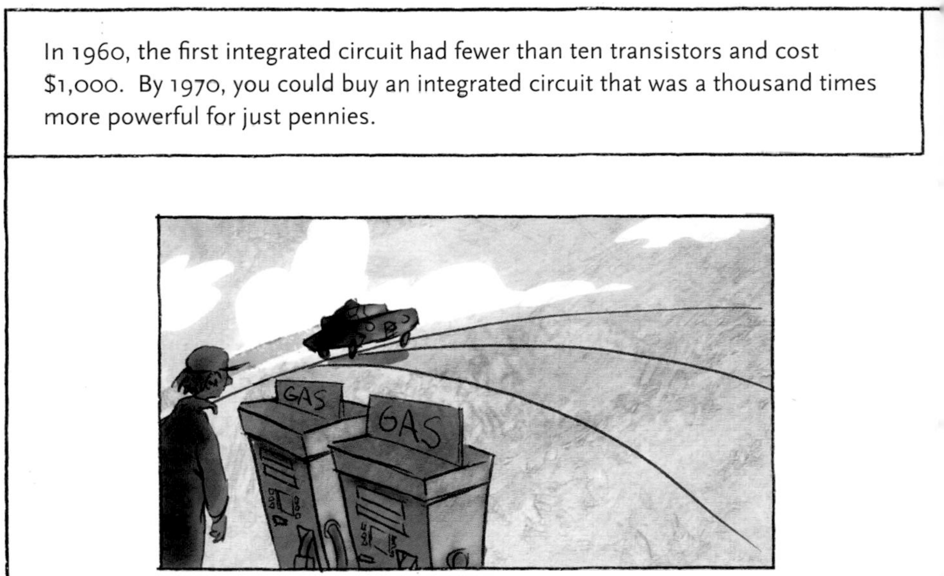
GAS
GAS

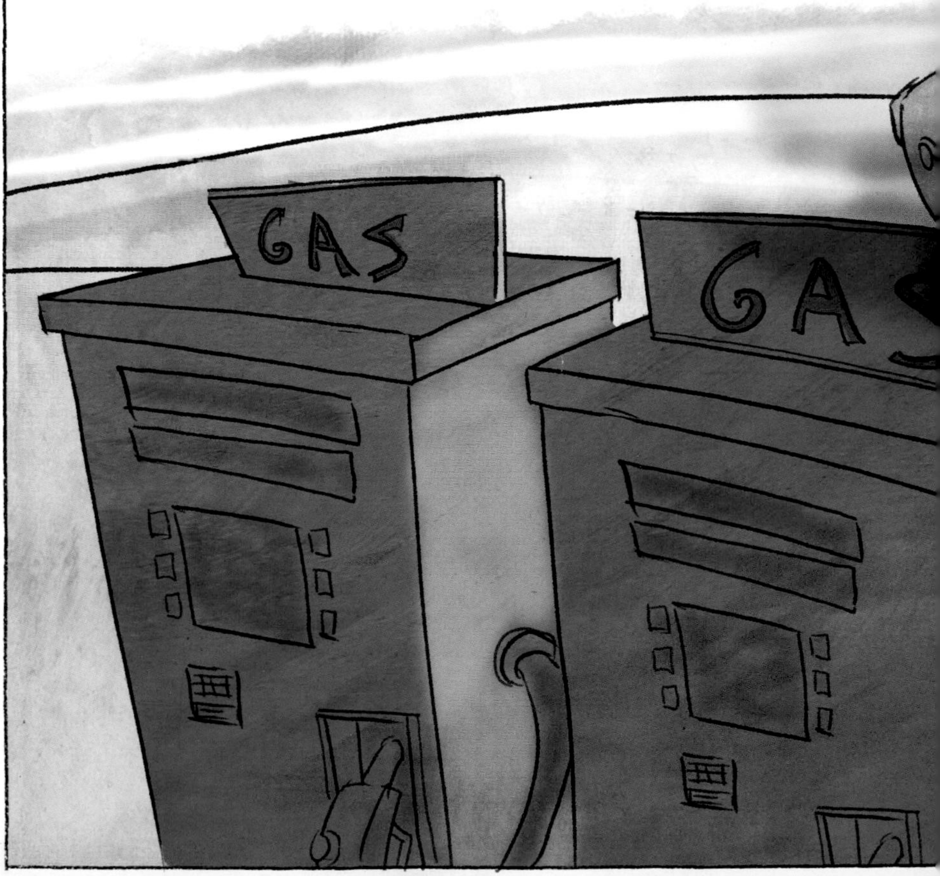
GAS

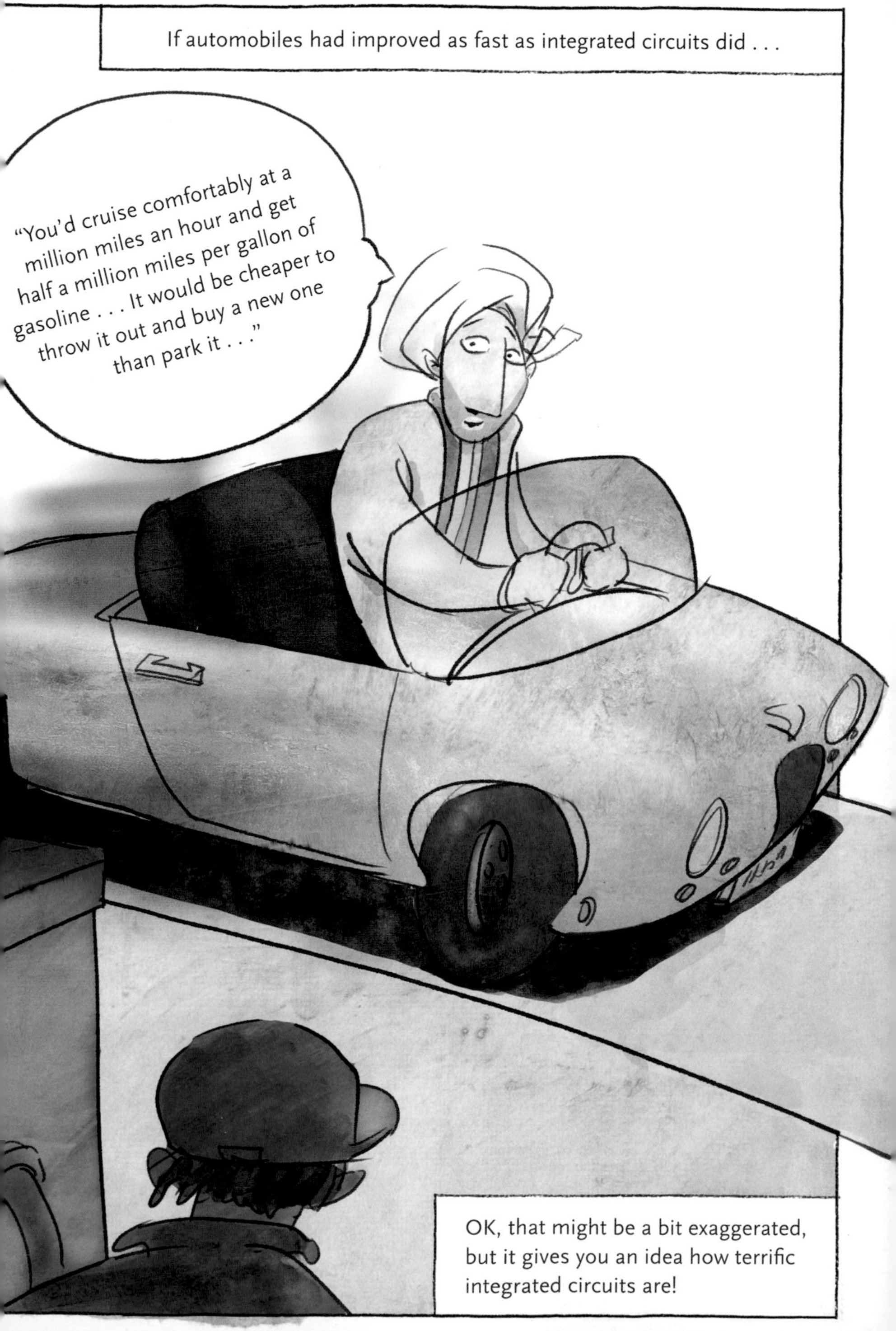
If automobiles had improved as fast as integrated circuits did . . .
"You'd cruise comfortably at a million miles an hour and get half a million miles per gallon of gasoline . . . It would be cheaper to throw it out and buy a new one than park it . . ."
OK, that might be a bit exaggerated, but it gives you an idea how terrific integrated circuits are!

Despite computers' astonishing power, some people questioned their *widespread* usefulness. Even Howard Aiken, the man behind the Harvard Mark I, doubted building more of them.

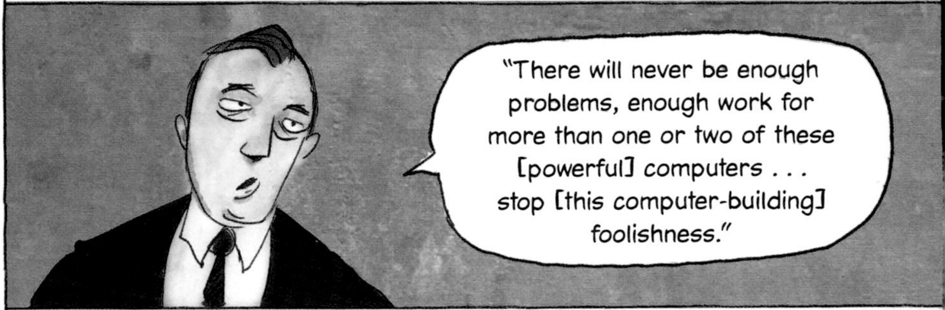
"There will never be enough problems, enough work for more than one or two of these [powerful] computers . . . stop [this computer-building] foolishness."

And besides, some people believed, there would never be enough smart people to operate them.

Others disagreed. Tom Watson Jr. of IBM was one of them. Despite the success the company enjoyed selling old-fashioned tabulating machines, he warned . . .

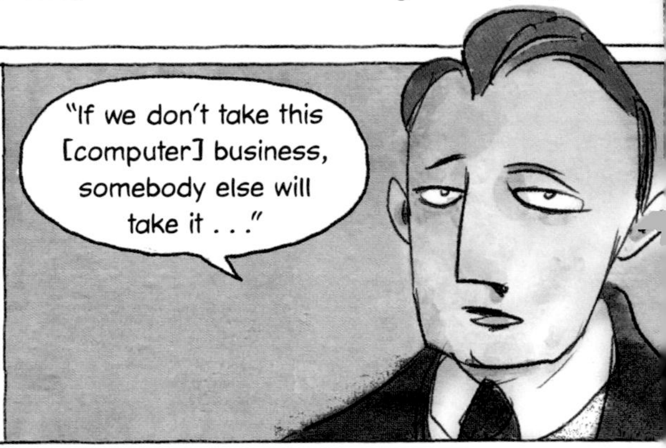
"If we don't take this [computer] business, somebody else will take it . . ."

In 1954, IBM started selling the IBM 650.

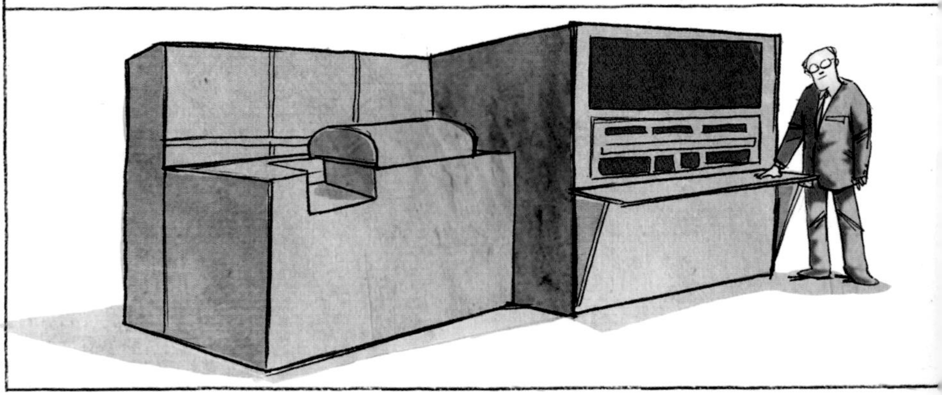

It was mass-produced and became known as the Model T of computers, a comparison to the popular early automobile that captured everyone's imagination. Many were bought by universities, inspiring a generation of computer programmers.

Early computers were fed programs and data via . . . punch cards! Each hole in a card represented a bit of data to be stored or an action to be performed. A stack of cards was used to make the computer accomplish a task. The computer would read the cards by shining light through the holes. And heaven forbid one of the holes in one of the cards was incorrectly entered. The whole program would go blooey! In 1956, engineers attached an electric keyboard to a computer, allowing direct connection between user and machine.

By 1960, scientific, government, and business people around the world were using about ten thousand computers of all kinds.

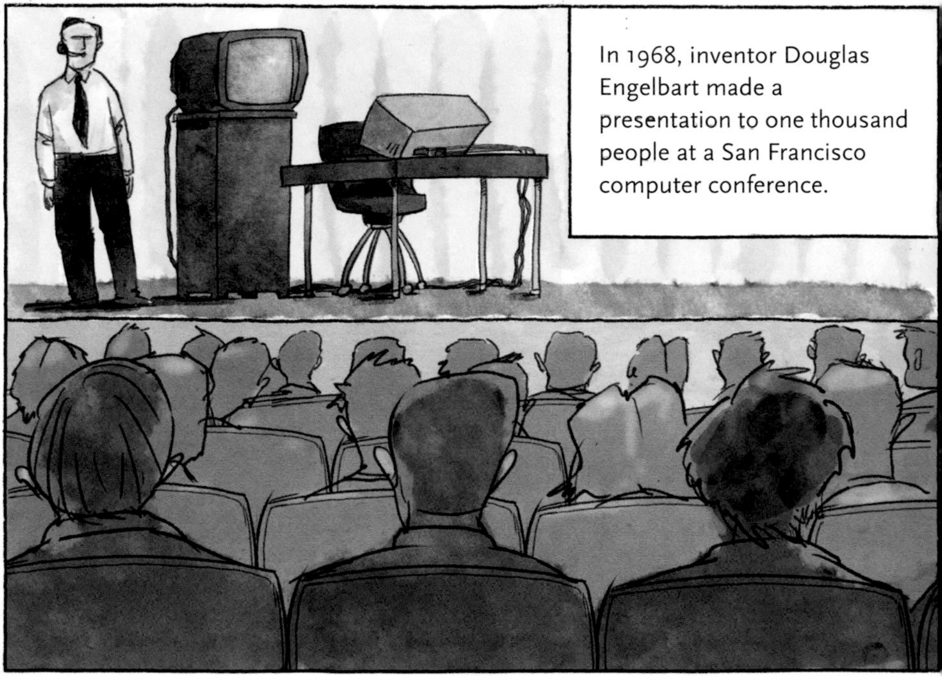
In 1968, inventor Douglas Engelbart made a presentation to one thousand people at a San Francisco computer conference.

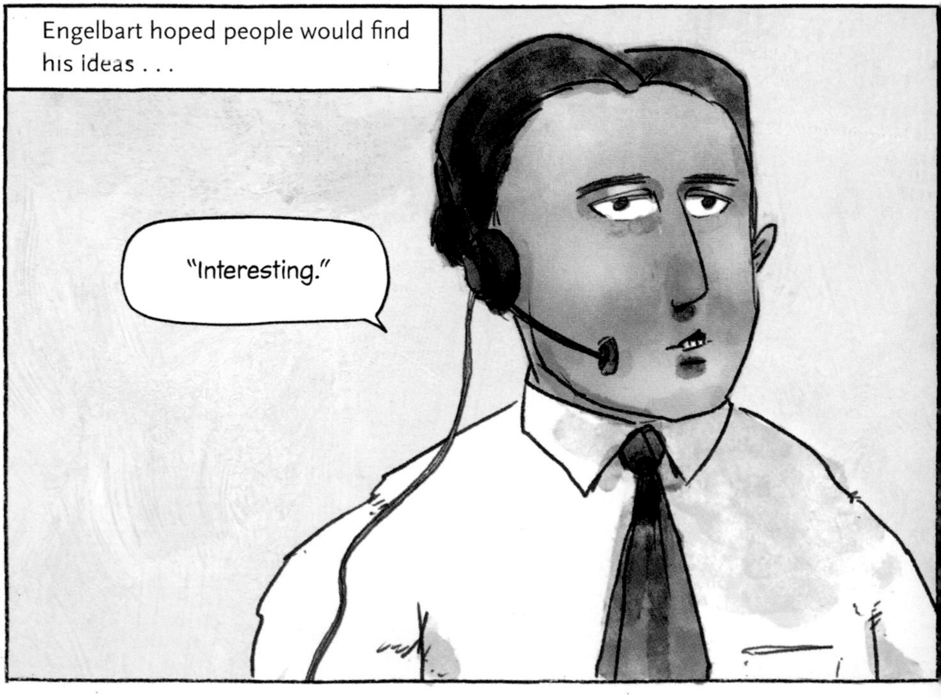
Engelbart hoped people would find his ideas . . .
"Interesting."

In fact, he had a few big ideas to share. Engelbart showed how people could interact between widely separated computers and how they could select items on a computer screen that links, or connects, to other information. He also showed how images and sound could be part of the interaction.

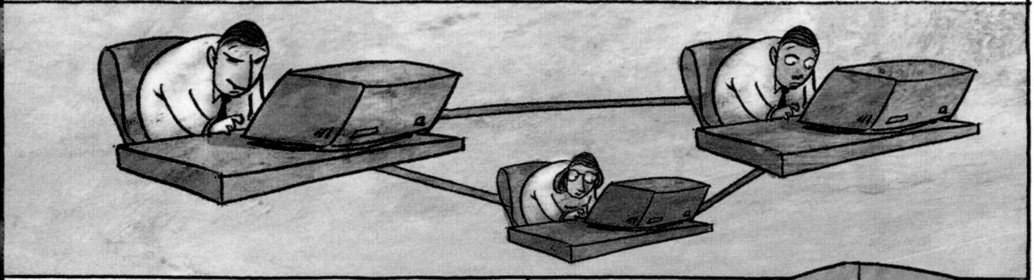

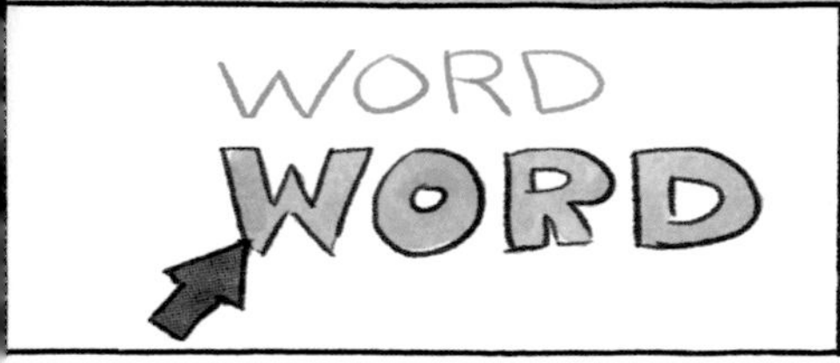
WORD
WORD

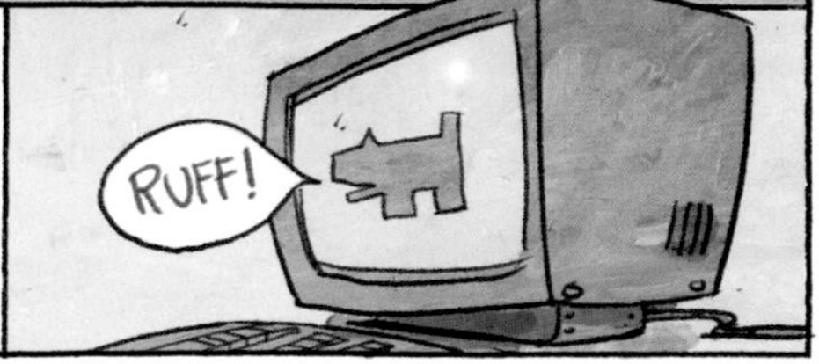
RUFF!

He used a small, handheld wooden device to move a cursor, or pointer, on the computer screen. The wire that connected it to the computer resembled a tail, prompting Engelbart and his colleagues to call it a mouse.

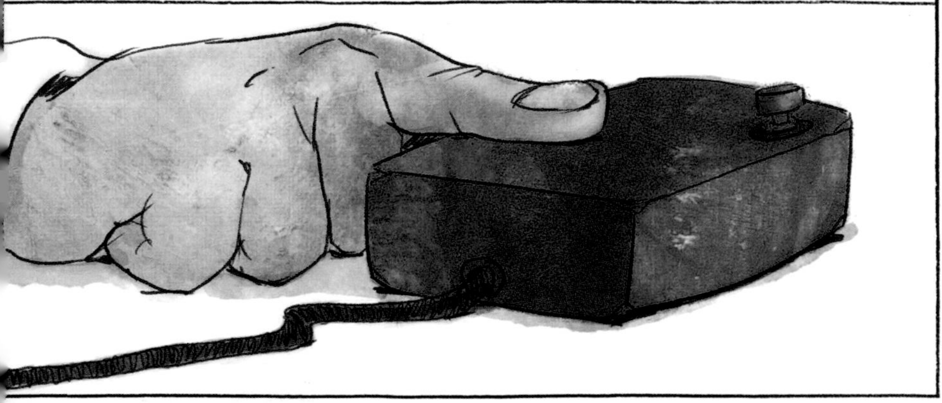

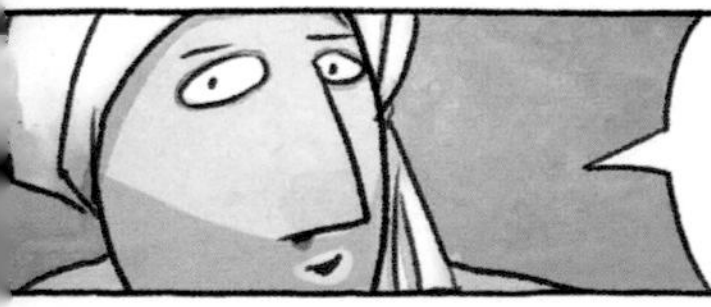

The demonstration was a glimpse into a future that would arrive thirty years later and has been called the Mother of All Demos.

The future of computers appeared rosy . . . but it wasn't. Many times, computers sat idle while programs were being written. The programs were called *software* to set them apart from the hardware, which are the bits and pieces of the actual machine.

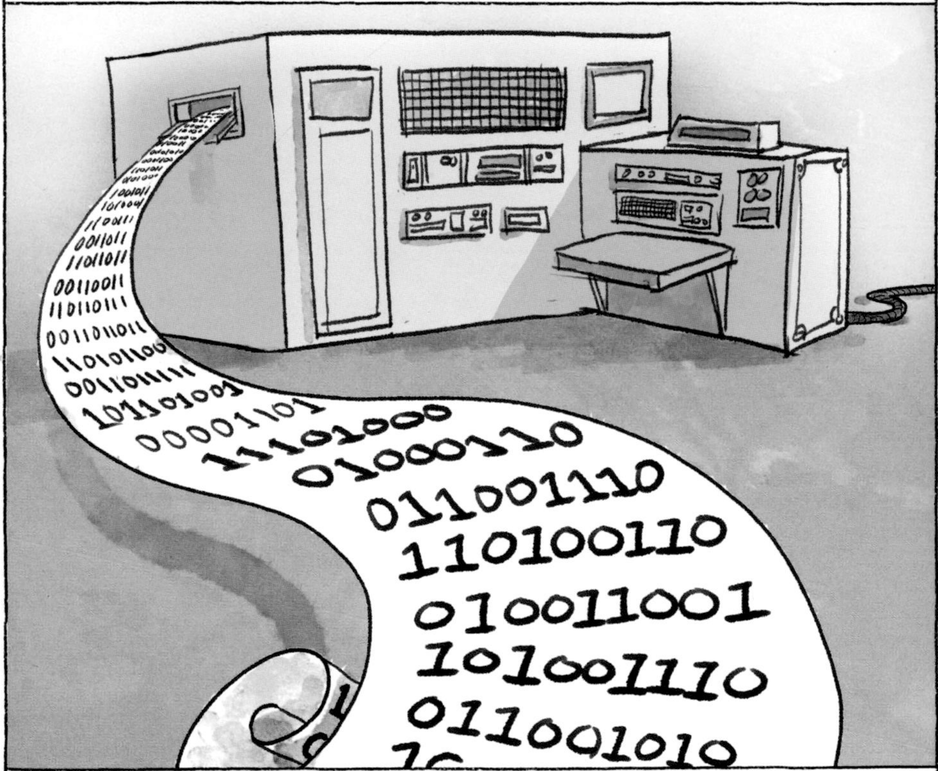

011001110
110100110
010011001
101001110
011001010

The very basic language a computer uses is called machine language. It consists of only the ones and zeros the switches understand.

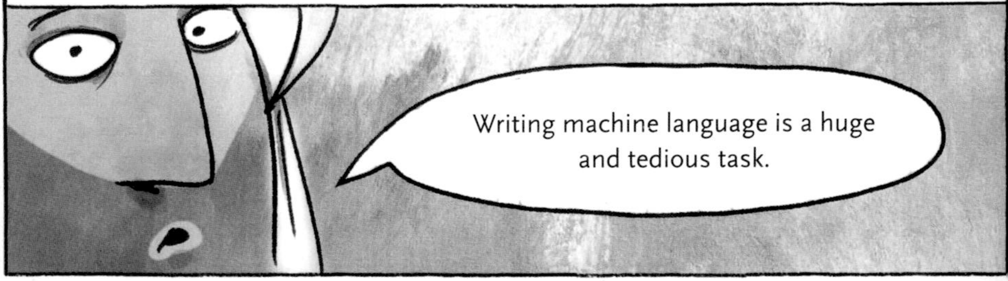

Writing machine language is a huge and tedious task.

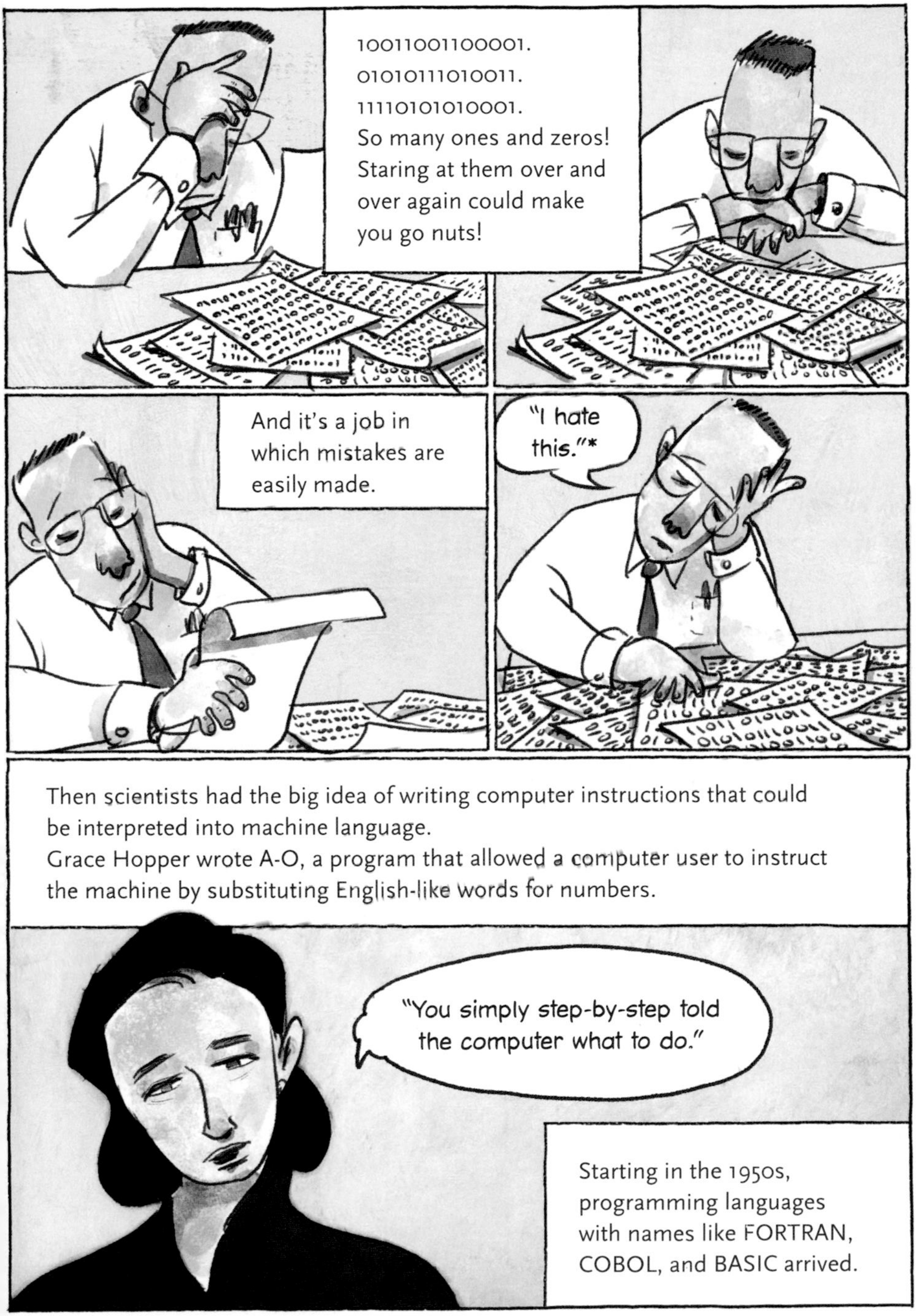
10011001100001.
01010111010011.
11110101010001.
So many ones and zeros! Staring at them over and over again could make you go nuts!
And it's a job in which mistakes are easily made.
"I hate this."*
Then scientists had the big idea of writing computer instructions that could be interpreted into machine language.
Grace Hopper wrote A-O, a program that allowed a computer user to instruct the machine by substituting English-like words for numbers.
"You simply step-by-step told the computer what to do."
Starting in the 1950s, programming languages with names like FORTRAN, COBOL, and BASIC arrived.

*Not a real quote

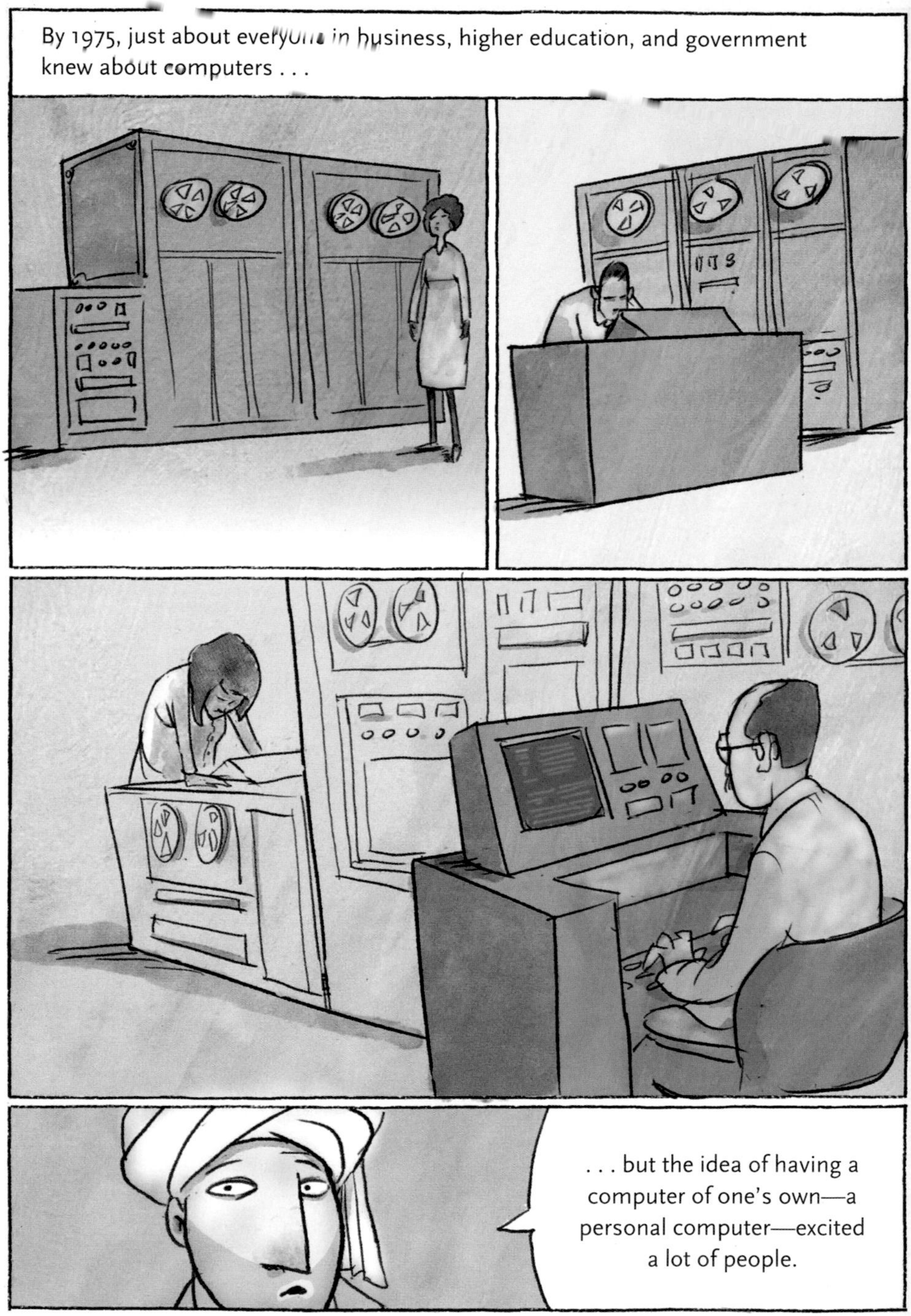
By 1975, just about everyone in business, higher education, and government knew about computers . . .
. . . but the idea of having a computer of one's own—a personal computer—excited a lot of people.

It gave engineer businessman Edward Roberts an idea.

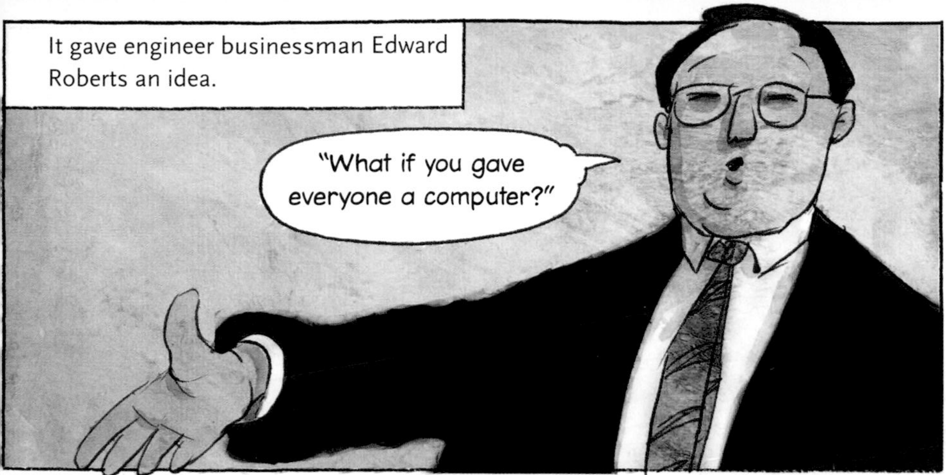
"What if you gave everyone a computer?"

He'd sold build-it-yourself toy rocket kits and build-it-yourself desk calculators. Now he decided to sell a build-it-yourself computer.

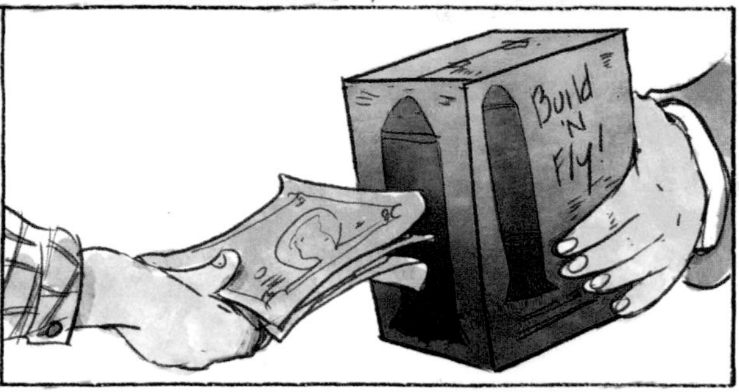
Build 'N Fly!

In all honesty, Roberts's Altair computer wasn't very good. Instead of a screen, it had flashing lights, and instead of a keyboard to enter data or programming, it had a row of switches. It was roughly the size of a shoebox.
Roberts hoped to sell two hundred of them.

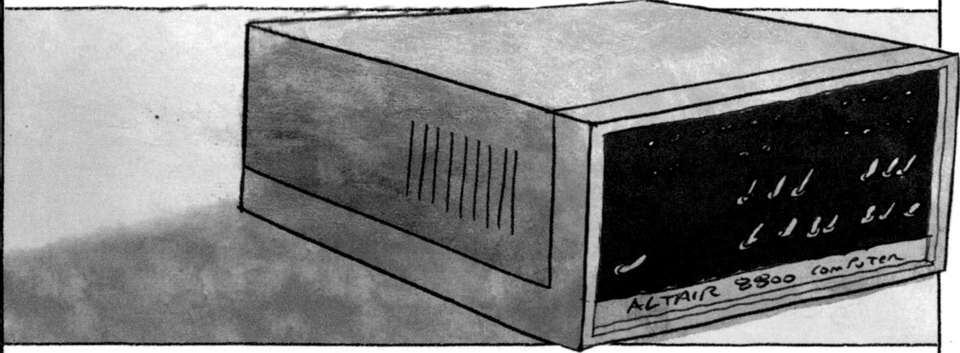
ALTAIR 8800 COMPUTER

Altair went on sale and Roberts was flooded with orders . . . he sold five thousand in the first few months!

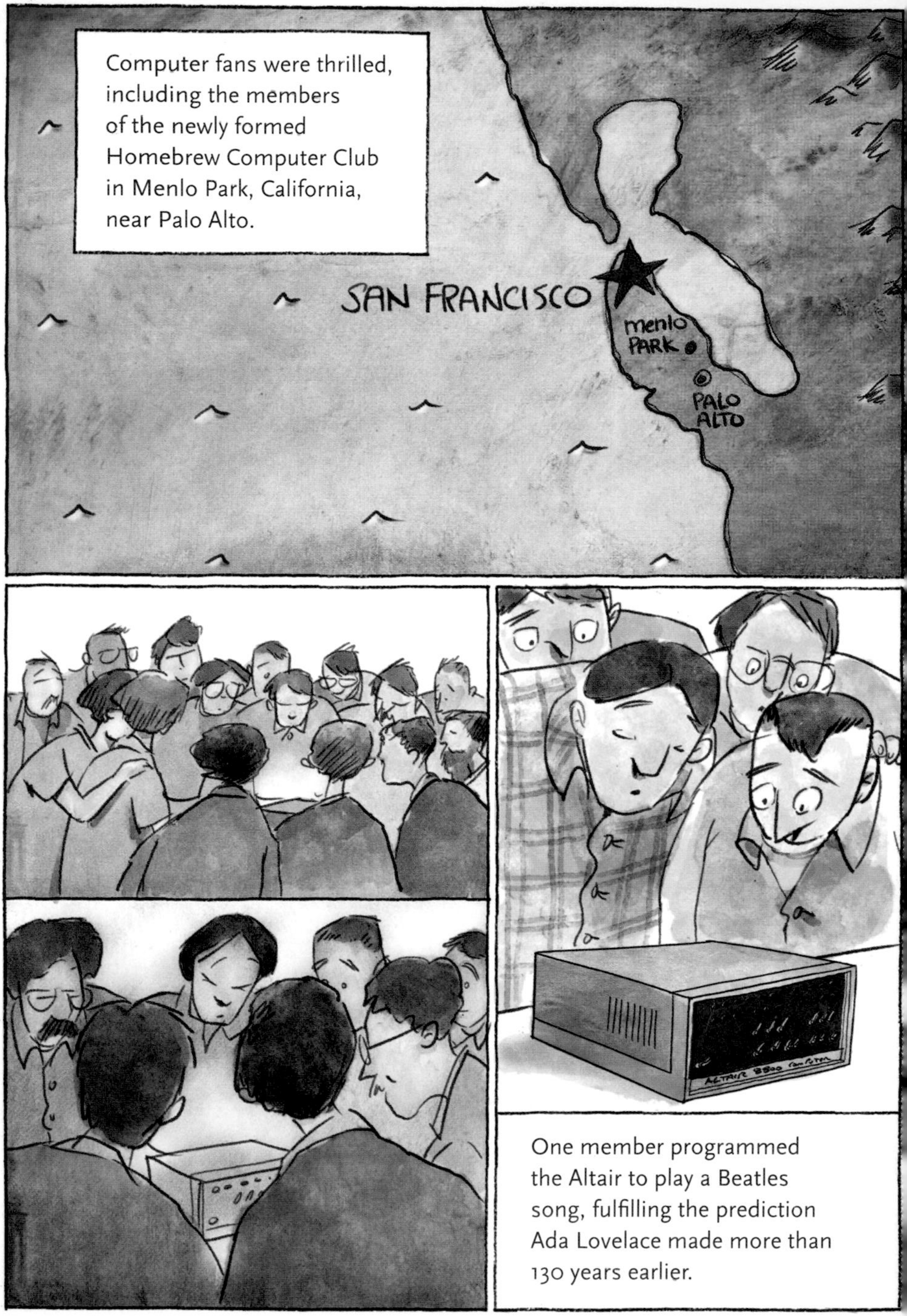
Computer fans were thrilled, including the members of the newly formed Homebrew Computer Club in Menlo Park, California, near Palo Alto.
SAN FRANCISCO
menlo PARK
PALO ALTO
One member programmed the Altair to play a Beatles song, fulfilling the prediction Ada Lovelace made more than 130 years earlier.

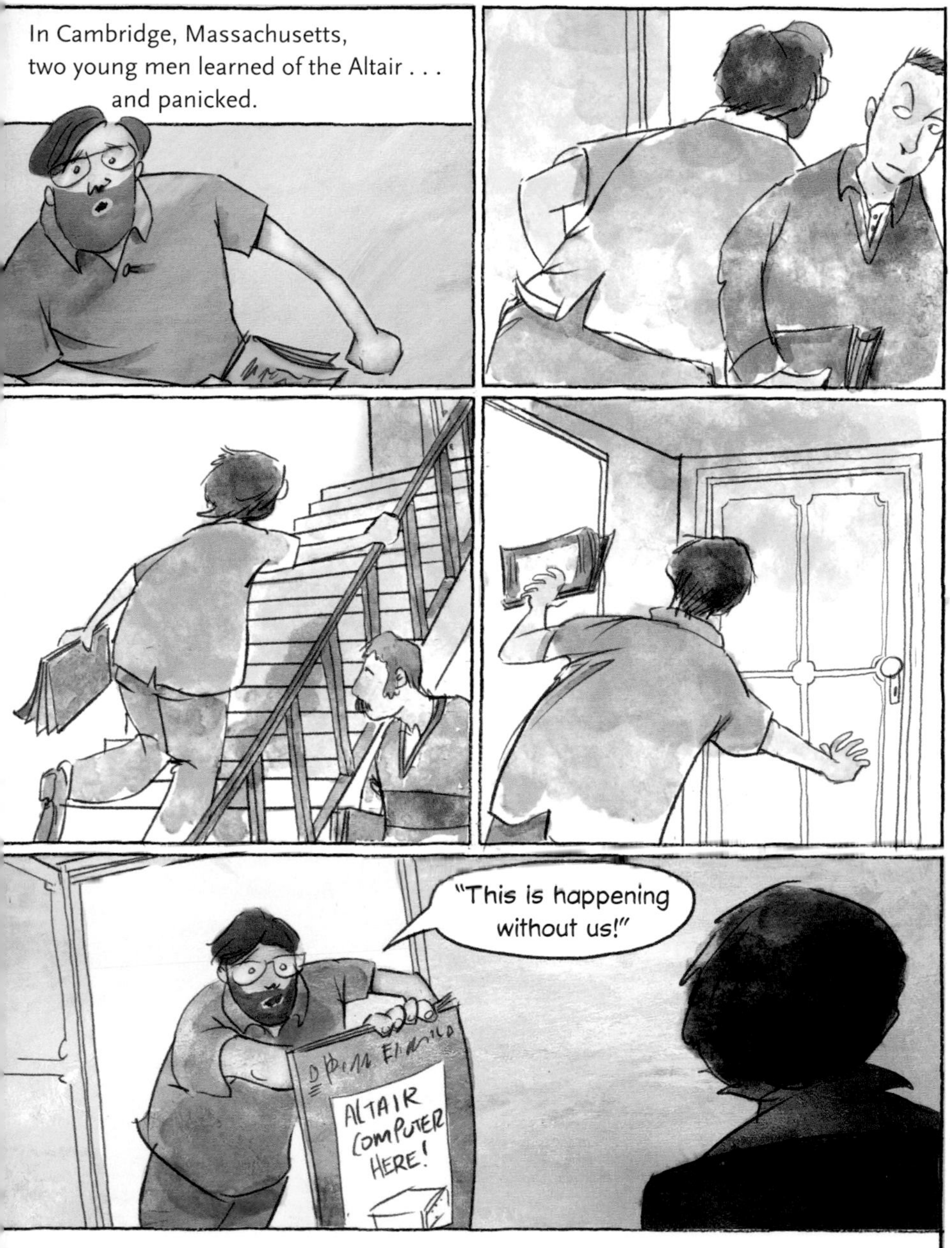
In Cambridge, Massachusetts, two young men learned of the Altair . . . and panicked.
"This is happening without us!"
ALTAIR COMPUTER HERE!

By *this*, he meant the dawn of the personal computer. They were a couple of *nerds* who loved the idea of a personal computer and worried they'd miss the coming personal computer revolution.

Twenty-one-year-old Paul Allen and nineteen-year-old Bill Gates had been childhood friends.

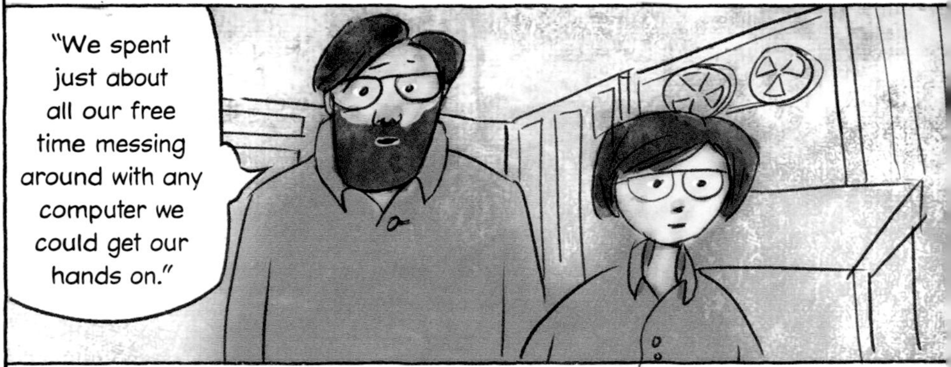
"We spent just about all our free time messing around with any computer we could get our hands on."

As teenagers, the self-taught programmers provided their coding skills to local companies, the government, and their own high school. Gates spent much of his last semester of high school not in class but coding for a nearby power company.

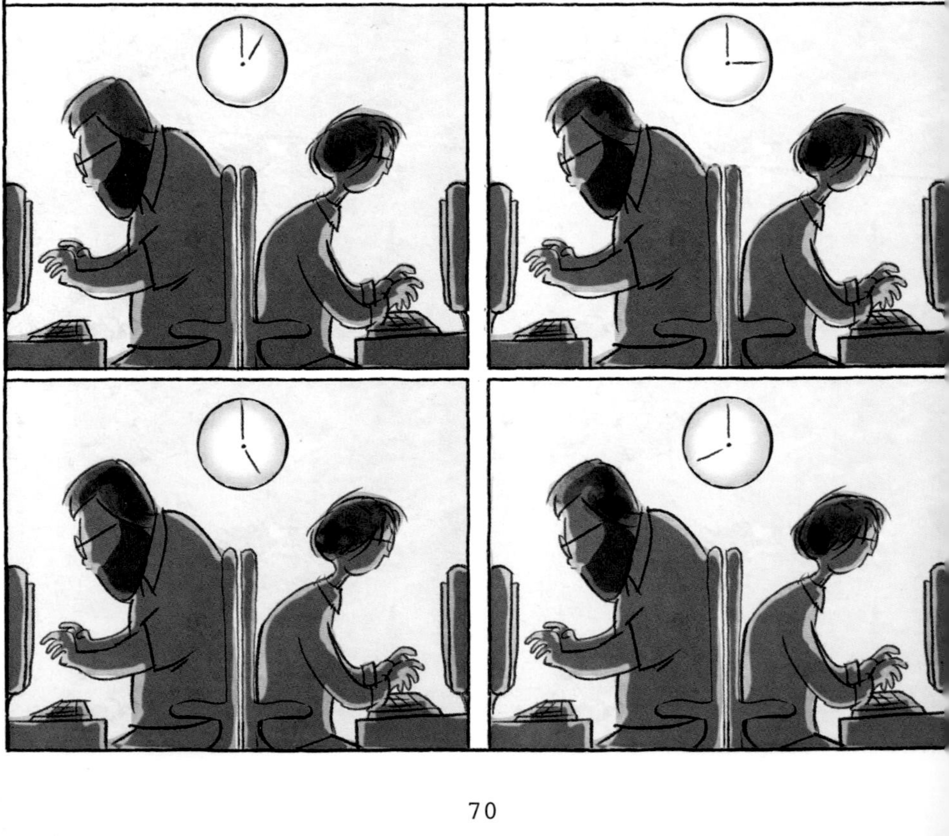

He and Allen would code hour after hour, even ignoring meals. For energy, Gates licked Tang (an orange-flavored powder to be mixed with water) off his hand.

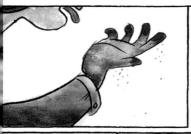

"His palm had a chronic orange tinge . . ."

After high school, Gates had entered Harvard University.

Allen had taken a job at a nearby technology company.

But upon learning of the Altair computer, the two friends spent eight weeks writing a program for it. After demonstrating the program to Roberts, Allen became Altair's director of software. Gates stayed at Harvard a while, but eventually also joined Altair. He never graduated from college.

"Hey, if we're really successful we could . . . grow to around thirty-five employees."

Seeing a bright future for themselves, the young men formed a company. They called their partnership Micro-Soft.

The Altair computer touched more people than just Gates and Allen. It also excited shy Steve Wozniak—Woz, for short—a young man with a knack for building electronic things.

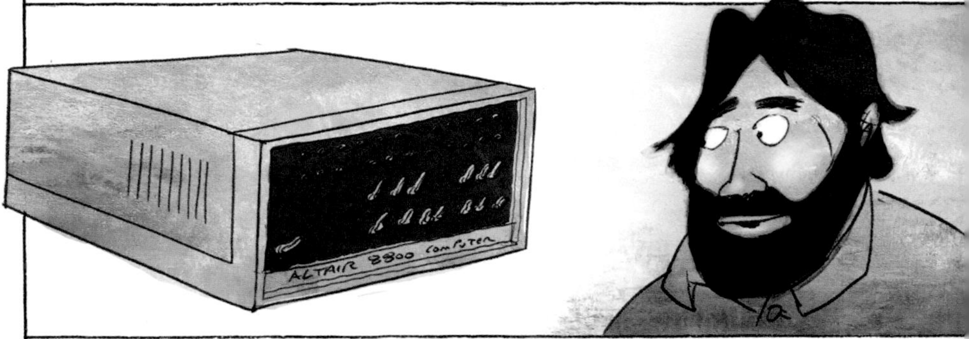
ALTAIR 8800 COMPUTER

As a child he'd built a crystal radio, an intercom system, and a shortwave radio.

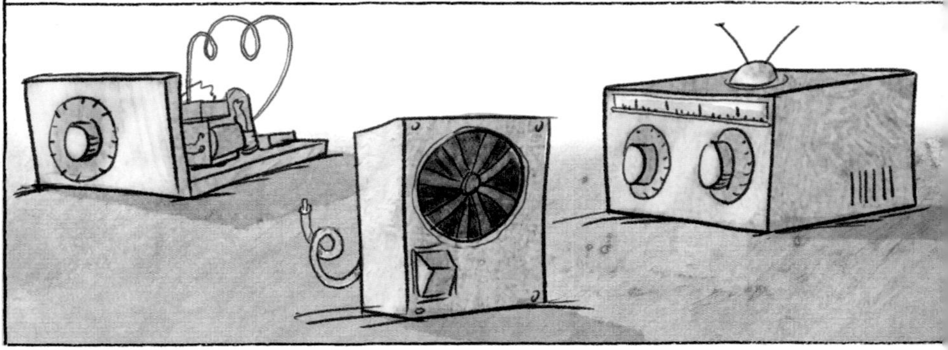

He attended the meeting of the Homebrew Computer Club the night the Altair was introduced.

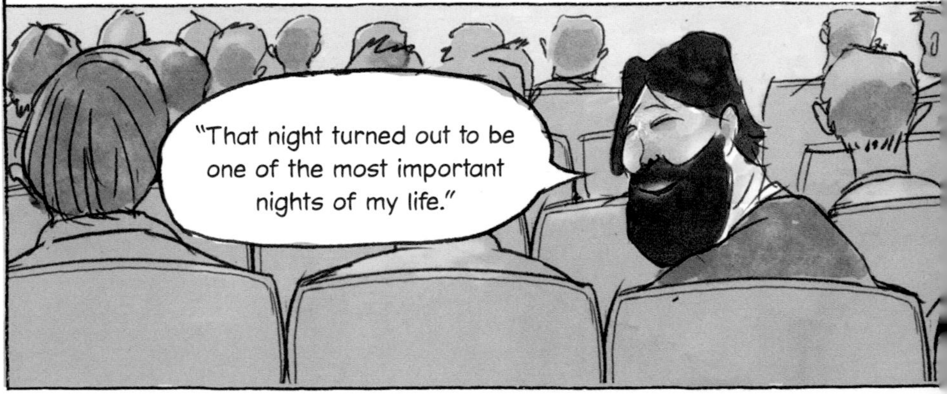
"That night turned out to be one of the most important nights of my life."

Woz saw the electronic possibilities for computer design. He had already built his own computer when he was twenty.

With no keyboard or screen, and driven by punch card instructions, it wasn't much better than the Altair. Still, it led him to a teenage neighbor who shared his interest in electronics.

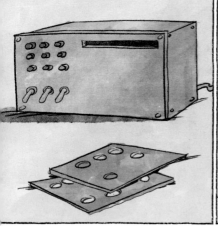

"He was kind of skinny and wiry and full of energy."

Steve Jobs.

Jobs started college and soon dropped out, but he stayed on campus to take courses that interested him.

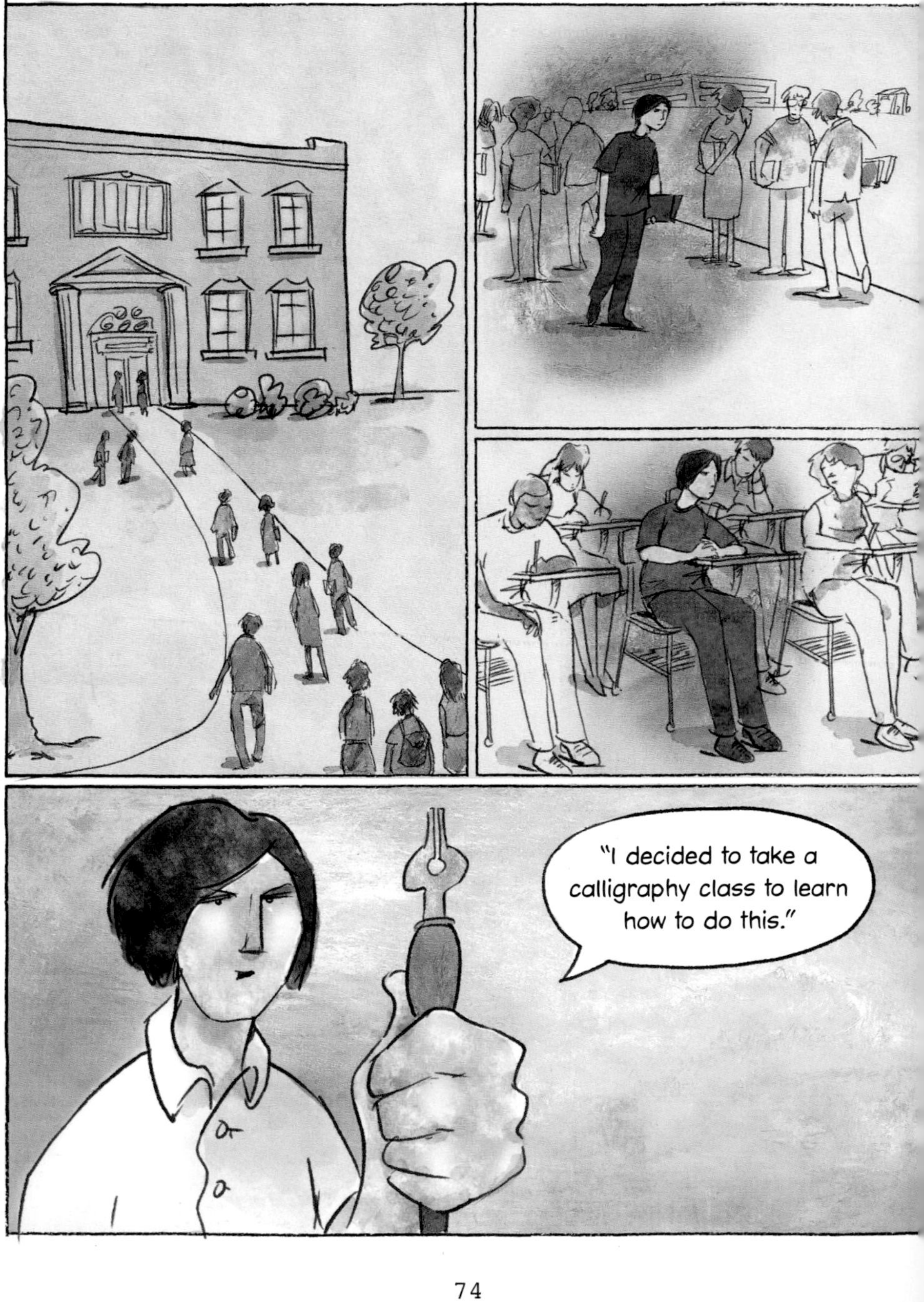
"I decided to take a calligraphy class to learn how to do this."

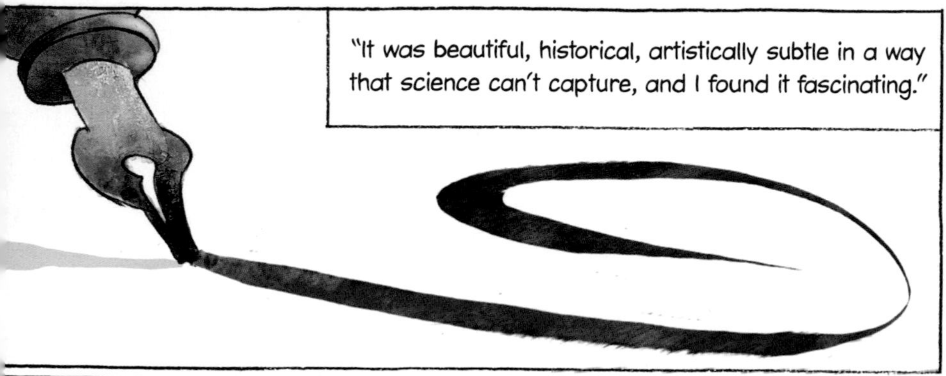
"It was beautiful, historical, artistically subtle in a way that science can't capture, and I found it fascinating."

None of this had any practical application for his life. But ten years later, when he was designing computers . . .

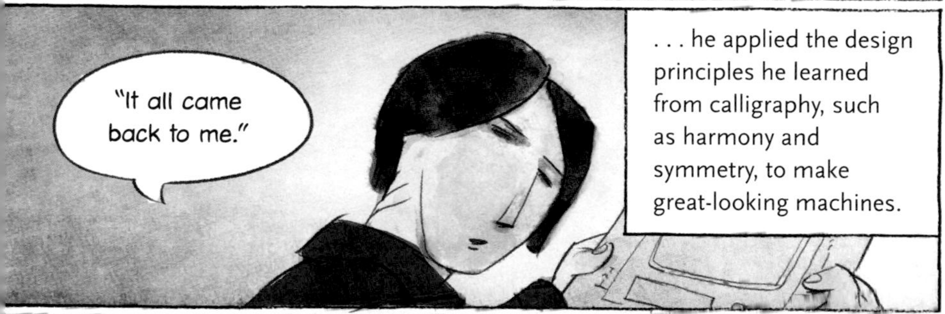
"It all came back to me."
. . . he applied the design principles he learned from calligraphy, such as harmony and symmetry, to make great-looking machines.

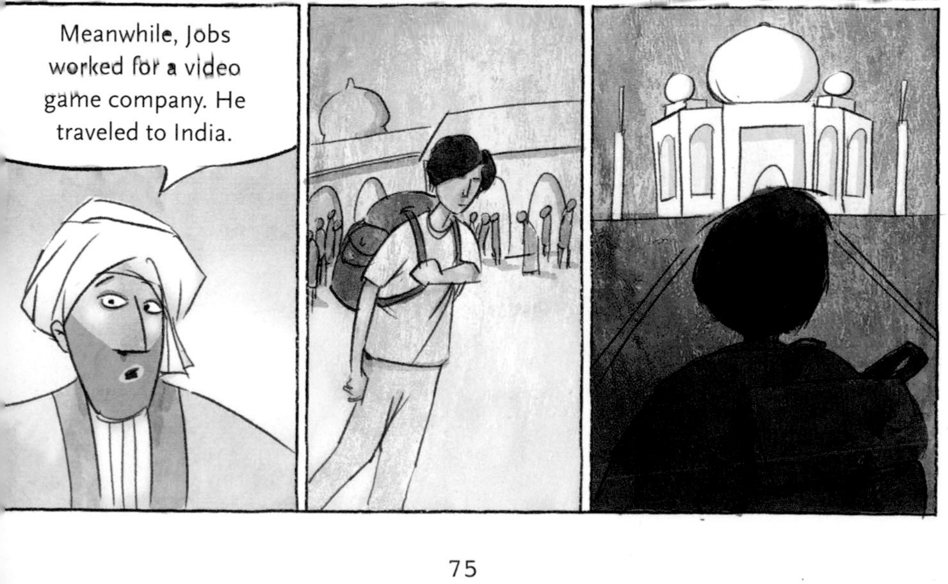
Meanwhile, Jobs worked for a video game company. He traveled to India.

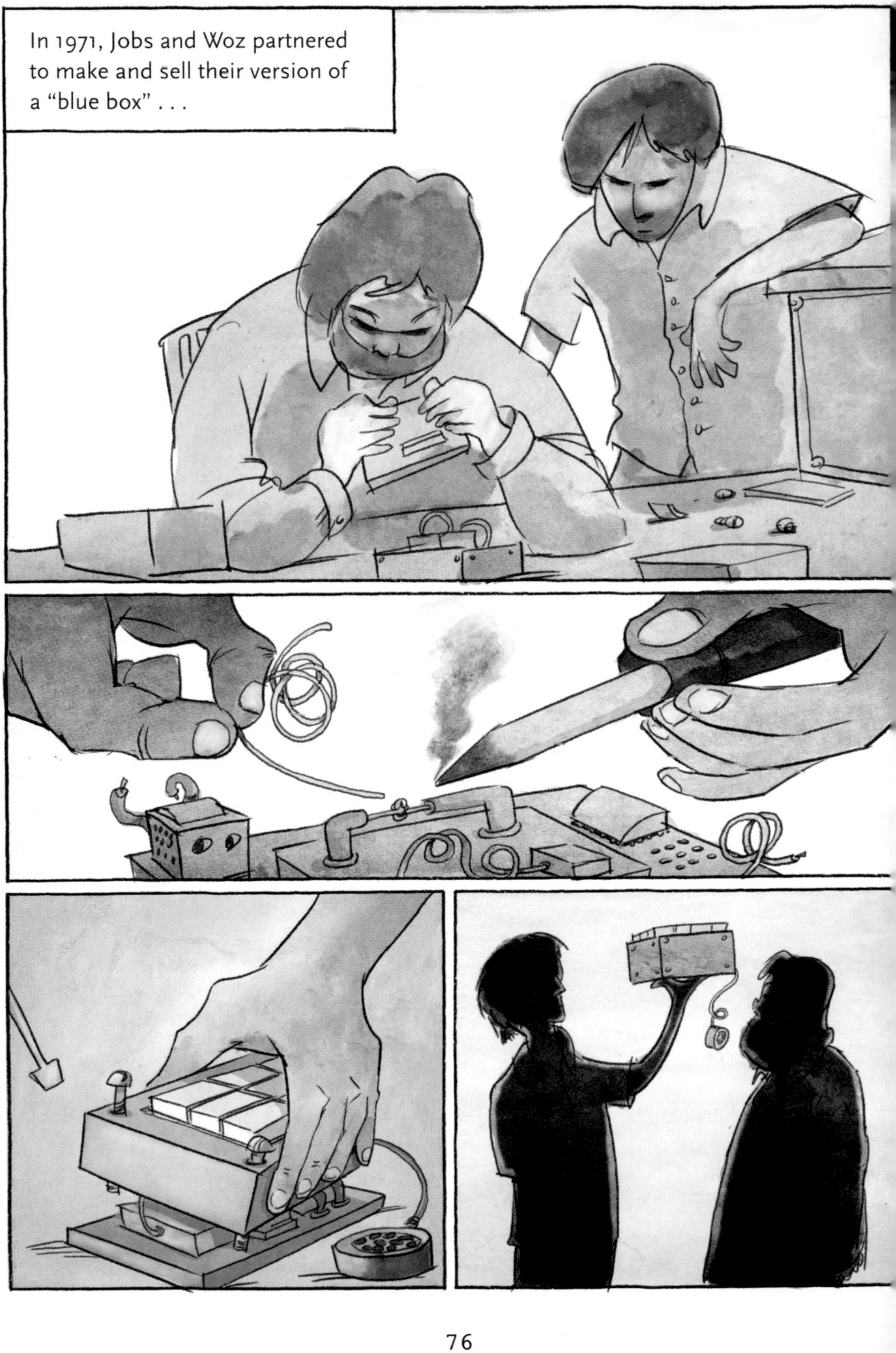
In 1971, Jobs and Woz partnered to make and sell their version of a "blue box" . . .

. . . an electronic device that allowed the user to make free telephone calls. (This was before cell phones!)

They were clever, popular . . . and illegal. Jobs and Woz could have landed in jail. Still . . .

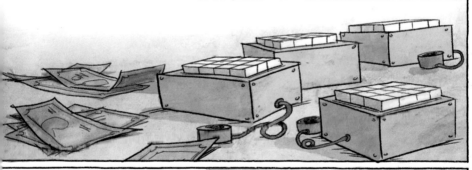

"It gave us a taste of what we could do with my engineering skills and his vision."

In 1976, the pair pooled $1,300 of their own money and started making the Apple I, using the Jobs family's garage as their manufacturing location.

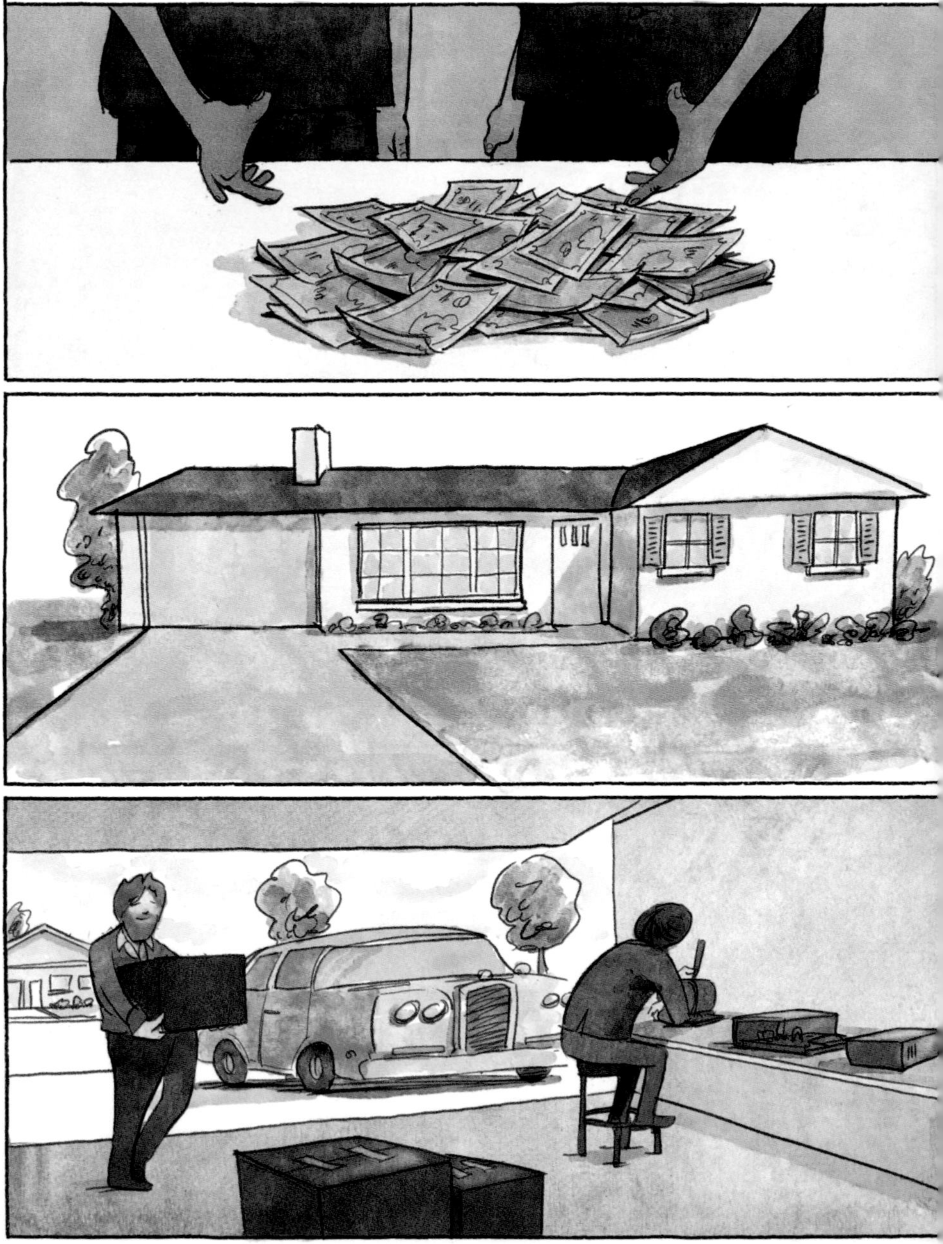

The Apple I didn't look anything like a modern computer. It was more of a wooden shingle covered in electronics.

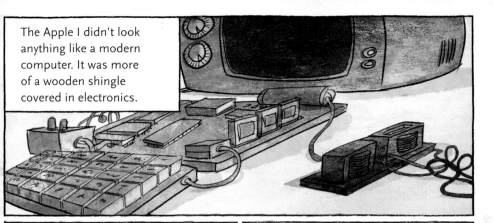

But hobbyists liked it and they sold nearly two hundred of them. Then Jobs had a big idea for a different kind of personal computer.

"My vision was to create the first fully packaged computer. We were no longer aiming for the handful of hobbyists . . . For every one of them were a thousand people who would want the machine to be ready to run."

The Apple II arrived and proved Jobs right. It seemed everyone wanted an Apple computer and it made the company one of the fastest growing in American history.

Widespread interest in personal computers didn't escape the notice of IBM, which had by 1971 grown into a multi-billion-dollar company with 270,000 employees. In 1981, they released the IBM Personal Computer—the IBM PC.

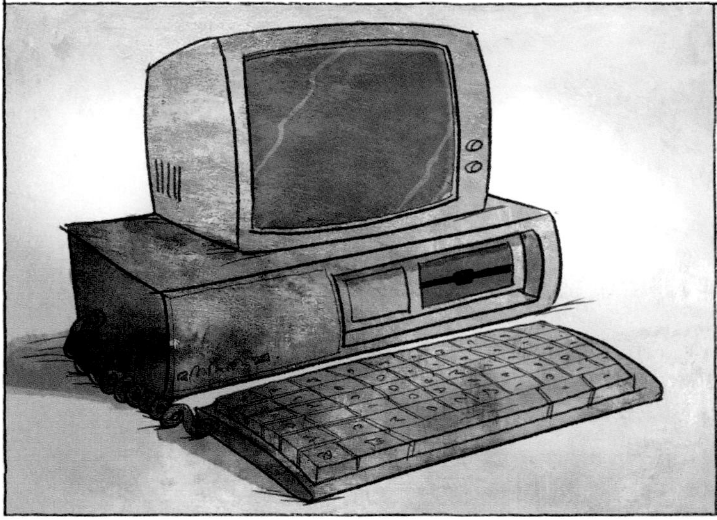

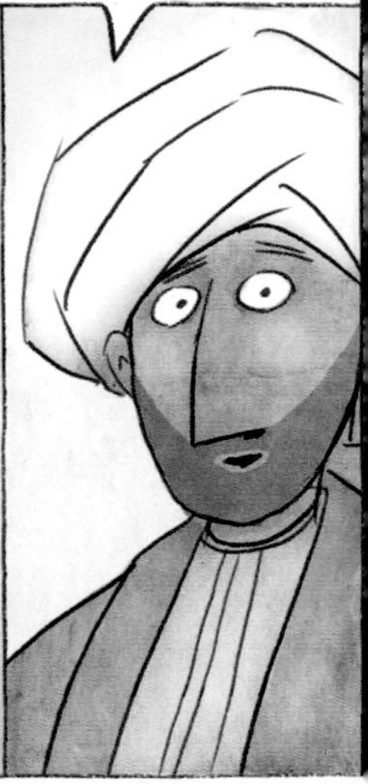

Of course, the computer needed an operating system, which is software to run it. IBM turned to . . . Bill Gates and Microsoft. They provided the software, asking only for a small royalty or payment from the sale of each computer on which it was installed.

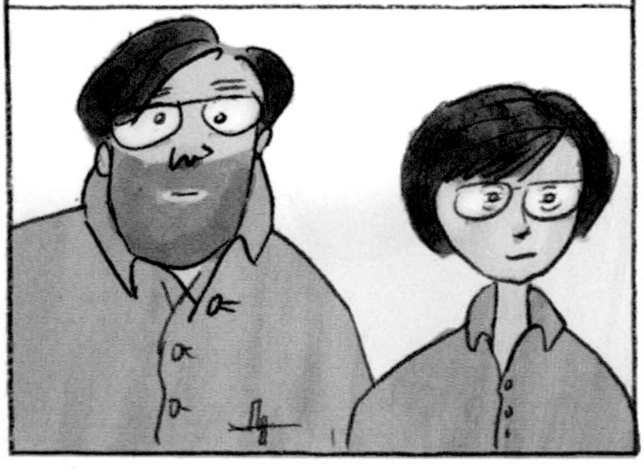

The IBM PC, and the machines that other companies built resembling it, became the most popular and influential personal computer in the world.

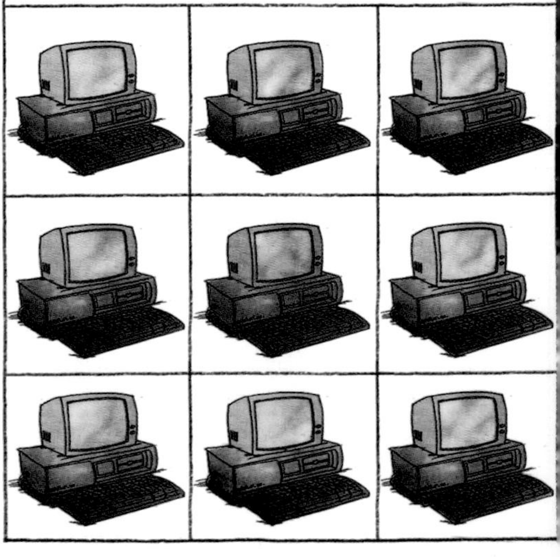

Microsoft grew to tens of thousands of employees.

And the money that Microsoft earned by providing PC software helped make Bill Gates the richest person in the world.

After a while, Allen left Microsoft and Woz left Apple to follow other paths.

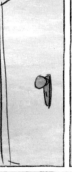

Steve Jobs strove to be a technology visionary and helped develop the Macintosh computer, the iPod, the iPad, and the iPhone. He also lent his talents to the building of animation company Pixar.

As personal computers became more popular, transistors became smaller and smaller.

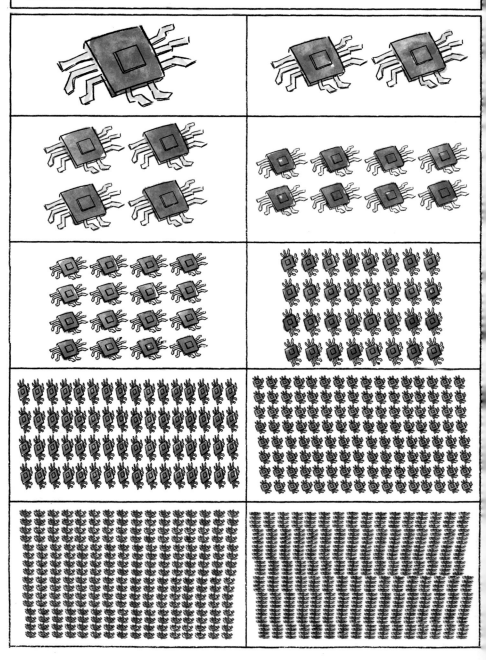

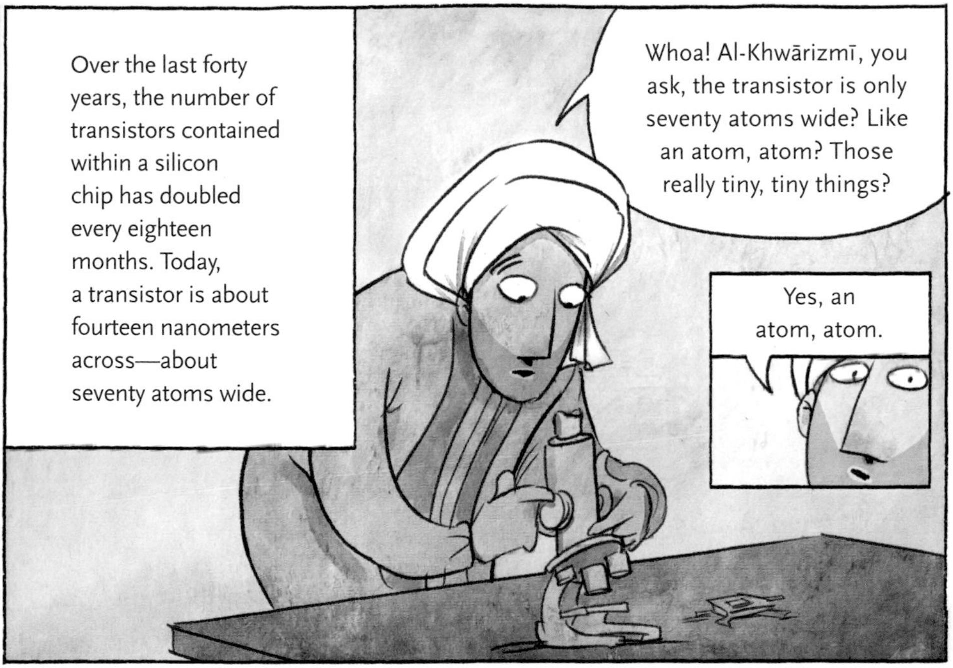
Over the last forty years, the number of transistors contained within a silicon chip has doubled every eighteen months. Today, a transistor is about fourteen nanometers across—about seventy atoms wide.
Whoa! Al-Khwārizmī, you ask, the transistor is only seventy atoms wide? Like an atom, atom? Those really tiny, tiny things?
Yes, an atom, atom.

Ever-shrinking transistors have allowed engineers to create some fantastic things . . . like the smartphone in your pocket or bag, which is really a computer that is also a phone. It has more computing power than the computer that flew Neil Armstrong and Buzz Aldrin to the surface of the moon.

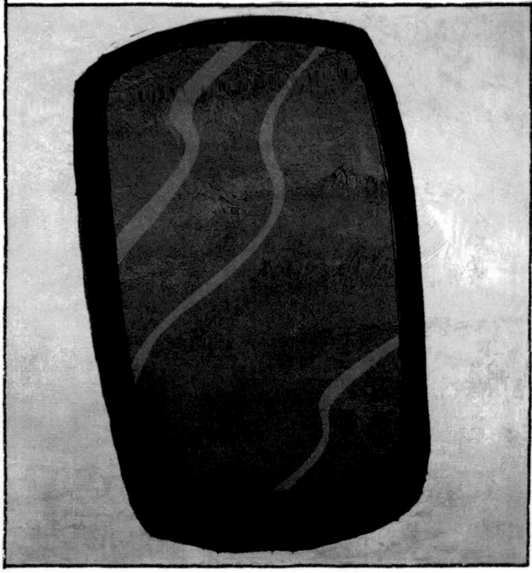

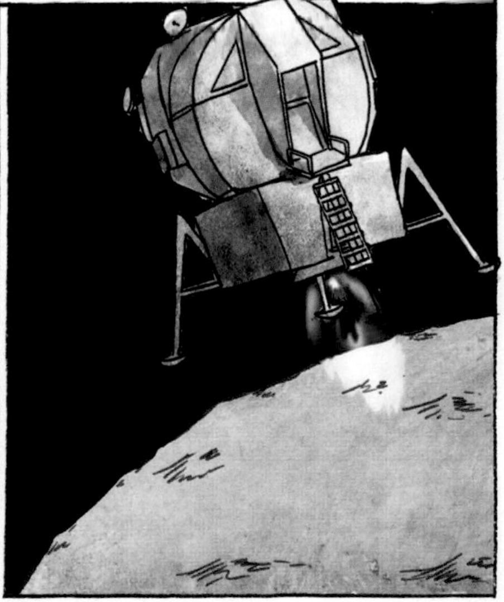

And with a rice-sized microchip placed under your skin . . .

you can automatically connect to a computer, or to a device run by a computer.

With a wave of your hand, you can pay for a vending-machine snack . . .

. . . or ride a train without the bother of holding a ticket.

A chip might also be used to monitor your health, warning you if your temperature is rising or if there's a problem with your heart.

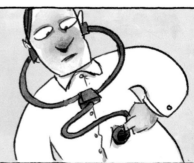

. . . open your front door . . .

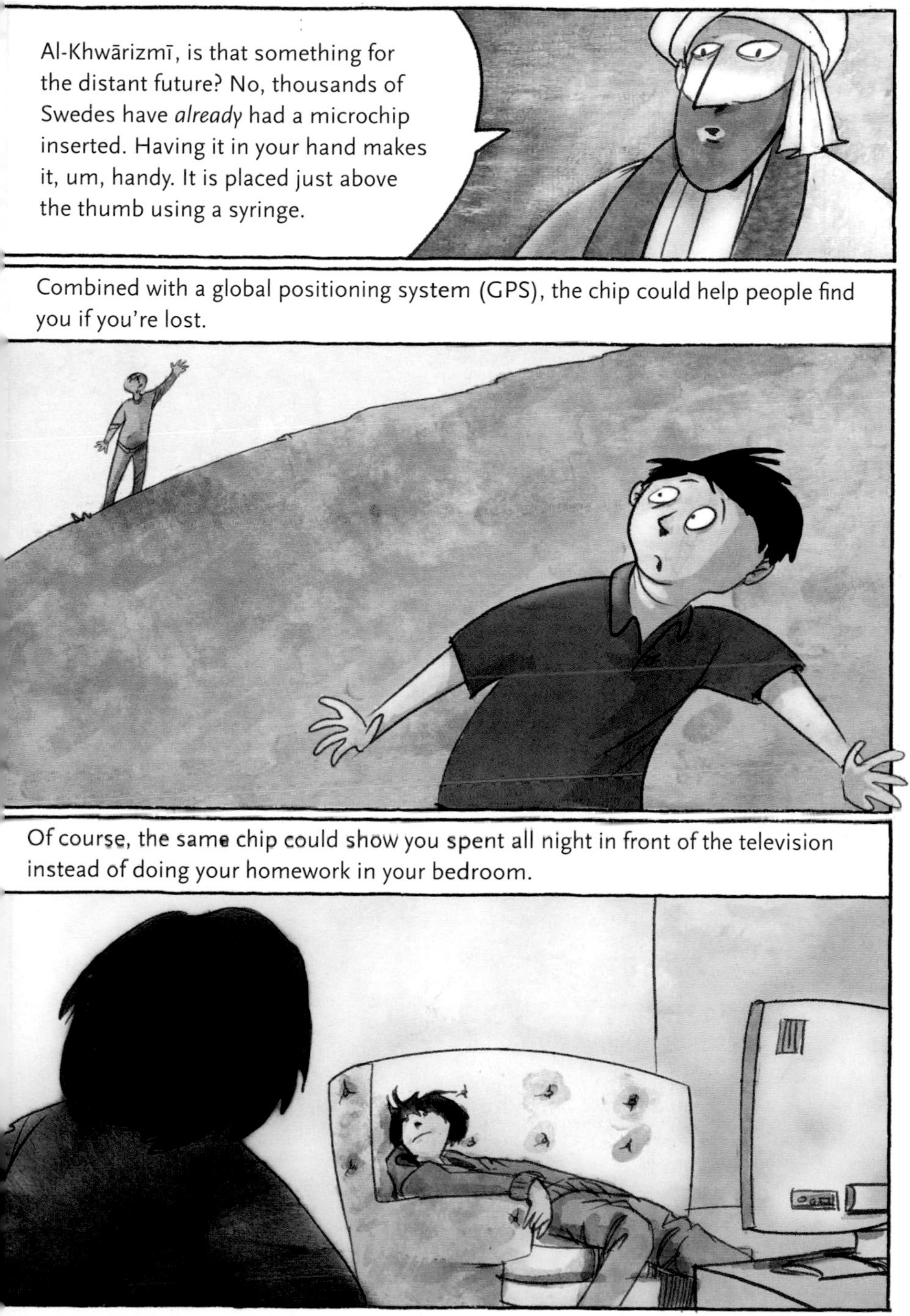
Al-Khwārizmī, is that something for the distant future? No, thousands of Swedes have *already* had a microchip inserted. Having it in your hand makes it, um, handy. It is placed just above the thumb using a syringe.
Combined with a global positioning system (GPS), the chip could help people find you if you're lost.
Of course, the same chip could show you spent all night in front of the television instead of doing your homework in your bedroom.

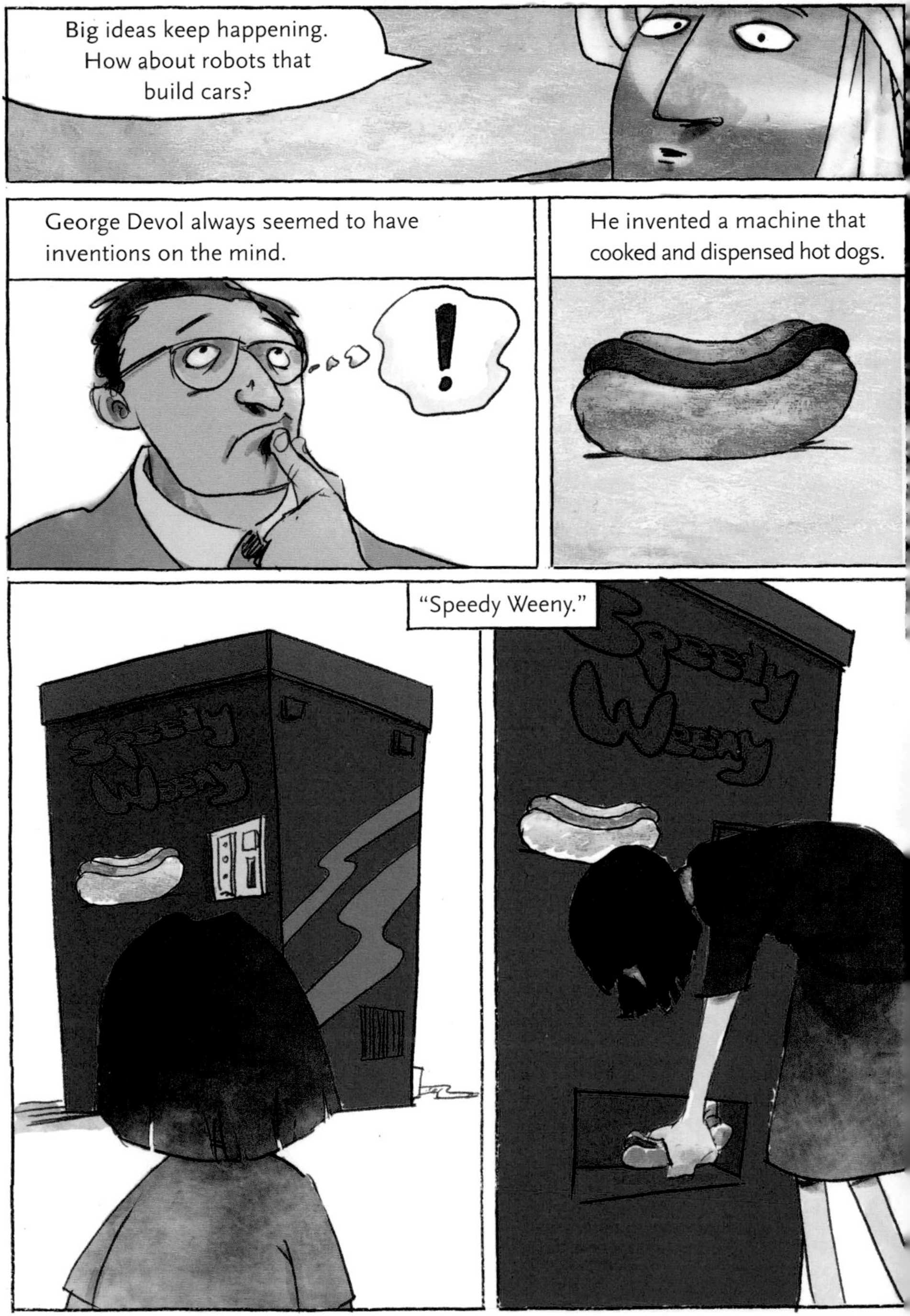

Big ideas keep happening. How about robots that build cars?
George Devol always seemed to have inventions on the mind.
!
He invented a machine that cooked and dispensed hot dogs.
"Speedy Weeny."
Speedy Weeny
Speedy Weeny

But Devol is better known for his industrial robot, the Unimate. The mechanical arm was designed to complete tedious and dangerous tasks that had to be repeated over and over. It could be programmed to remember up to two hundred commands.

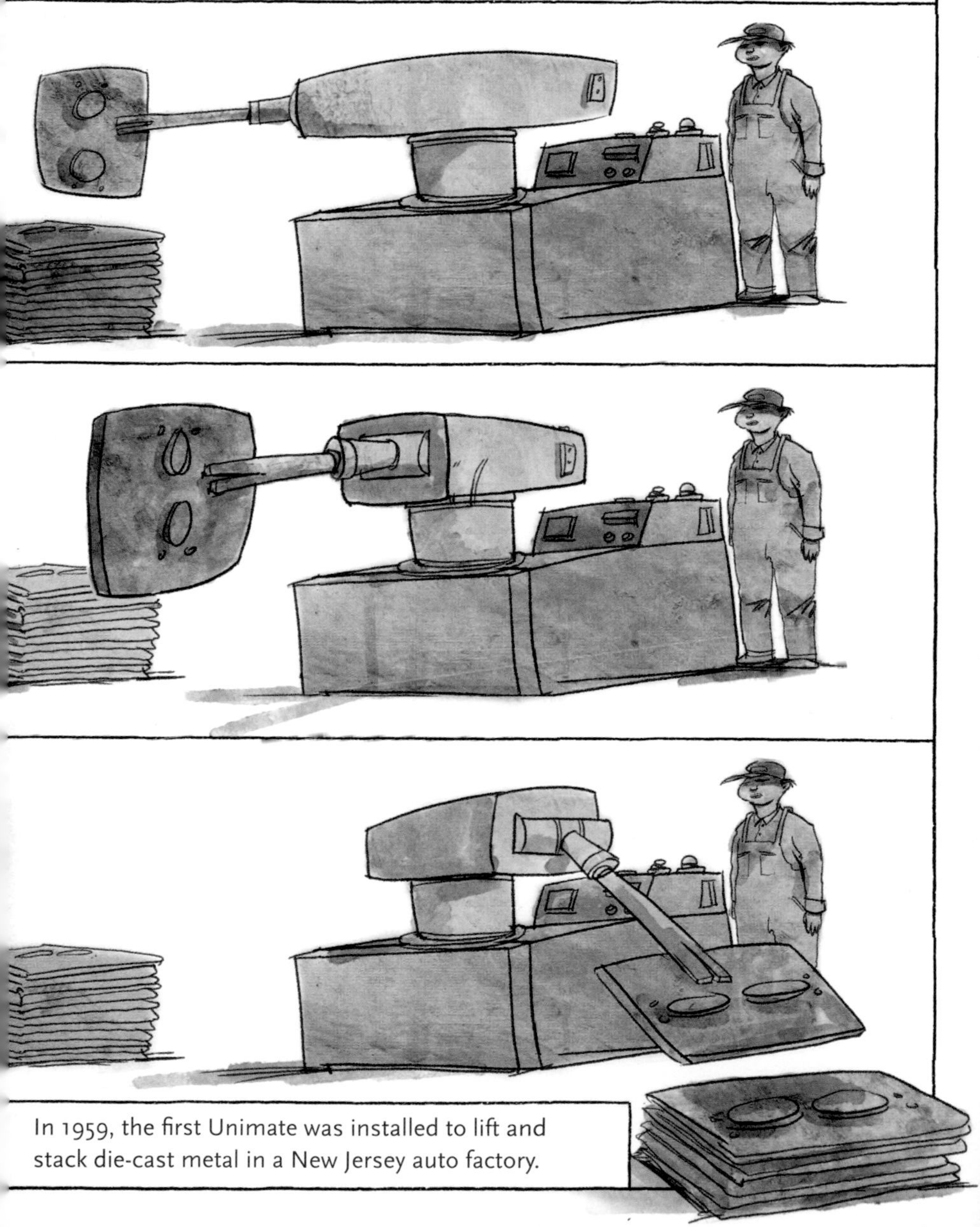

In 1959, the first Unimate was installed to lift and stack die-cast metal in a New Jersey auto factory.

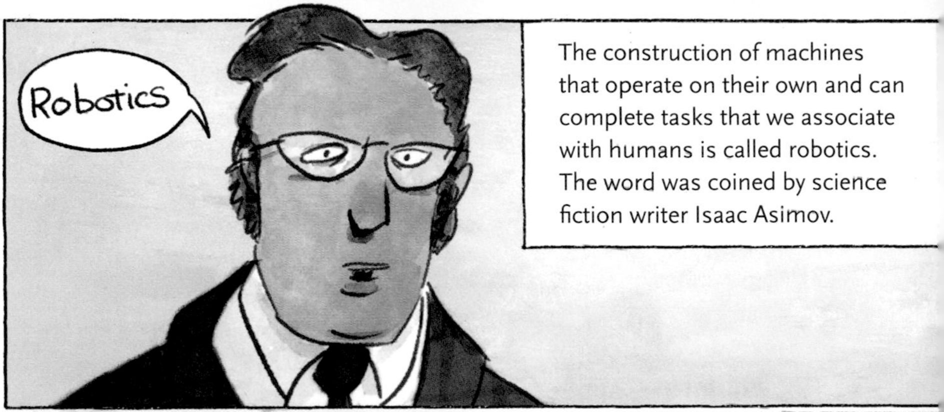
Robotics
The construction of machines that operate on their own and can complete tasks that we associate with humans is called robotics. The word was coined by science fiction writer Isaac Asimov.

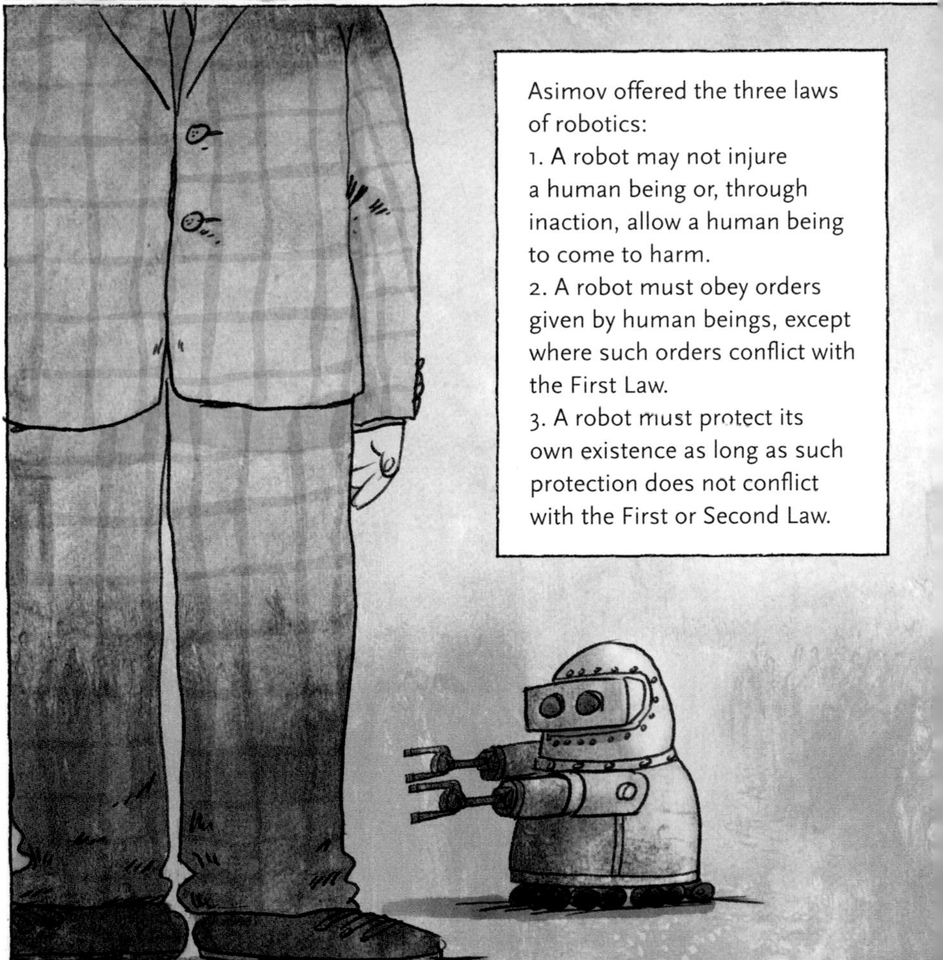
Asimov offered the three laws of robotics:
1. A robot may not injure a human being or, through inaction, allow a human being to come to harm.
2. A robot must obey orders given by human beings, except where such orders conflict with the First Law.
3. A robot must protect its own existence as long as such protection does not conflict with the First or Second Law.

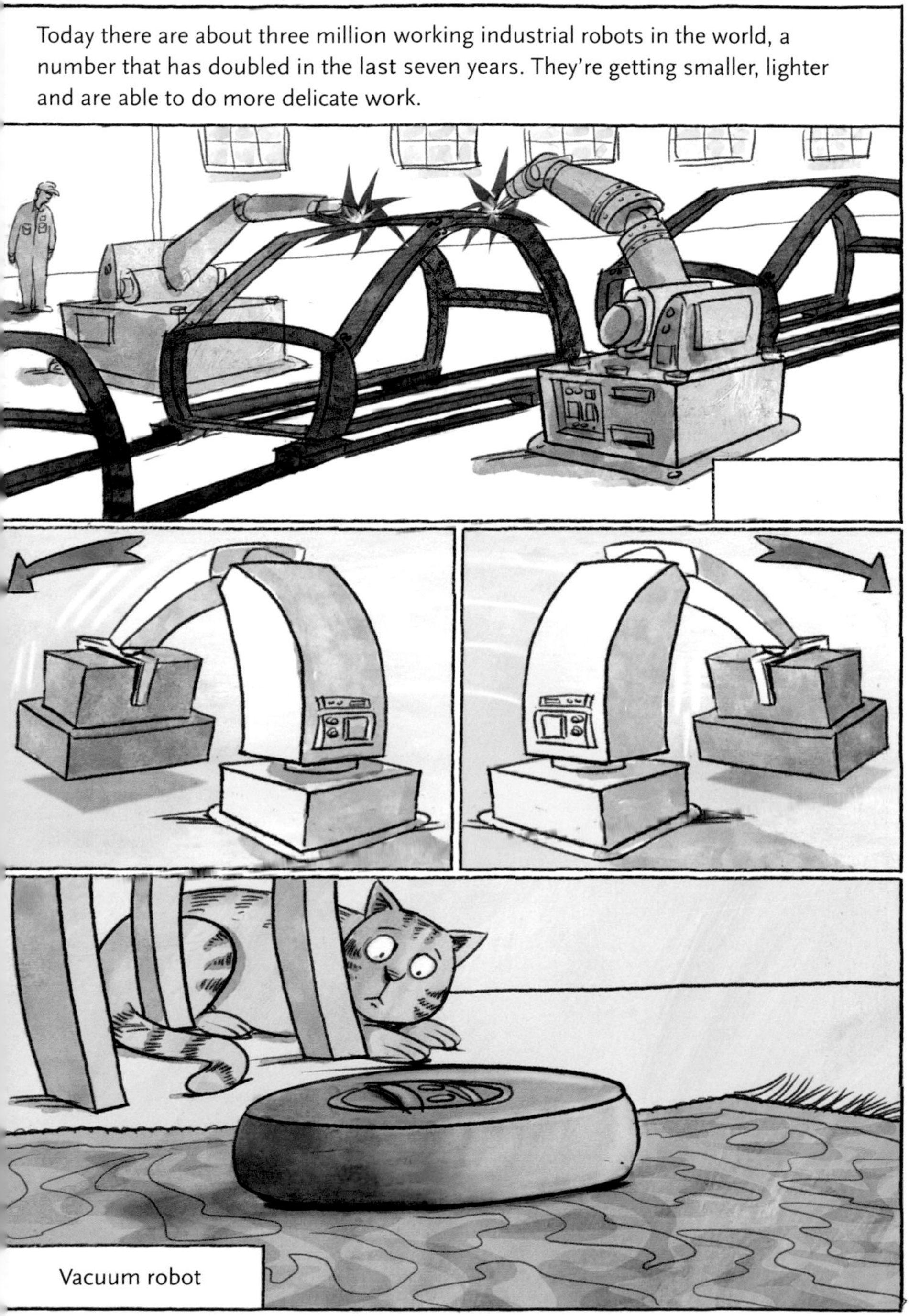
Today there are about three million working industrial robots in the world, a number that has doubled in the last seven years. They're getting smaller, lighter and are able to do more delicate work.
Vacuum robot

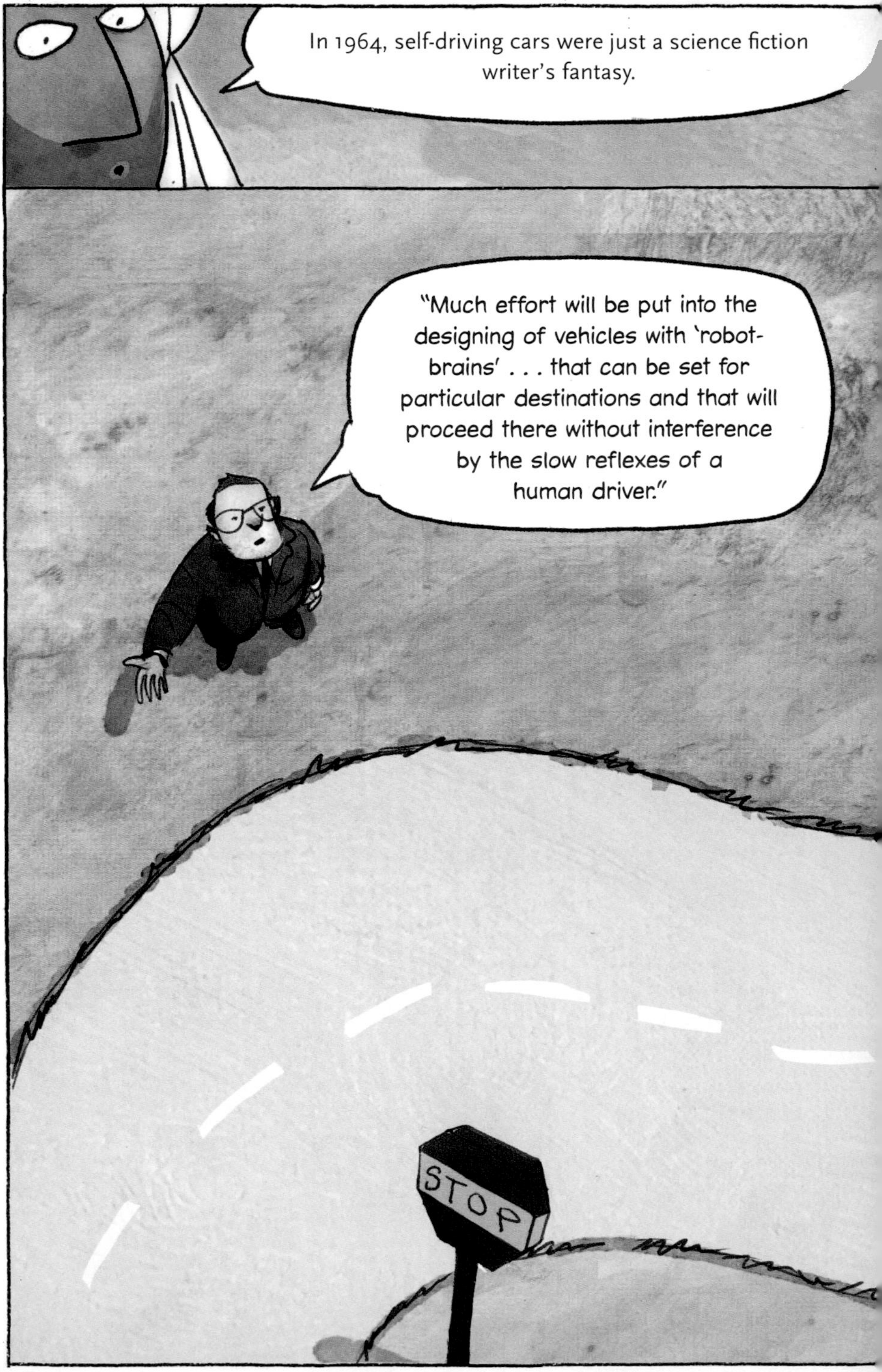
In 1964, self-driving cars were just a science fiction writer's fantasy.
"Much effort will be put into the designing of vehicles with 'robot-brains' . . . that can be set for particular destinations and that will proceed there without interference by the slow reflexes of a human driver."
STOP

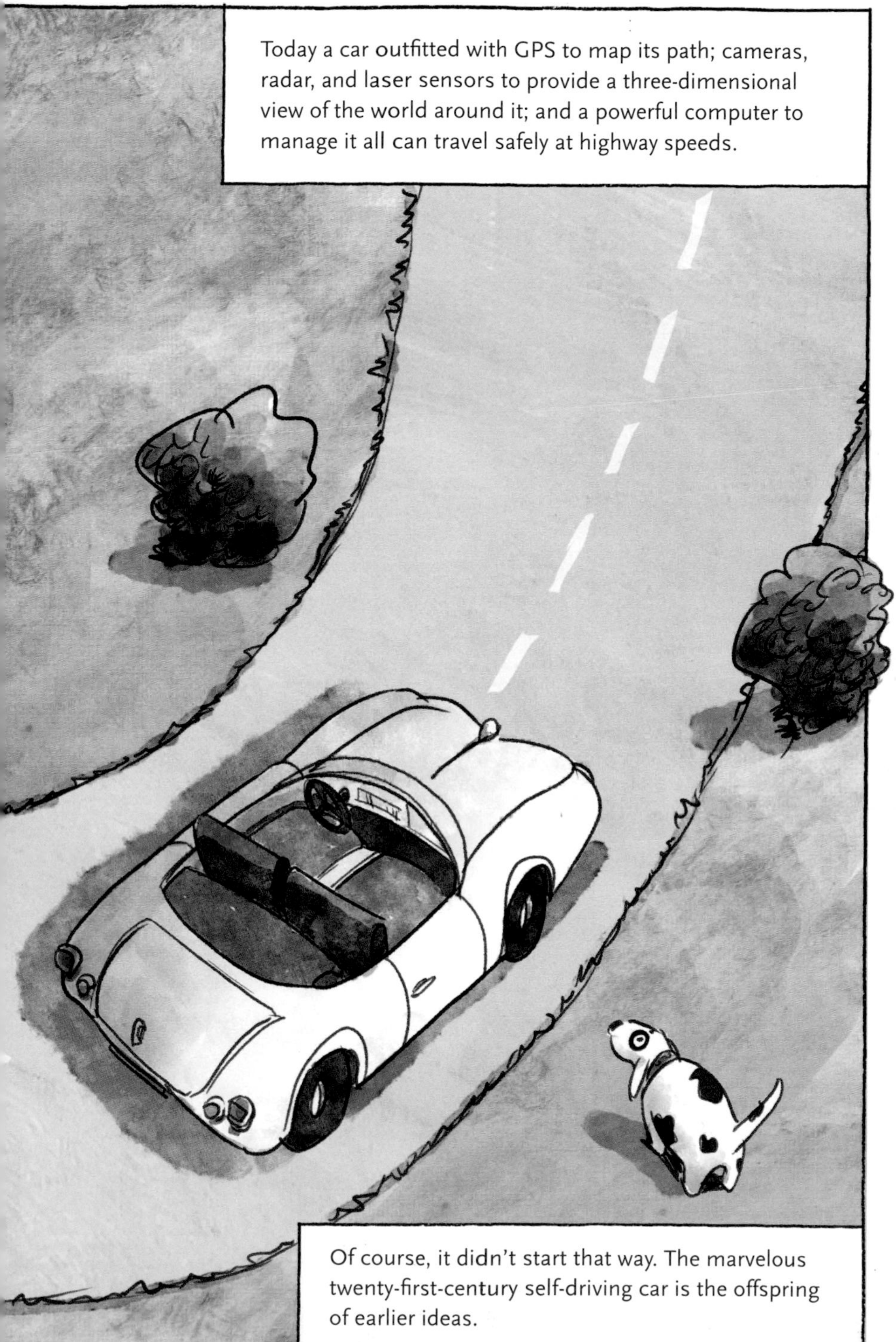
Today a car outfitted with GPS to map its path; cameras, radar, and laser sensors to provide a three-dimensional view of the world around it; and a powerful computer to manage it all can travel safely at highway speeds.
Of course, it didn't start that way. The marvelous twenty-first-century self-driving car is the offspring of earlier ideas.

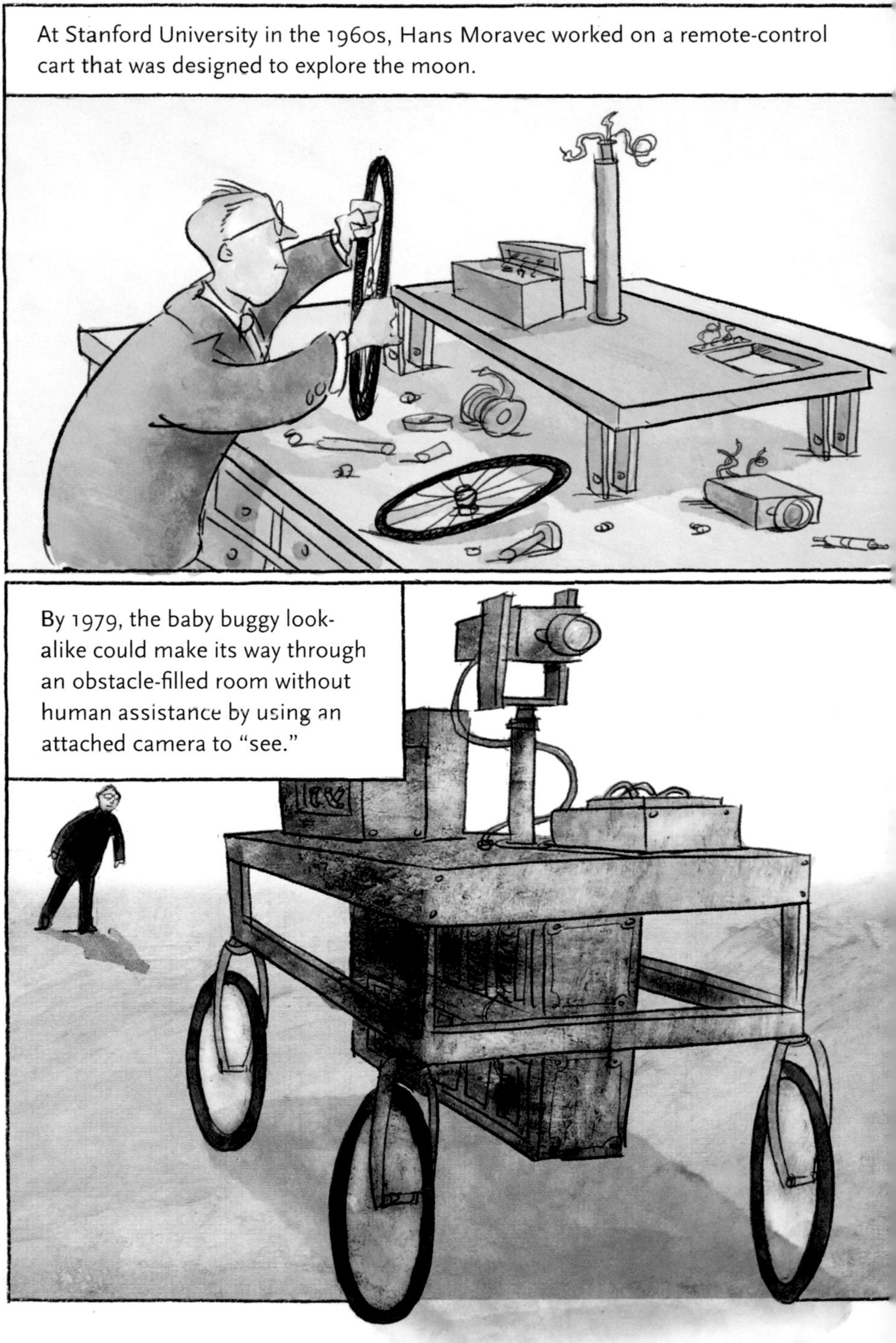
At Stanford University in the 1960s, Hans Moravec worked on a remote-control cart that was designed to explore the moon.
By 1979, the baby buggy look-alike could make its way through an obstacle-filled room without human assistance by using an attached camera to "see."

Its computer needed ten to fifteen minutes to make sense of nearby objects before lurching forward in 3-ft (1-m) spurts. The 90-ft (30-m) trip across the room took five hours.

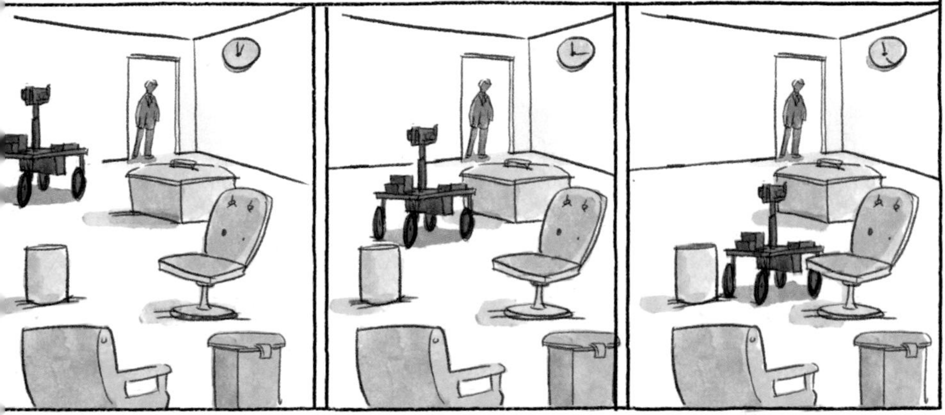

Once, while the unattended cart sat in a parking lot before testing, it escaped and drove itself through traffic on a nearby road.

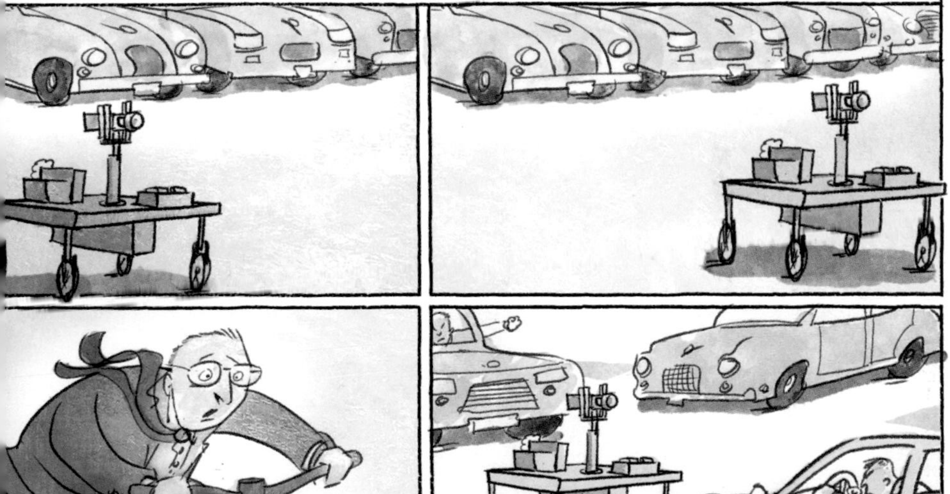

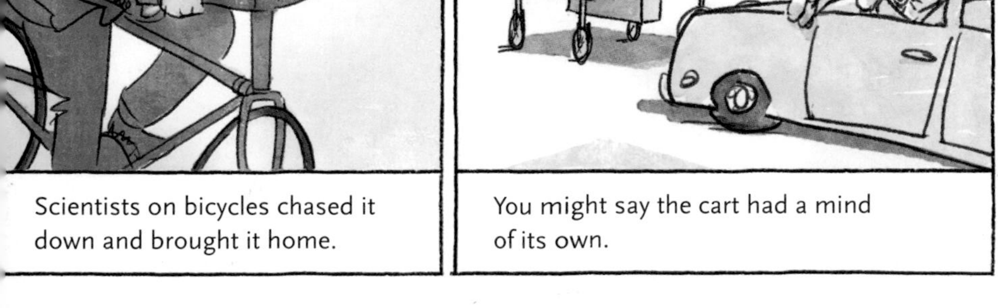

Scientists on bicycles chased it down and brought it home.

You might say the cart had a mind of its own.

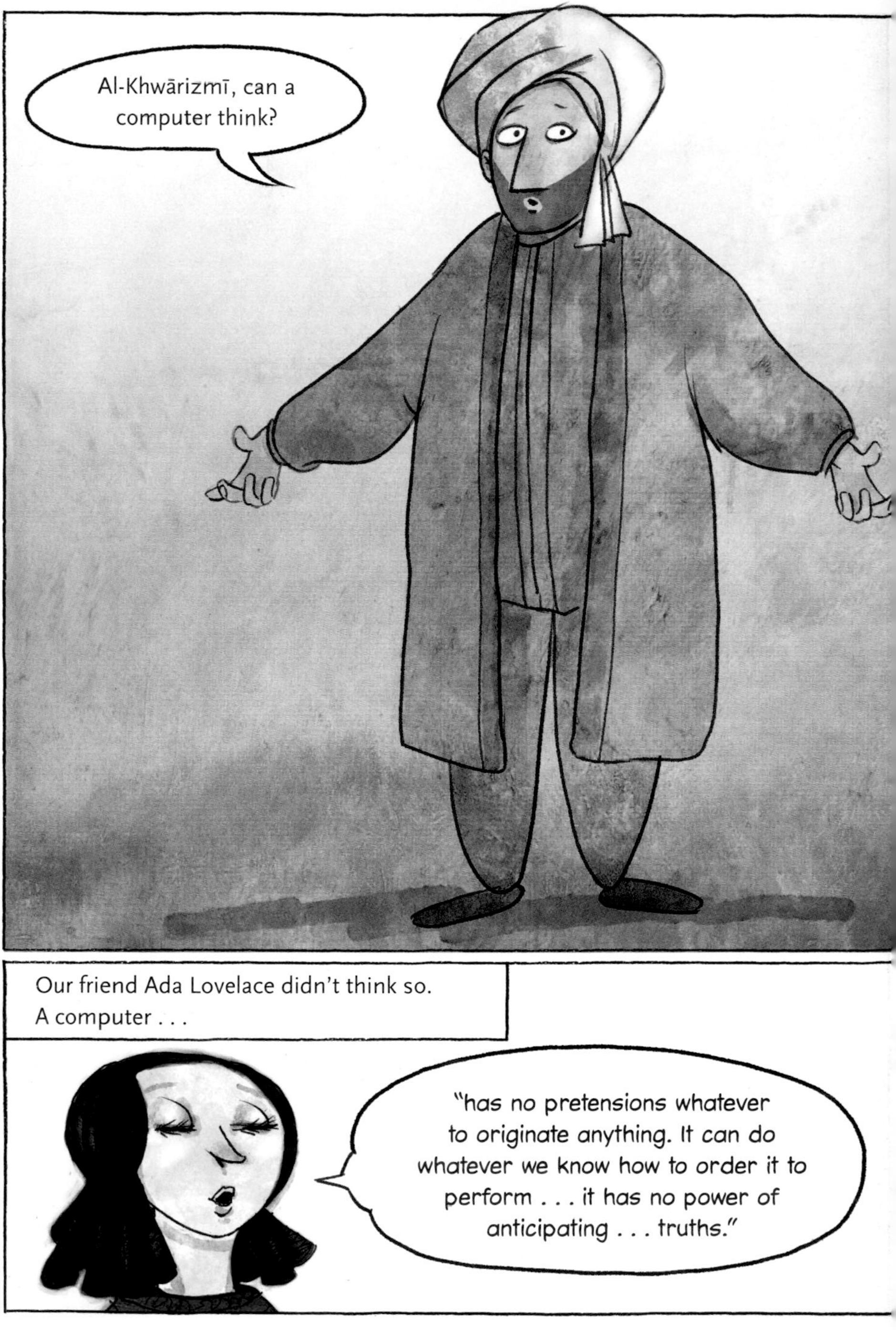
Al-Khwārizmī, can a computer think?
Our friend Ada Lovelace didn't think so. A computer . . .
"has no pretensions whatever to originate anything. It can do whatever we know how to order it to perform . . . it has no power of anticipating . . . truths."

In 1950 Alan Turing, one of the scientists who worked on England's Colossus computer, called this "Lady Lovelace's Objection." Turing seemed to disagree with Ada.

Since a computer can change the course of its operation—that is, modify its behavior—depending on the results of early calculations, can't it be said that the computer "learned"?

Powerful computers, playing games like chess and go, have been programmed to keep track of successful moves and failures. By playing many, many games, sometimes in the millions, they collect a treasure trove of successful moves that allow them to beat the best human players.

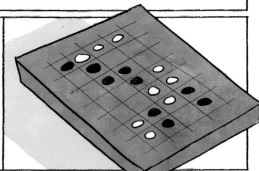

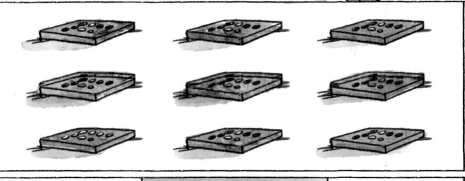

To this, Turing said,

"I feel that one is obliged to regard the machine as showing intelligence."

Turing then wrote,

"I propose to consider the question, 'Can machines think?'"

Right away, Turing saw the problem of defining "think." Solving an addition problem is thinking, as is mapping the best route to Grandma's house. But thinking can also be deciding whether Bigfoot exists, or choosing the right person to marry, or creating the words and pictures for a graphic novel.

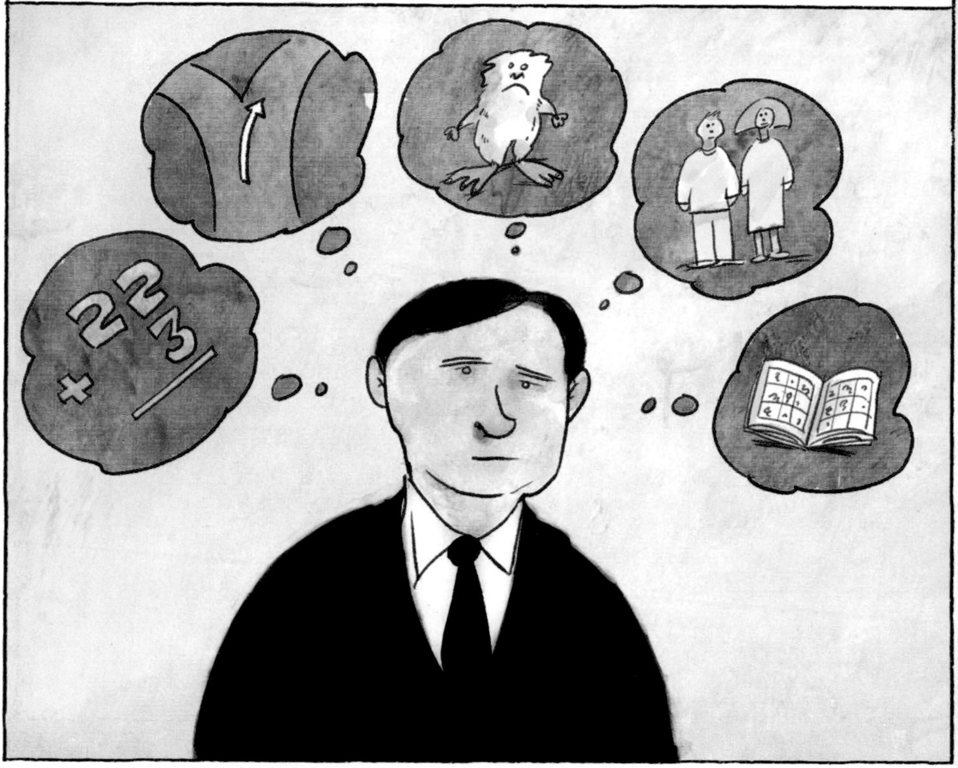

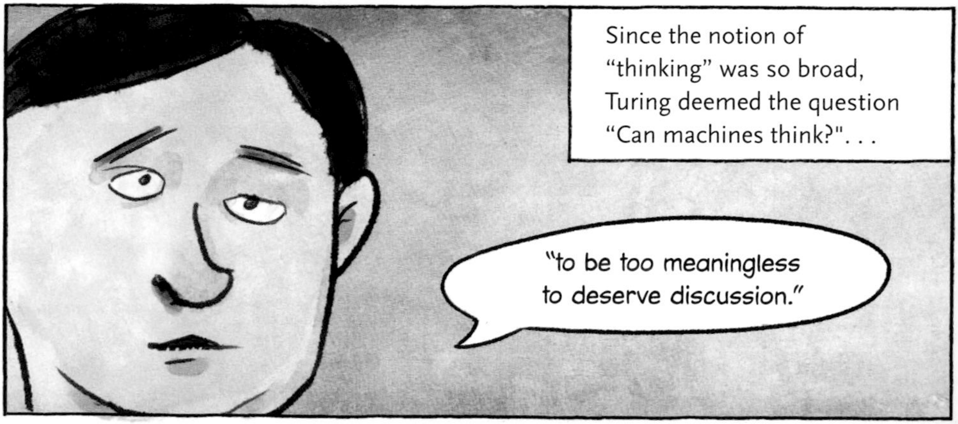

Since the notion of "thinking" was so broad, Turing deemed the question "Can machines think?". . .
"to be too meaningless to deserve discussion."

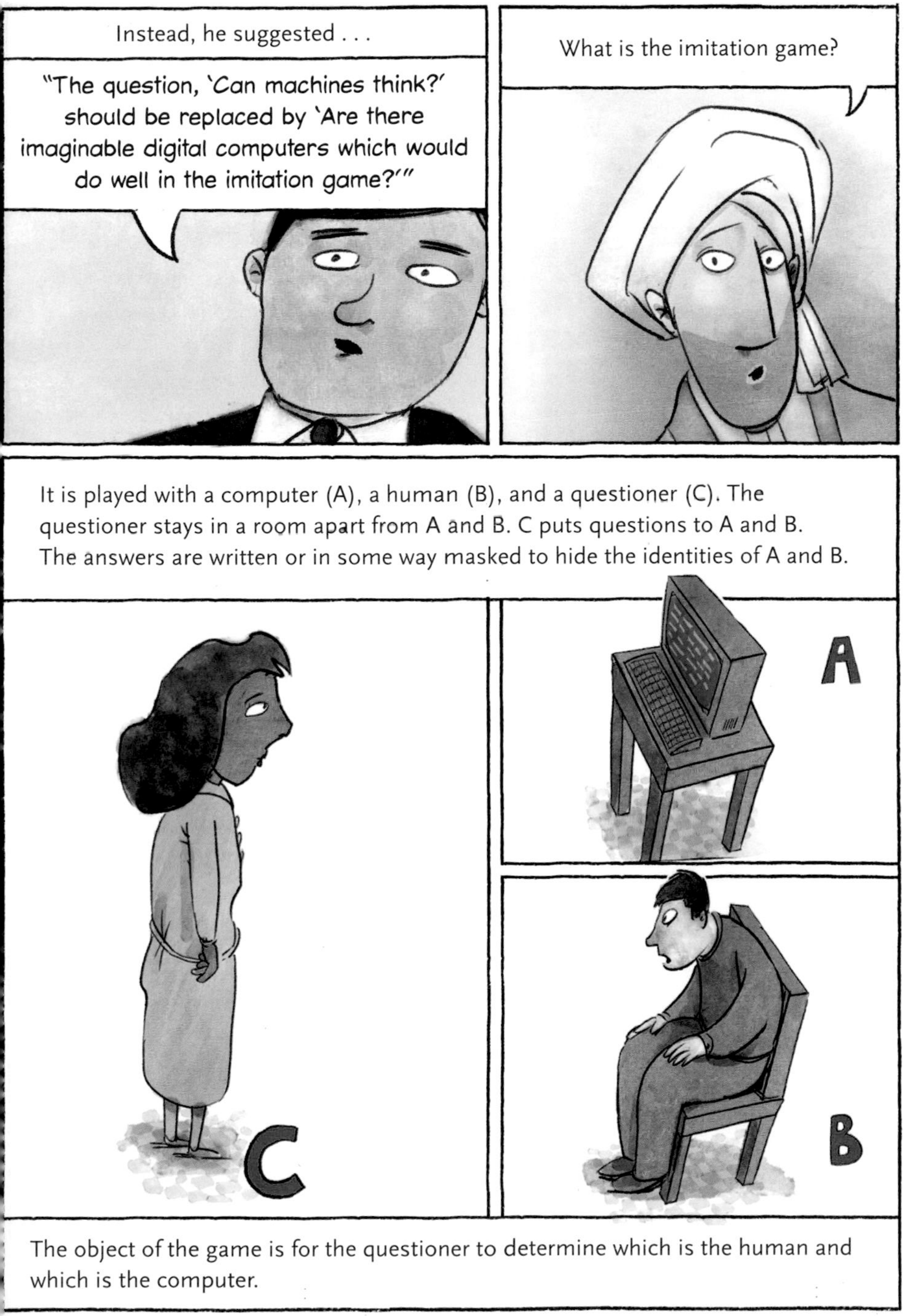
Instead, he suggested . . .
"The question, 'Can machines think?' should be replaced by 'Are there imaginable digital computers which would do well in the imitation game?'"
What is the imitation game?
It is played with a computer (A), a human (B), and a questioner (C). The questioner stays in a room apart from A and B. C puts questions to A and B. The answers are written or in some way masked to hide the identities of A and B.
C
A
B
The object of the game is for the questioner to determine which is the human and which is the computer.

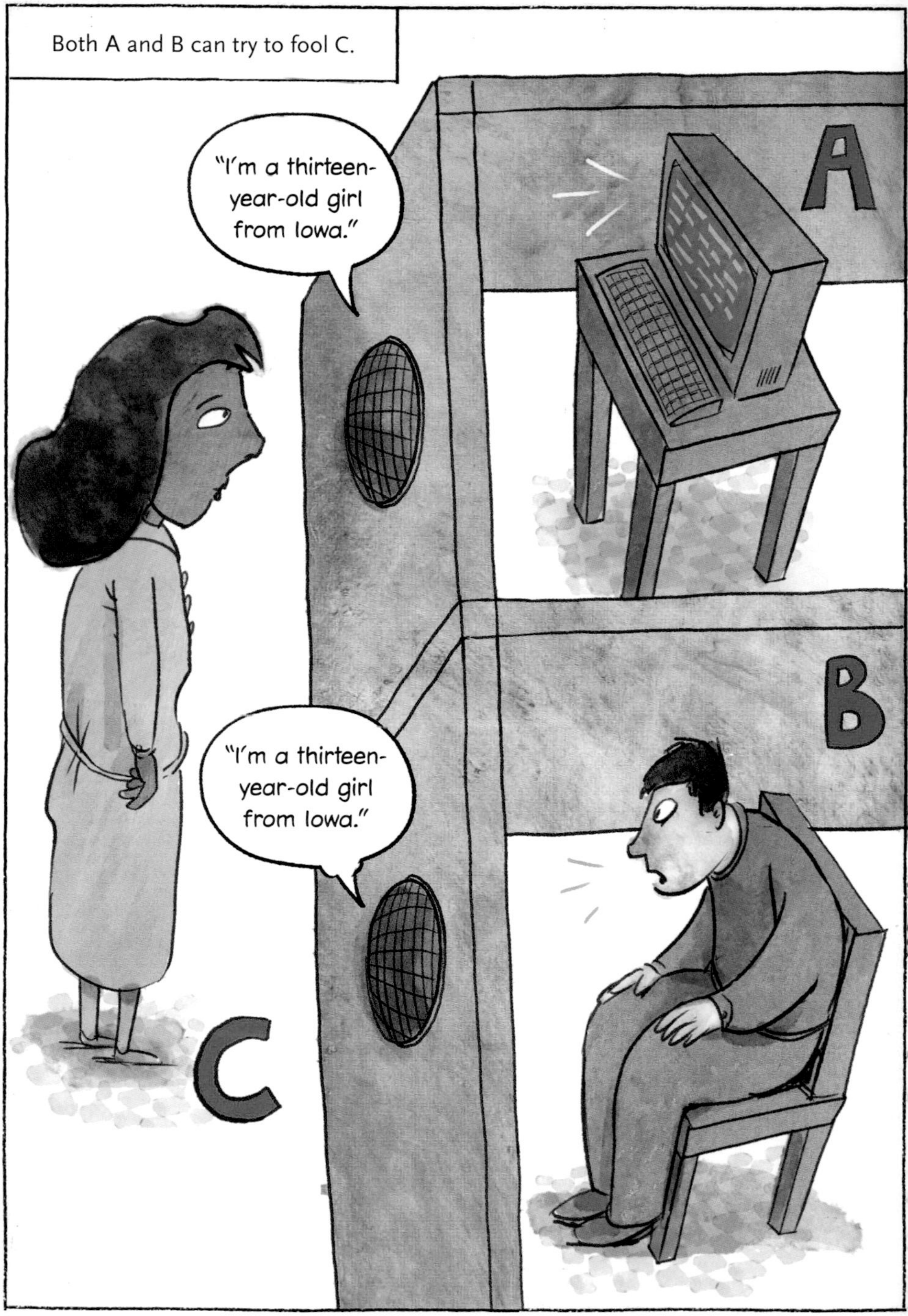
Both A and B can try to fool C.
"I'm a thirteen-year-old girl from Iowa."
A
"I'm a thirteen-year-old girl from Iowa."
B
C

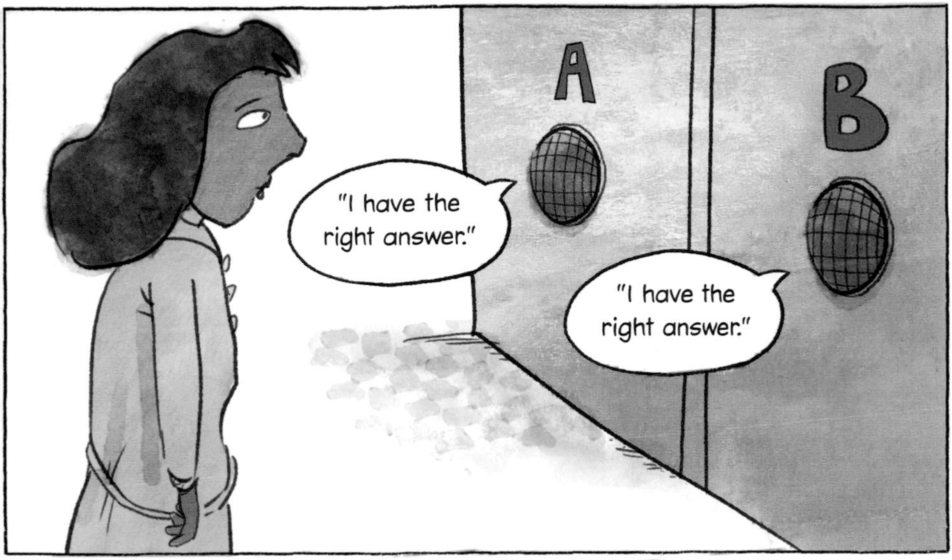
A
B
"I have the right answer."
"I have the right answer."

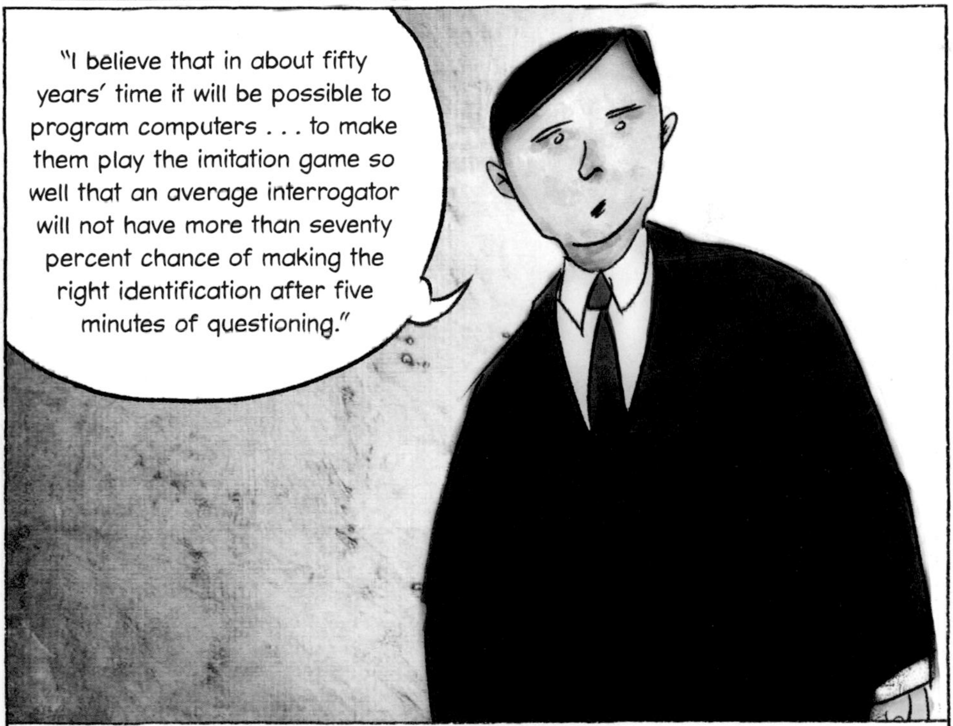
"I believe that in about fifty years' time it will be possible to program computers . . . to make them play the imitation game so well that an average interrogator will not have more than seventy percent chance of making the right identification after five minutes of questioning."

By 2000, Turing's prediction had not come true. And even today, we are not likely to be fooled into believing a computer is human.

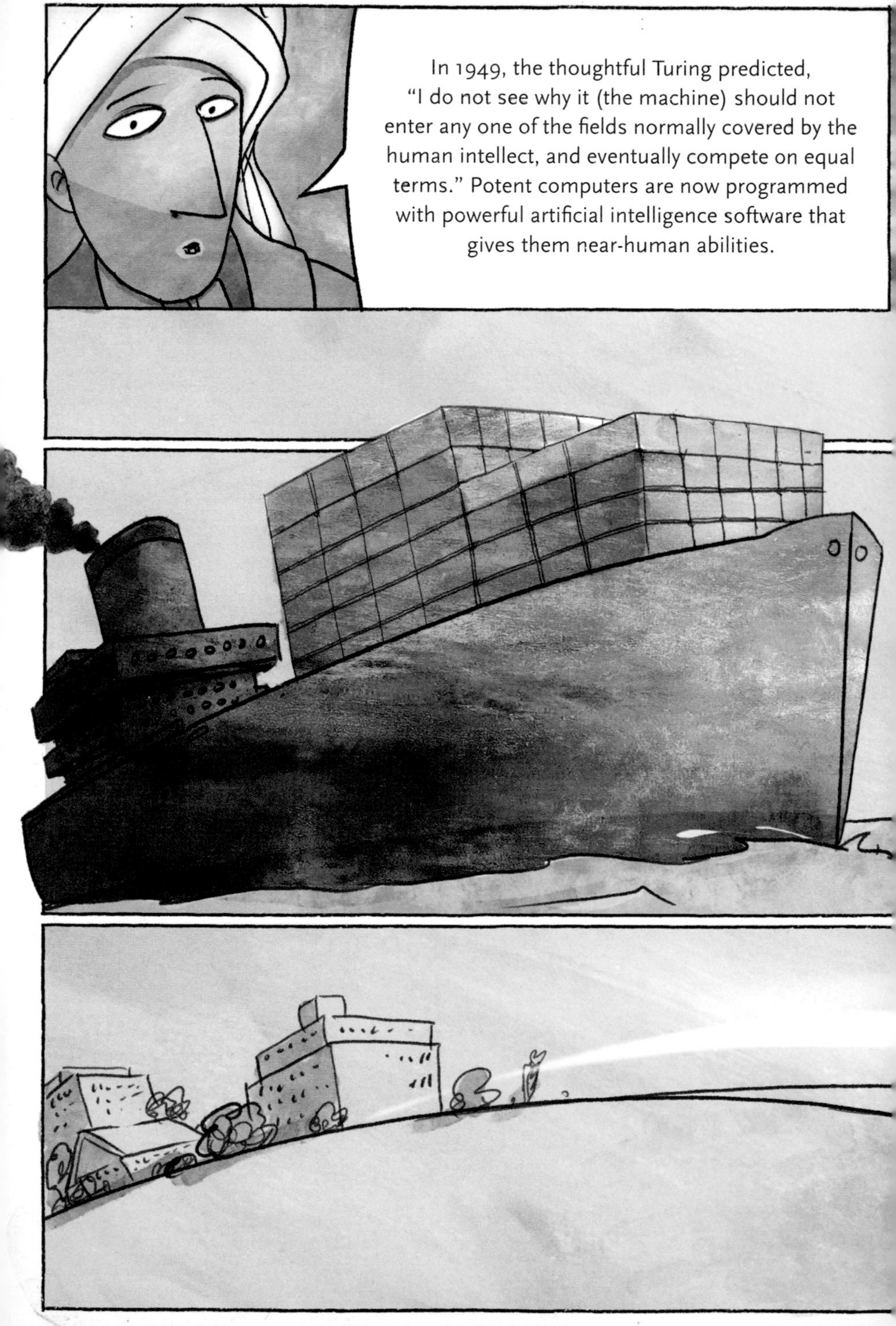
In 1949, the thoughtful Turing predicted, "I do not see why it (the machine) should not enter any one of the fields normally covered by the human intellect, and eventually compete on equal terms." Potent computers are now programmed with powerful artificial intelligence software that gives them near-human abilities.

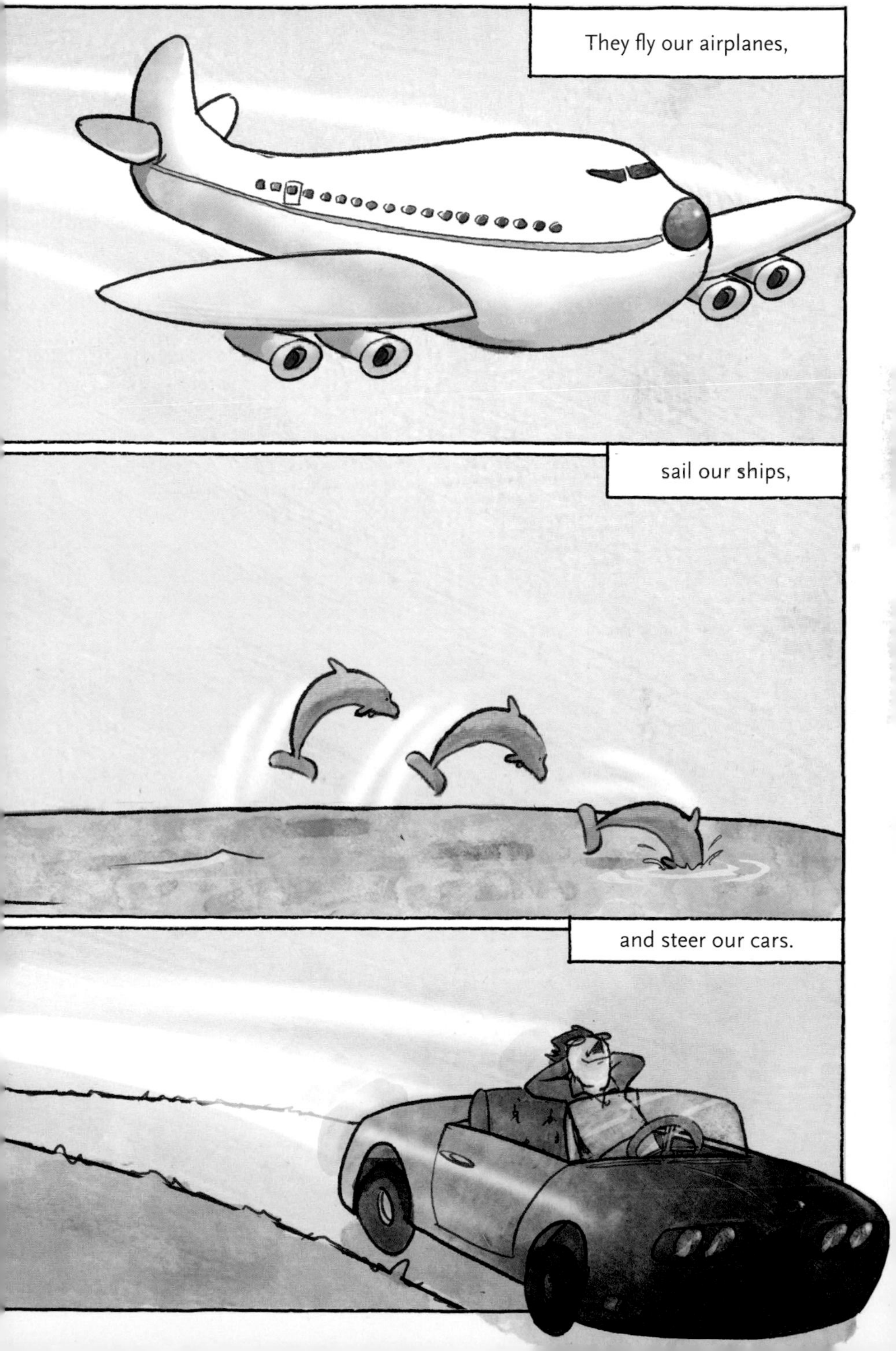
They fly our airplanes,
sail our ships,
and steer our cars.

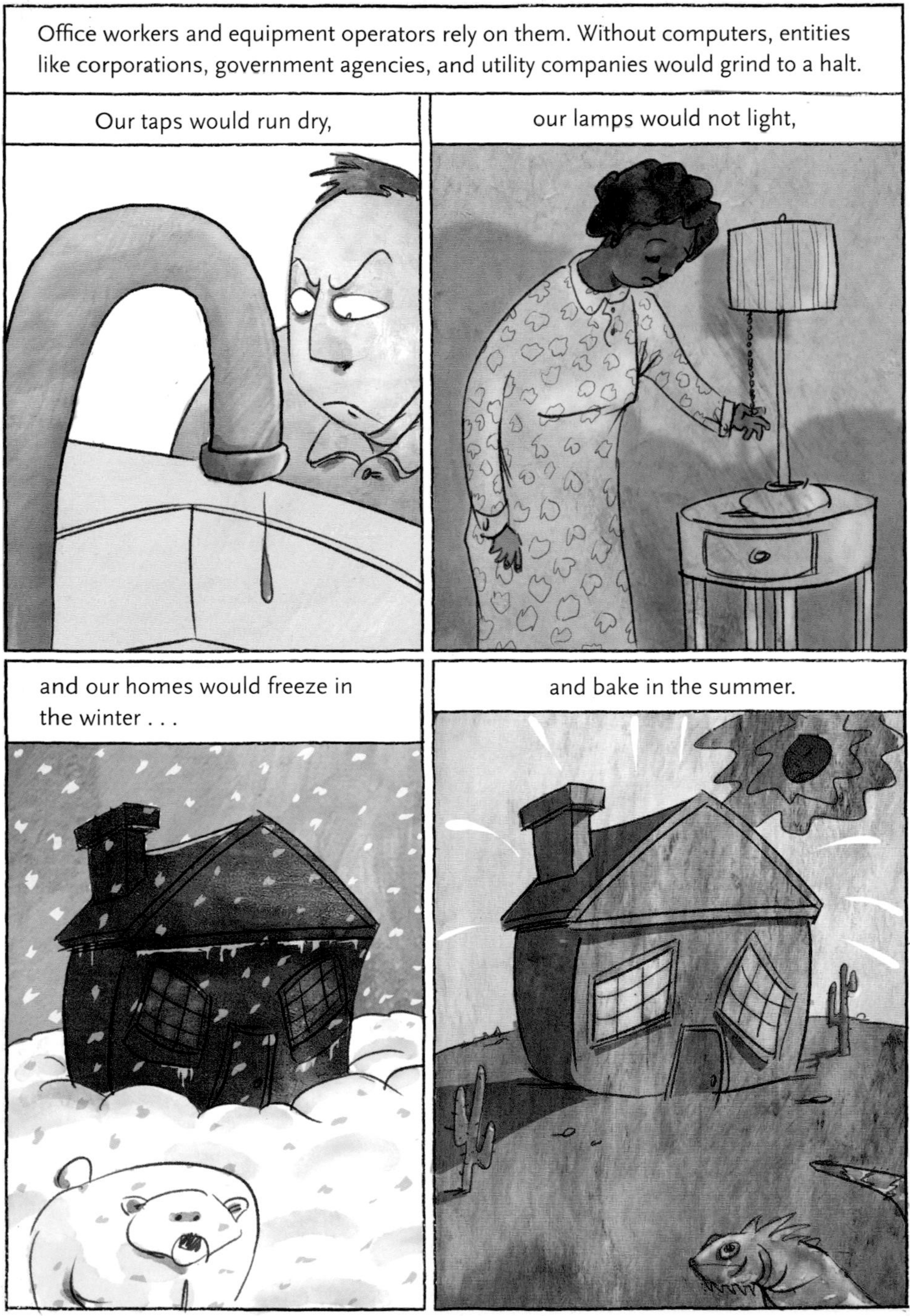
Office workers and equipment operators rely on them. Without computers, entities like corporations, government agencies, and utility companies would grind to a halt.
Our taps would run dry,
our lamps would not light,
and our homes would freeze in the winter . . .
and bake in the summer.

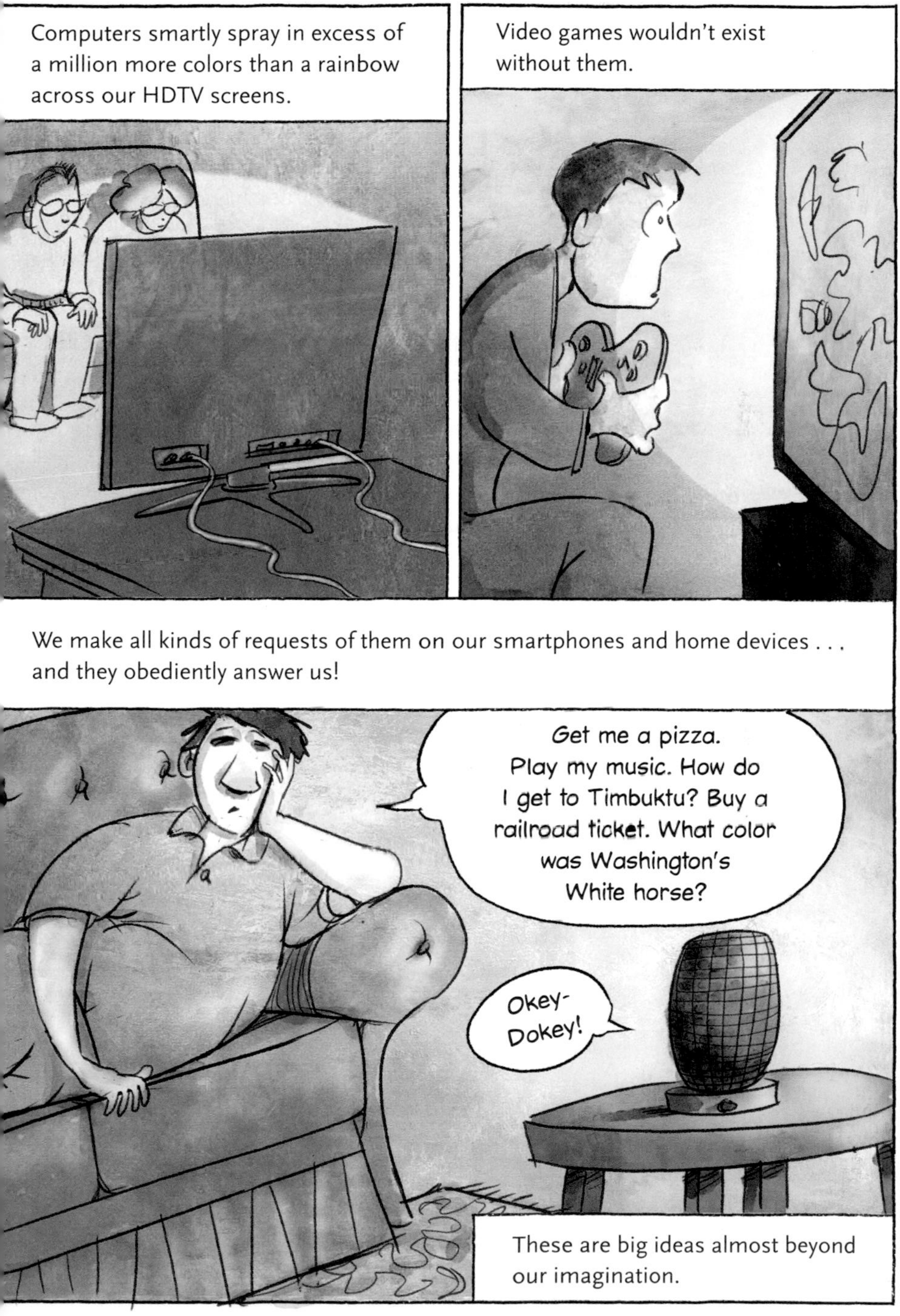
Computers smartly spray in excess of a million more colors than a rainbow across our HDTV screens.
Video games wouldn't exist without them.
We make all kinds of requests of them on our smartphones and home devices . . . and they obediently answer us!
Get me a pizza. Play my music. How do I get to Timbuktu? Buy a railroad ticket. What color was Washington's White horse?
Okey-Dokey!
These are big ideas almost beyond our imagination.

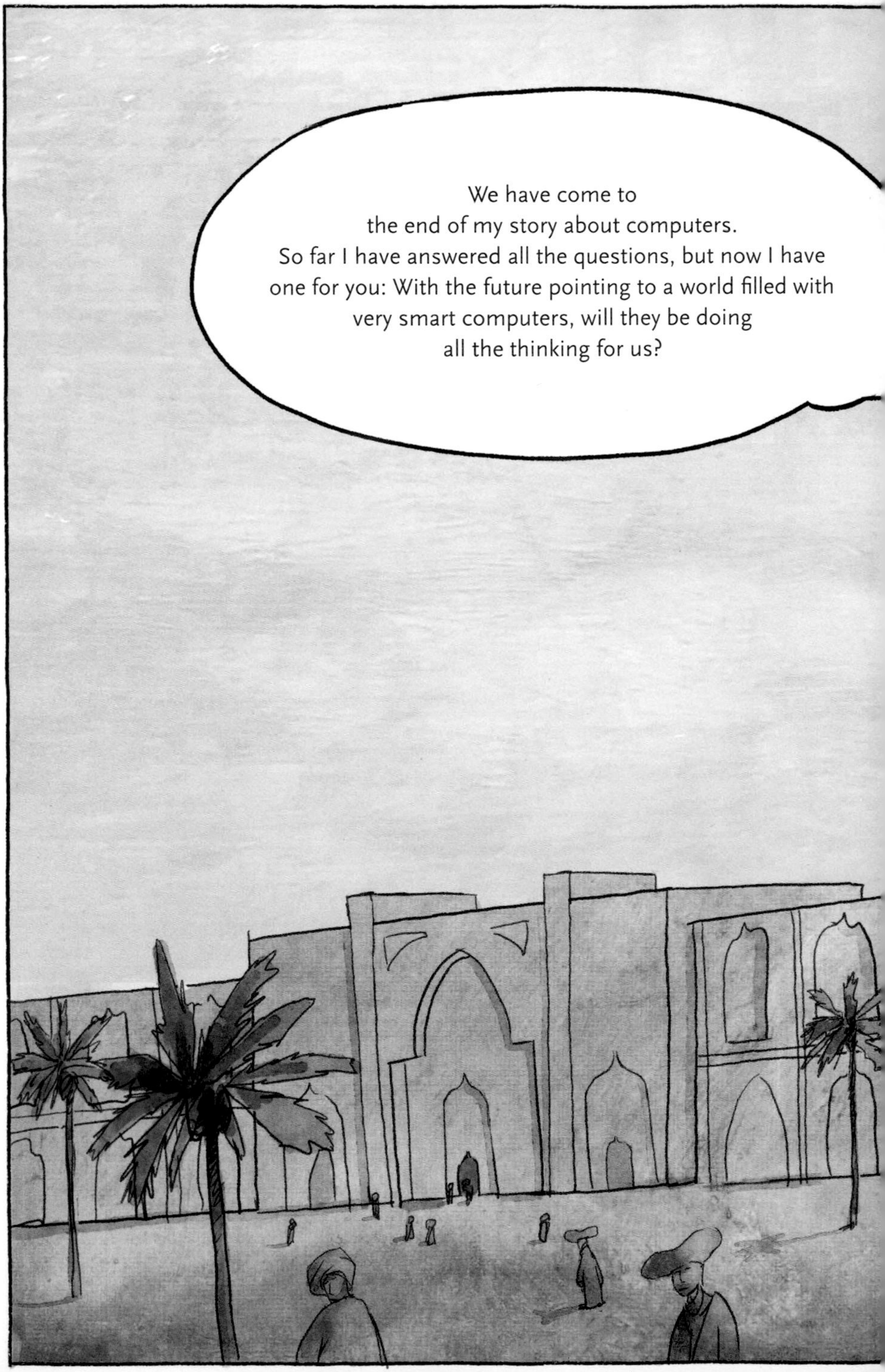
We have come to the end of my story about computers. So far I have answered all the questions, but now I have one for you: With the future pointing to a world filled with very smart computers, will they be doing all the thinking for us?

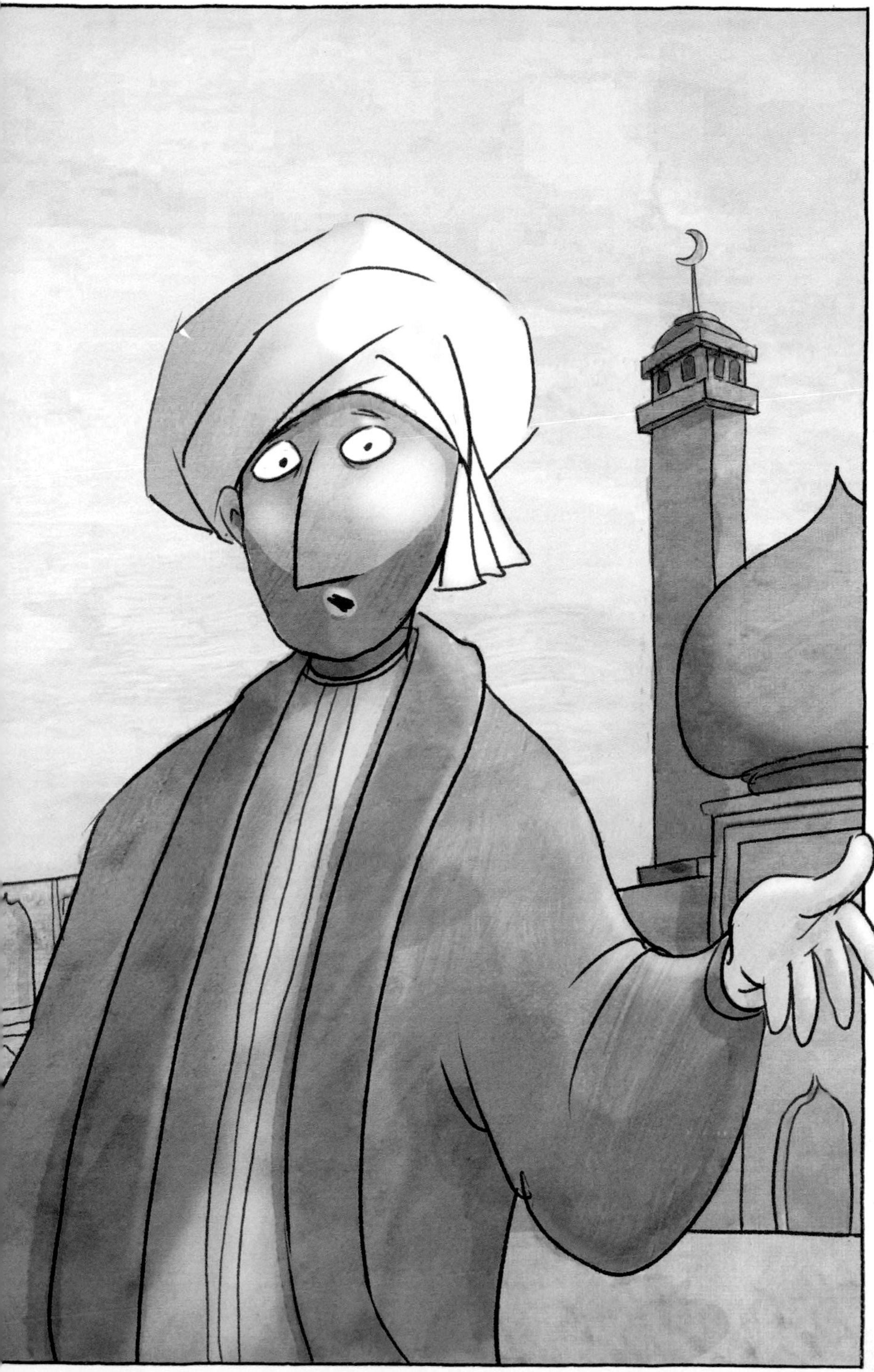

A BIT ABOUT BINARY

We talked about the importance of ones and zeroes to computer operations. Let's see how ones and zeroes can express any number. But first, let's look at writing numbers using zero through nine. It is called the decimal or base ten system, and is the way we are most familiar with.

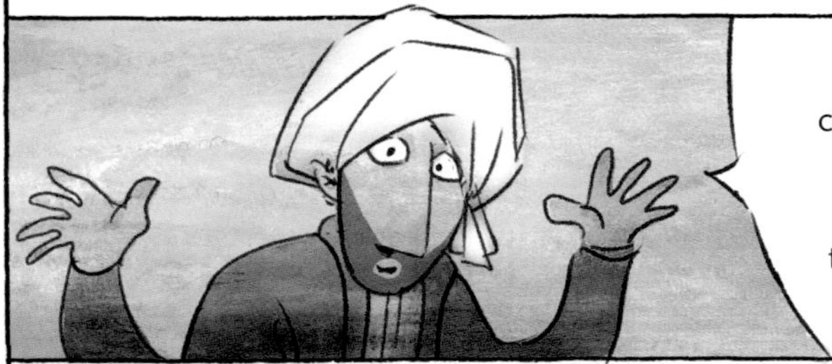

It's likely we are most comfortable using the base ten system because we have ten fingers. It's easy to imagine the earliest people using their fingers to count.

In the decimal system, numbers are placed in columns. Moving to the left, each column is ten times greater than the neighboring column. The value of each column:

1000	100	10	1

When we write 4302, for example, we are saying there are four groups of a thousand, three groups of hundreds, no groups of tens, and two ones. Or:

4 × 1000	3 × 100	0	2 × 1
4000	300	0	2

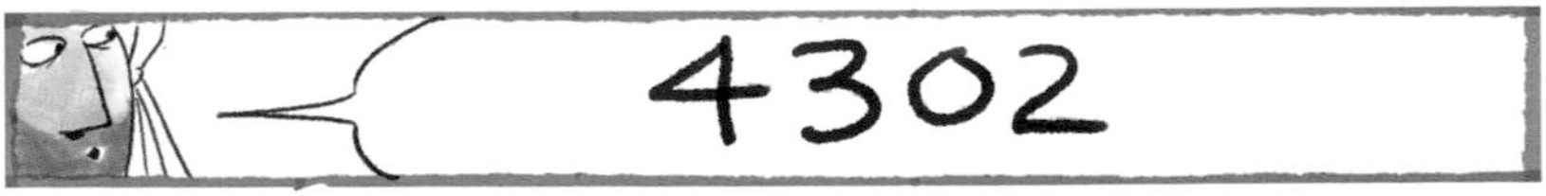
4302

In the base 2 system, columns to the left are double the preceding column's value. The value of each column:

256	128	64	32	16	8	4	2	1

And there can be only one or none of that amount in the column.

So the binary way of saying 362: There is one (256) + none (128) + one (64) + one (32) + none (16) + one (8) + none (4) + one (2) + none (1) The total of all those numbers equals 362.

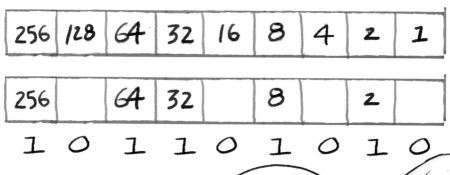

256	128	64	32	16	8	4	2	1
256		64	32		8		2	
1	0	1	1	0	1	0	1	0

The binary expression of 362 is 101101010.

Each of the columns of ones and zeros in the binary system is called a bit.

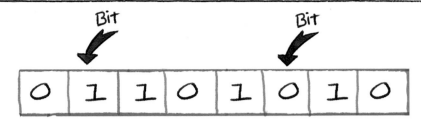

So an 8-bit computer, for example, is a computer that is limited to representing numbering up to 255 . . . which is the total of all the 8-bit columns.
(1+2+4+8+16+32+64+128=255)

| 128 | 64 | 32 | 16 | 8 | 4 | 2 | 1 | = 255 |

| 128 | 64 | 32 | 16 | 8 | 4 | 2 | 1 | = BYTE |

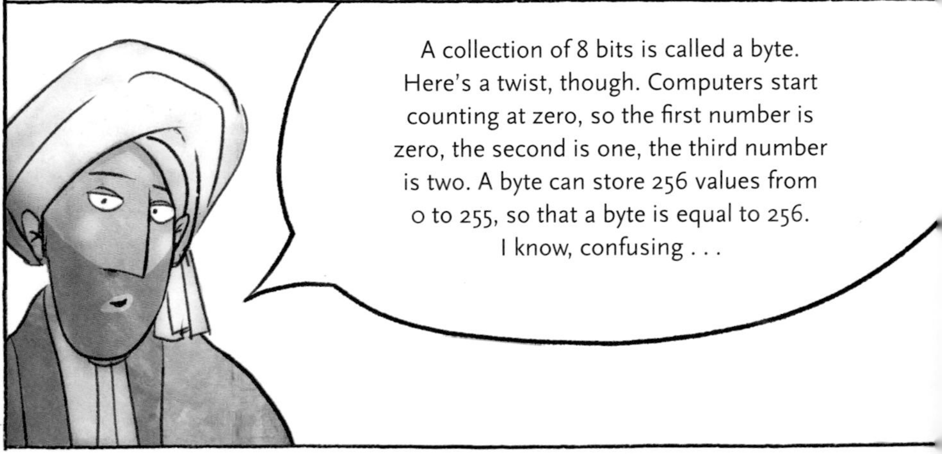

A collection of 8 bits is called a byte. Here's a twist, though. Computers start counting at zero, so the first number is zero, the second is one, the third number is two. A byte can store 256 values from 0 to 255, so that a byte is equal to 256. I know, confusing . . .

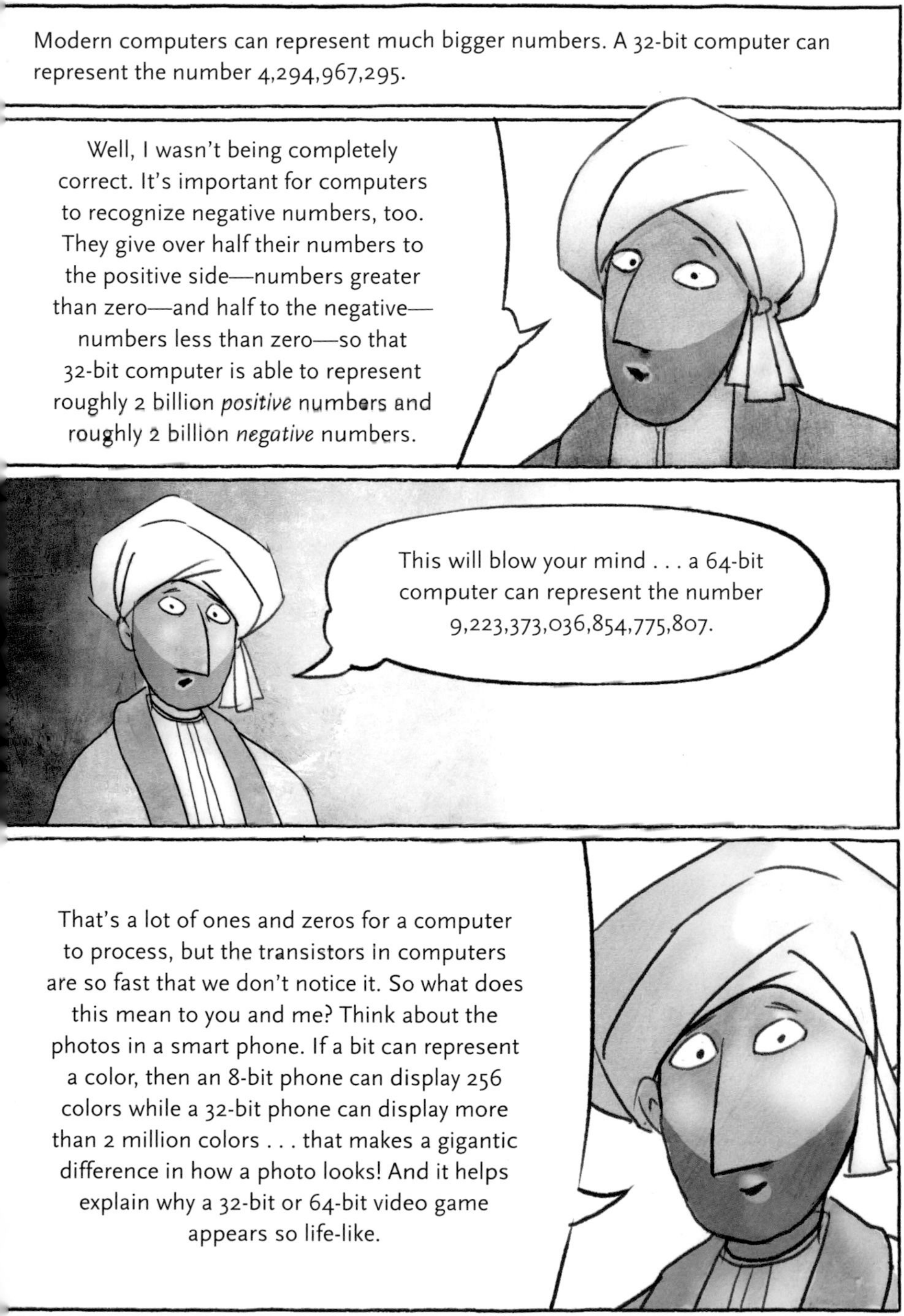
Modern computers can represent much bigger numbers. A 32-bit computer can represent the number 4,294,967,295.
Well, I wasn't being completely correct. It's important for computers to recognize negative numbers, too. They give over half their numbers to the positive side—numbers greater than zero—and half to the negative—numbers less than zero—so that 32-bit computer is able to represent roughly 2 billion *positive* numbers and roughly 2 billion *negative* numbers.
This will blow your mind . . . a 64-bit computer can represent the number 9,223,373,036,854,775,807.
That's a lot of ones and zeros for a computer to process, but the transistors in computers are so fast that we don't notice it. So what does this mean to you and me? Think about the photos in a smart phone. If a bit can represent a color, then an 8-bit phone can display 256 colors while a 32-bit phone can display more than 2 million colors . . . that makes a gigantic difference in how a photo looks! And it helps explain why a 32-bit or 64-bit video game appears so life-like.

SELECT TIMELINE OF COMPUTING

Machines That Think! is an introductory history of mainframe and personal computers, with a dollop of software history. They are reliant on mechanical and electrical devices—some ancient and many of which originated in Arabic and Asian countries—and on mathematics, again much of which saw its early advancements in those same regions. But the focus here is on those devices that were strictly tasked with the job of computing, that is, of adding, subtracting, multiplying, and dividing. It is the tale of the employment of numbers to accomplish all manner of wonders beyond simple sums. With that in mind, I have constructed the following timeline.

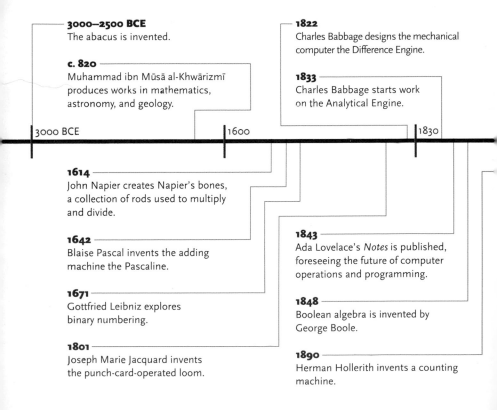

3000–2500 BCE
The abacus is invented.

c. 820
Muhammad ibn Mūsā al-Khwārizmī produces works in mathematics, astronomy, and geology.

3000 BCE

1822
Charles Babbage designs the mechanical computer the Difference Engine.

1833
Charles Babbage starts work on the Analytical Engine.

1600

1830

1614
John Napier creates Napier's bones, a collection of rods used to multiply and divide.

1642
Blaise Pascal invents the adding machine the Pascaline.

1671
Gottfried Leibniz explores binary numbering.

1801
Joseph Marie Jacquard invents the punch-card-operated loom.

1843
Ada Lovelace's *Notes* is published, foreseeing the future of computer operations and programming.

1848
Boolean algebra is invented by George Boole.

1890
Herman Hollerith invents a counting machine.

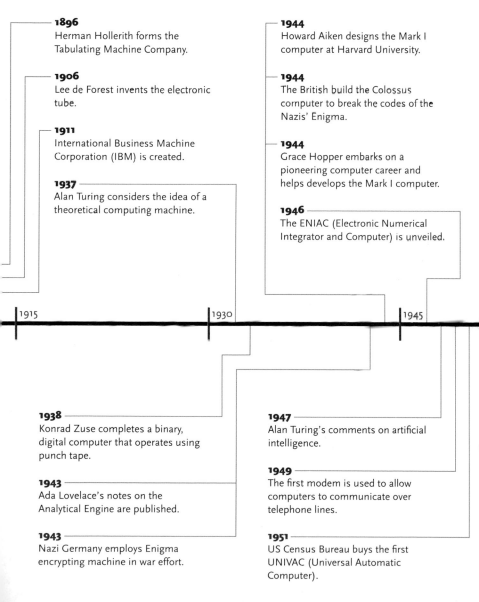

1896
Herman Hollerith forms the Tabulating Machine Company.

1906
Lee de Forest invents the electronic tube.

1911
International Business Machine Corporation (IBM) is created.

1937
Alan Turing considers the idea of a theoretical computing machine.

1944
Howard Aiken designs the Mark I computer at Harvard University.

1944
The British build the Colossus computer to break the codes of the Nazis' Enigma.

1944
Grace Hopper embarks on a pioneering computer career and helps develops the Mark I computer.

1946
The ENIAC (Electronic Numerical Integrator and Computer) is unveiled.

1915

1930

1945

1938
Konrad Zuse completes a binary, digital computer that operates using punch tape.

1943
Ada Lovelace's notes on the Analytical Engine are published.

1943
Nazi Germany employs Enigma encrypting machine in war effort.

1947
Alan Turing's comments on artificial intelligence.

1949
The first modem is used to allow computers to communicate over telephone lines.

1951
US Census Bureau buys the first UNIVAC (Universal Automatic Computer).

1951
The IBM 650 computer employs a magnetic data storage drum.

1956
MIT experiments with direct input to computer using a keyboard.

1958
Jack Kilby and Robert Noyce produce first integrated circuit or silicon chip.

1960
Common Business Oriented Language (COBOL) is created.

1972
C programming language is created.

1974
Xerox introduces the PARC Alto computer, which employs a Graphical User Interface (GUI).

1975
Altair introduces the personal computer.

1945

1960

1975

1962
Atlas computer employs virtual memory.

1963
American Standard Code for Information Interchange (ASCII) allows computers of different manufacturers to share data.

The computer mouse is patented by Douglas Engelbart.

1967
IBM creates the floppy disk.

1983
Apple introduces the Lisa computer.

1983
The internet, a "network of networks" owned by the US government, is launched.

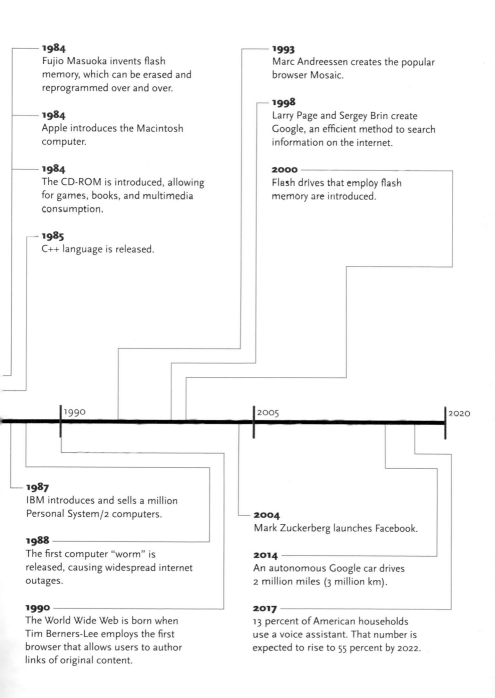

1984
Fujio Masuoka invents flash memory, which can be erased and reprogrammed over and over.

1984
Apple introduces the Macintosh computer.

1984
The CD-ROM is introduced, allowing for games, books, and multimedia consumption.

1985
C++ language is released.

1993
Marc Andreessen creates the popular browser Mosaic.

1998
Larry Page and Sergey Brin create Google, an efficient method to search information on the internet.

2000
Flash drives that employ flash memory are introduced.

1990

2005

2020

1987
IBM introduces and sells a million Personal System/2 computers.

1988
The first computer "worm" is released, causing widespread internet outages.

1990
The World Wide Web is born when Tim Berners-Lee employs the first browser that allows users to author links of original content.

2004
Mark Zuckerberg launches Facebook.

2014
An autonomous Google car drives 2 million miles (3 million km).

2017
13 percent of American households use a voice assistant. That number is expected to rise to 55 percent by 2022.

WHO WAS MUHAMMAD IBN MŪSĀ AL-KHWĀRIZMĪ?

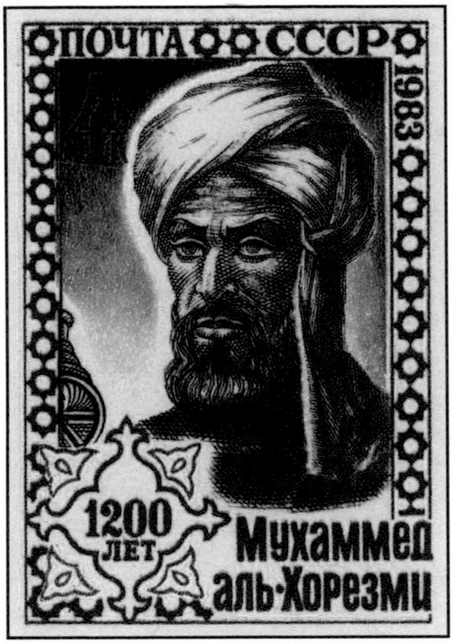
ПОЧТА СССР
1983
1200 ЛЕТ
Мухаммед
аль-Хорезми

There is no known image of al-Khwārizmī. Many academic books and histories use this portrait, which was printed on a postage stamp issued by the Soviet Union in 1983. The stamp celebrates al-Khwārizmī's achievements. He was born in Persia, the part that is now known as Uzbekistan, and which had been part of the Soviet Union.

Al-Khwārizmī (780–850 CE) was a Persian mathematician and astronomer. His book on algebra—an equation-solving system created by the ancient Babylonians—found its way to the Western world in the twelfth century and became a cornerstone of modern mathematics. At the same time, another of his works introduced Hindu numerals to the West. It's nearly impossible to think of the world without 0, 1, 2, 3, 4, 5, 6, 7, 8, and 9. Early scholars were ignorant of their true source, instead taking note of al-Khwārizmī's whereabouts and dubbing the numerals *Arabic*. Today, they are commonly referred to as Hindu-Arabic numerals to reflect their Hindu origin and the significant contribution of Arabic mathematicians to their evolution.

Western scholars knew only of al-Khwārizmī's works that had been translated into Latin. Consequently, he is also known by the Latin version of his name, Algoritmi. "Algoritmi" wrote an essay describing the procedure of following steps to solve a problem, and from his Latin name the word *algorithm* originates.

Although many of the early advancements of computers were the product of Western scientists and engineers, we should remember that we owe a debt to Persian mathematician Muhammad ibn Mūsā al-Khwārizmī.

NOTES

Page 20—"sacrificed to improvements in mechanism." Isaacson, Walter. *The Innovators*, p. 9.

Page 20—"Mad, bad, and dangerous to know." Castle, Terry. "Mad, Bad, and Dangerous to Know."

Page 21—"poetical science." Isaacson, p. 7.

Page 29—"The Analytic Engine does not occupy common . . ." Isaacson, p. 27.

Page 29—"The Engine can arrange and combine . . ." Swade, Doron. *The Difference Engine*, p.170.

Page 39—"There was this large mass of machinery . . ." Isaacson, p. 90.

Page 49—"Here, figure out how the machine works . . ." Isaacson, p. 98.

Page 49—"We learned to diagnose problems better . . ." Ibid.

Page 50—"If the ENIAC's administrators had known . . ." Isaacson, p.100.

Page 54—"We discovered something important today." Isaacson, p.144.

Page 56—"With transistors, [engineers] . . ." Palfreman, Jon, dir. *The Machine That Changed the World*.

Page 56—"How do you wire them all . . ." Palfreman.

Page 59—"You'd cruise comfortably at a . . ." Palfreman.

Page 60—"There will never be enough problems . . ." Augartin, Stan. *Bit by Bit*, p.155–6.

Page 60—"If we don't take this . . ." Palfreman.

Page 62—"Interesting." "The Mother of All Demos," YouTube.

Page 65—"You simply step by step told the computer what to do." Isaacson, p. 92.

Page 67—"What if you gave everyone a . . ." Lohr, Steve. "H. Edward Roberts, PC Pioneer, Dies at 68."

Page 69—"This is happening without us!" Isaacson, p. 332.

Page 70—"We spent just about all our free time . . ." Gates.

Page 71—"His palm had a chronic orange tinge . . ." Isaacson, p. 327.

Page 71—"Hey, if we're really . . ." Pilkington, Ed. "Paul Allen: I think Bill Gates was surprised by my book."

Page 72—"That night turned out to be . . ." Isaacson, p. 334.

Page 73—"He was kind of skinny and wiry and full of energy." Issacson, p. 346.

Page 74—"I decided to take a calligraphy class . . ." Chokshi.

Page 75—"It was beautiful . . ." Chokshi.

Page 75—"It all came back to me." Chokshi, Niraj. "The Trappist Monk Whose Calligraphy Inspired Steve Jobs—and Influenced Apple's Design."

Page 77—"It gave us a taste of what we could do . . ." Isaacson, p. 347.

Page 79—"My vision was to create the first fully packaged . . ." Isaacson, p. 352.

Page 90—"Much effort will be put . . ." Bogost, Ian. "The Secret History of the Robot Car."

Page 94—". . . has no pretensions whatever to originate . . ." Isaason, p. 29.

Page 95—"I feel that one is obliged to regard the . . ." Isaacson, p.124.

Page 95—"I propose to consider the question, 'Can machines think?'" Turing, A. M. "Computing Machinery and Intelligence."

Page 96—". . . to be too meaningless to deserve discussion." Ibid.

Page 97—"The question, 'Can machines think?' should be replaced . . ." Ibid.

Page 99—"I believe that in about fifty years' time . . ." Ibid.

Page 100—"I do not see why . . ." Computer History Museum.

SELECTED BIBLIOGRAPHY

Books

Augarten, Stan. *Bit by Bit: An Illustrated History of Computers*. New York: Ticknor and Fields, 1984.

Babbage, Charles. *A Chapter on Street Noise*. London: John Murray, 1864. play.google .com/books/reader?id=RilcAAAAcAAJ&pg=GBS.PA1

Babbage, Charles. *Passages from the Life of a Philosopher*. London: Longman, Green, Longman, Roberts & Green, 1864. archive.org/details/passagesfromlifoobabbgoog

Curley, Robert, ed. *Computing: From the Abacus to the IPAD*. New York: Britannica Educational Publishing, 2012.

Dyson, George. *Turing's Cathedral*. New York: Pantheon Books, 2012.

Hafner, Katie, and Matthew Lyon. *Where the Wizards Stayed Up Late*. New York: Simon & Schuster, 1996.

Ifrah, Georges. *The Universal History of Computing*. New York: Wiley & Sons, 2001.

Isaacson, Walter. *The Innovators: How a group of hackers, geniuses, and geeks created the digital revolution*. New York: Simon & Schuster, 2014.

Mahoney, Michael Sean. *Histories of Computing*. Cambridge: Harvard University Press, 2011.

Manes, Stephen, and Paul Andrews. *Gates*. New York: Doubleday, 1993.

Markoff, John. *What the Dormouse Said*. New York: Viking, 2005

Muir, Jane. *Of Men and Numbers: The Story of the Great Mathematicians*. New York: Dover Publications, 1996.books.google.com/books?id=uV3rJkmnQhsC&printsec =frontcover#v=onepage&q&f=false

Pullman, J. M. *The History of the Abacus*. New York: Frederick A. Praeger. 1968.

Seife, Charles. *Zero: The Biography of a Dangerous Idea*. New York: Penguin, 2000.

Swade, Doron. *The Difference Engine: Charles Babbage and the Quest to Build the First Computer*. New York: Penguin, 2001.

Articles

Alfred, Randy. "Nov. 4, 1953: UNIVAC Gets Election Right, But CBS Balks." *Wired*, November 4, 2010. www.wired.com/2010/11/1104cbs-tv-univac-election/

Bogost, Ian. "The Secret History of the Robot Car." *The Atlantic*, November 14, 2014. www. theatlantic.com/magazine/archive/2014/11/the-secret-history-of-the-robot-car/380791/

Bridgeport Post. "Bethel Firm Produces 'Robot' To Speed Factory Automation." February 23, 1961, p15. www.newspapers.com/clip/19396064/early_unimate_robotic_arm_article/

Castle, Terry. "Mad, Bad, and Dangerous to Know." *New York Times*, April 13, 1997. archive.nytimes.com/www.nytimes.com/books/97/04/13/reviews/970413.13castlet.html

Chokshi, Niraj. "The Trappist Monk Whose Calligraphy Inspired Steve Jobs—and Influenced Apple's Design." *Washington Post*, March 8, 2016. www.washingtonpost.com /news/arts-and-entertainment/wp/2016/03/08/the-trappist-monk-whose-calligraphy -inspired-steve-jobs-and-influenced-apples-designs/?utm_term=.356870064439

Christian, Brian. "Mind vs. Machine." *The Atlantic*, March 2011. www.theatlantic.com /magazine/archive/2011/03/mind-vs-machine/308386/

Computerworld. "Moth in the Machine: Debugging the Origins of 'Bug.'" September 3, 2011. www.computerworld.com/article/2515435/app-development/moth-in-the-machine --debugging-the-origins-of--bug-.html

Gates, Bill. "What I loved about Paul Allen." *Gatesnotes*. October 16, 2018. www.gatesnotes.com/About-Bill-Gates/Remembering-Paul-Allen

Geselowitz, Michael N. "The Jacquard Loom; Driver of the Industrial Revolution." *The Institute*, July 18, 2016. theInstitute.ieee.org/tech-history/technology-history/the-jacquard -loom-a-driver-of-the-industrial-revolution

Hagarty, James R. "Meet the New Generation of Robots for Manufacturing." *Wall Street Journal*, June 2, 2015. www.wsj.com/articles/meet-the-new-generation-of-robots-for -manufacturing-1433300884

Hazari, Arnab. "Electronics Are About to Reach Their Limit in Processing Power—but There Is a Solution." *Quartz*, January 5, 2017. qz.com/852770/theres-a-limit-to-how-small -we-can-make-transistors-but-the-solution-is-photonic-chips/

Holley, Peter. "This Firm Already Microchips Employees. Could Your Ailing Relative Be Next?" *Washington Post*, August 23, 2018. www.washingtonpost.com /technology/2018/08/23/this-firm-already-microchips-employees-could-your-ailing -relative-be-next/?utm_term=.0dc845d65dfe

Hollings, Christopher, Ursula Martin, and Adrian Rice. "How Ada Lovelace's Notes on the Analytical Engine Created the First Computer Program." Science Focus, June 15, 2018. www.sciencefocus.com/future-technology/how-ada-lovelaces-notes-on-the-analytical -engine-created-the-first-computer-program/

International Federation of Robotics. "Robots Double Worldwide by 2020." May 30, 2018. ifr.org/ifr-press-releases/news/robots-double-worldwide-by-2020

Kelly, Kevin. "The Three Breakthroughs That Have Finally Unleashed AI on the World." *Wired*, October 27, 2014. www.wired.com/2014/10/future-of-artificial-intelligence/

Knight, Will. "This Robot Could Transform Manufacturing." *Technology Review*, September 18, 2013. www.technologyreview.com/s/429248/this-robot-could-transform-manufacturing/

Lohr, Steve. "H. Edward Roberts, PC Pioneer, Dies at 68." *New York Times*, April 2, 2010. www.nytimes.com/2010/04/03/business/03roberts.html

Markoff, John. "Apple Visionary Redfined Digital Age." *New York Times*, October 5, 2011. www.nytimes.com/2011/10/06/business/steve-jobs-of-apple-dies-at-56.html

Moravic, H. P. "The Stanford Cart and the CMU Rover." IEEE.org. ieeexplore.ieee.org /document/1456952/

Pearce, Jeremy. "George C. Devol, Inventor of Robotic Arm, Dies at 99." *New York Times*, August 15, 2011. www.nytimes.com/2011/08/16/business/george-devol-developer-of -robot-arm-dies-at-99.html

Pilkington, Ed. "Paul Allen: I think Bill Gates was surprised by my book. He'll want an intense discussion about it." *The Guardian*, May 2, 2011. www.theguardian.com /technology/2011/may/02/paul-allen-microsoft-bill-gates-ideas

Popova, Maria. "When Babbage and Dickens Waged a War on Noise." *Brain Pickings* (blog), undated. www.brainpickings.org/2012/11/28/discord-babbage-noise/

Prakash, Neha. "Did You Know the First Computer Mouse Was Wooden!" Mashable, October 5, 2012. mashable.com/2012/10/05/mouse-history/#1zwXrCCCiEq

Simonite, Tom. "This More Powerful Version of Alphago Learns On Its Own." *Wired*, October 18, 2017. www.wired.com/story/this-more-powerful-version-of-alphago-learns-on-its-own

Turing, A. M. "Computing Machinery and Intelligence." *Mind 49*: 433-460. www.csee .umbc.edu/courses/471/papers/turing.pdf

Tweney, Dylan. "Dec 9, 1968: The Mother of All Demos." *Wired*, December 10, 2010. www .wired.com/2010/12/1209computer-mouse-mother-of-all-demos/

Weiss, Haley. "Why You're Probably Getting A Microchip Implant Someday." *Atlantic*, September 21, 2018. www.theatlantic.com/technology/archive/2018/09/how-i-learned-to -stop-worrying-and-love-the-microchip/570946/

Television

BBC. "Artificial Intelligence." www.bbc.com/future/tags/artificialintelligence

Chedd-Angier. *Scientific American Frontiers*. "Episode 3: Contests." chedd-angier.com /frontiers/season4.html

"The Mother of All Demos, Presented by Douglas Engelbart (1968)." PC Music, December 9, 1968. www.youtube.com/watch?v=yJDv-zdhzMY

Palfreman, Jon, dir. "Episode II—Inventing the Future." *The Machine That Changed the World*. Produced by New Television Workshop, WGBH Boston, 1992. www.youtube.com /watch?v=krlZf5H7Hp4&t=4s&list=PLTWacCXLFE_n1my1AiB-9ZbiobUu3bnMx&index=4

Palfreman, Jon, dir. "Episode III—The Paperback Computer." *The Machine That Changed the World*. Produced by New Television Workshop, WGBH Boston, 1992. www.youtube .com/watch?v=iwEpKy_7mYM&list=PLTWacCXLFE_n1my1AiB-9ZbiobUu3bnMx&index=4

Palfreman, Jon, dir. "Episode IV—The Thinking Machine." *The Machine That Changed the World*. Produced by New Television Workshop, WGBH Boston, 1992. www.youtube.com /watch?v=tXMaFhO6dIY&index=6&list=PLTWacCXLFE_n1my1AiB-9ZbiobUu3bnMx

PBS Digital Studios. "Boolean Logic and Logic Gates." CrashCourse, March 8, 2017. www .youtube.com/watch?v=gI-qXk7XojA

PBS Digital Studios. "Representing Number and Letters with Binary." CrashCourse, March 15, 20917. www.youtube.com/watch?v=1GSjbWtoc9M

Puiu, Tibi. "Your Smartphone Is Millions of Times More Powerful Than All of NASA's Combined Computing in 1969." ZME Science, September 19, 2017. www.zmescience .com/research/technology/smartphone-power-compared-to-apollo-432/

Pullen, John Patrick. "You Asked: How Do Driverless Cars Work?" *Time*, February 24, 2018. time.com/3719270/you-asked-how-do-driverless-cars-work/

Press, Gil. "The Turing Test and the Turing Machine." *Forbes*, November 5, 2017. www.forbes.com/sites/gilpress/2017/11/05/the-turing-test-and-the-turing -machine/#403d32aa1a14

Websites

American Museum of Natural History. "House of Wisdom." www.amnh.org/exhibitions /traveling-the-silk-road/take-a-journey/baghdad/house-of-wisdom

Computer History Museum. "Direct Keyboard Input to Computers." www .computerhistory.org/timeline/1956/

Computer History Museum. "Prototype Engelbart Mouse (replica)." www .computerhistory.org/revolution/input-output/14/350/1546

AUTHOR'S NOTE[*]

I'm not the first to say that Big Ideas stands on the shoulders of earlier, lesser-known big ideas. But repeating it doesn't make it any less true. Or less exciting! The Big Ideas That Changed the World series celebrates the hard-won succession of ideas that ultimately remade the world.

Computers occupy such a commanding role in our lives that we can be forgiven for thinking they have always been with us. That said, the present generation has no memory of a time before omnipresent computers. It is for them that this book is written. For "older" readers—people roughly forty and older—the book will be a reminder that advances in computing don't mark a finish but are way stations on a journey into the future.

While the early history of computers and computing is represented by accomplishments of the commonly referred to "Western" world, many of these achievements of engineering and gadgetry originated and were advanced in Arabic and Asian countries. This also meant the ascendancy of white males at the expense of women and people of color. For a long time, cultural norms steered bright women away from mathematics, computing, or *any* academic endeavor, for that matter. As late as the 1970s, young women were directed away from college and toward the workforce, where they were expected to pursue secretarial and administrative jobs instead of executive ones. At that time, homemaking was prioritized over careers. People of color faced outright discrimination that limited education opportunities and caused denial of jobs to qualified candidates. Women of color suffered both gender and race discrimination.

The domination of the West in the sciences has ended. India, Japan, Korea, and China, to name just a few countries, are leading players in computers, computing, and artificial intelligence. Tech giants such as Facebook and Google employ people of all races, religions, and gender identity. But to say there are no troubling aspects to the tech world would be a mistake. White males still earn the bulk of computer-science degrees. At this writing, the number of American women studying computer science is falling; a disheartening observation, given blossoming career opportunities.

Though the modern world rushes at a hectic, *rat-a-tat-tat* pace, I don't believe the gears of history are moving any faster than they had in the past. Bear with me: About twenty years passed after Columbus landed in the Caribbean before Ponce de Leon "discovered" Florida. About thirty years passed after the invention of the steam engine before there was a full-scale, viable steam locomotive. Neil Armstrong landed on the moon fifty years ago, and *we haven't been back since.*

The world of modern computing—of mainframes, software, personal computers, smartphones, tablets, personal assistants, and more—is only about sixty years old. That puts us in the infancy of the Information Age. We still await our "Florida," our "steam engine," our "return to the moon." When it arrives, it will be beyond belief! (But beware, things both good and bad can be beyond belief.)

Big Ideas is not the end point but just one stop on a continuum of ideas, big and small, that stretch across time. Whether an inspired success or a tragic failure, the ideas are a trail I'll follow in this series. And, like other trips, the pleasure will not be in the destination but in the journey.

*In the fall of 2019, reports surfaced of a novel, superfast computer that had completed a complex calculation in three and a half minutes that the most powerful supercomputer on the planet up until now would have needed ten thousand years to finish.

Is this a watershed moment in the world of computers?

INDEX

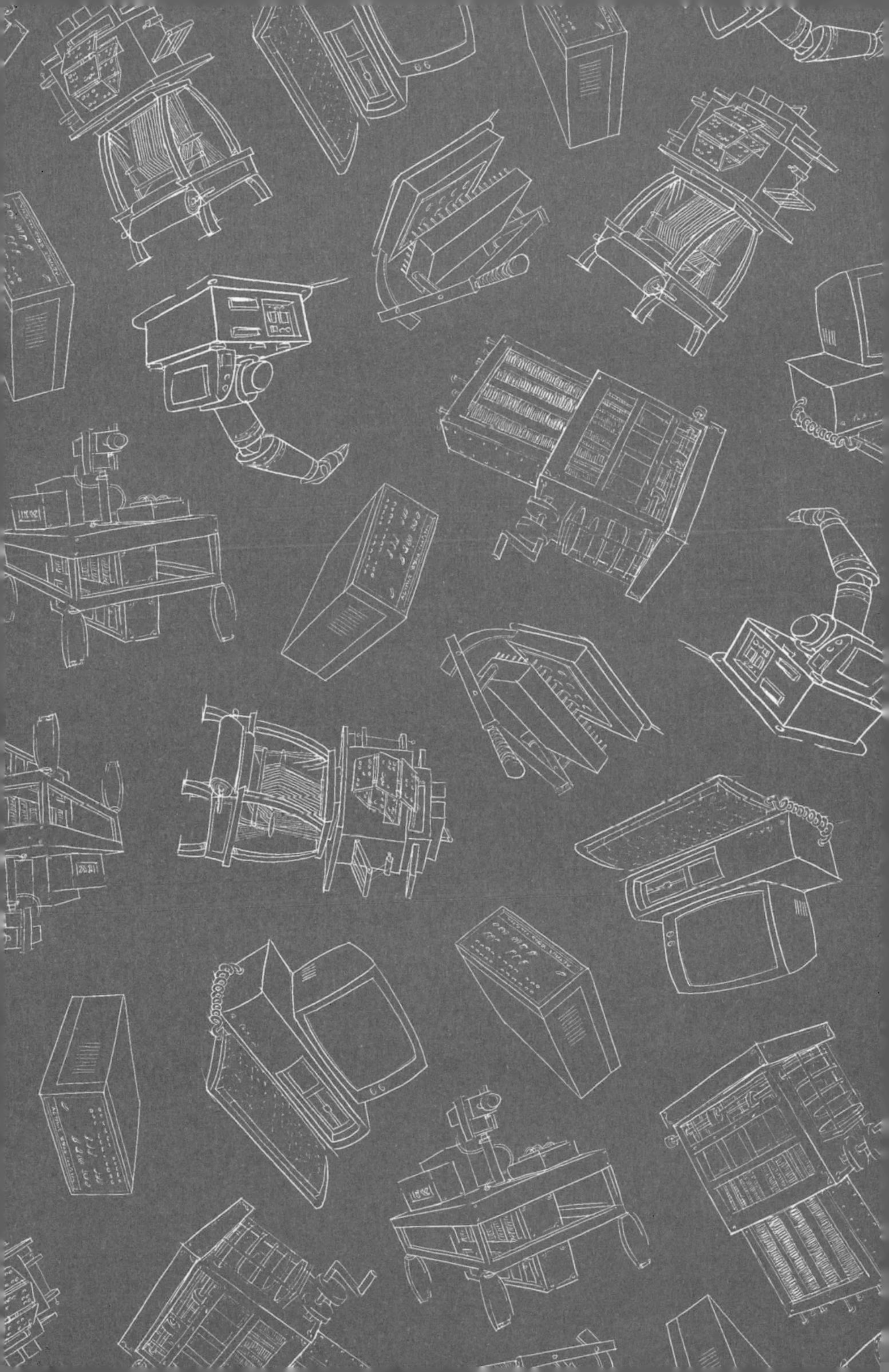

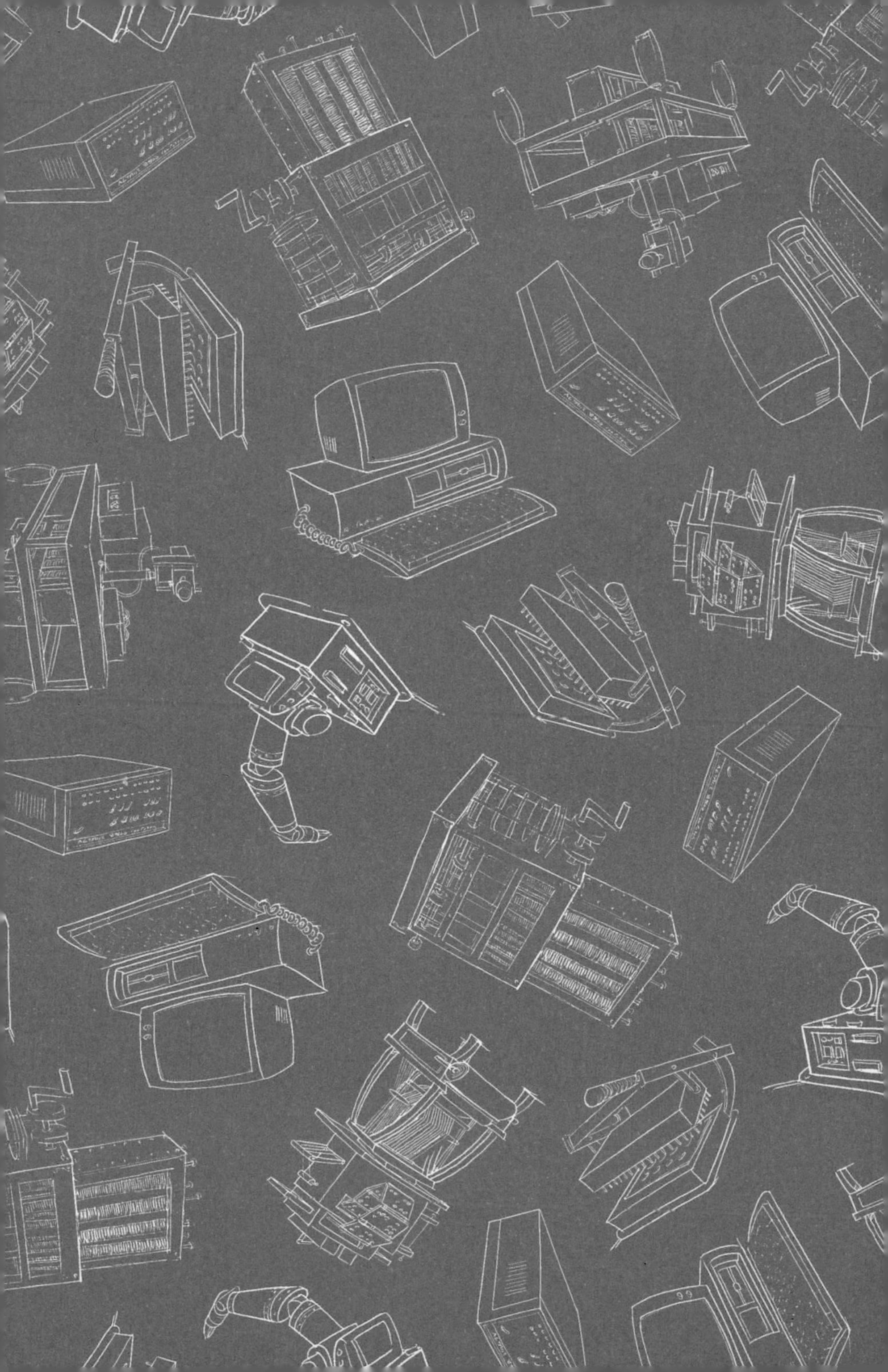